The Recollections of Skinner of Skinner's Horse

Lietenant Colonel James Skinner C.B.

The Recollections of Skinner of Skinner's Horse

James Skinner and his 'Yellow Boys' Irregular Cavalry in the Wars of India between the British, Mahratta, Rajput, Mogul, Sikh and Pindarree Forces

Told in his own words by

James Skinner

With additional material by J.Bailley Fraser

LEONAUR

The Recollections of Skinner of Skinner's Horse: James Skinner and his 'Yellow Boys' Irregular Cavalry in the Wars of India between the British, Mahratta, Rajput, Mogul, Sikh and Pindarree Forces

Originally published in *1851* under the
title *Military Memoir of Lieut-Col. James Skinner*

Published by Leonaur Ltd

Material original to this edition and its origination in
this form copyright © 2006 Leonaur Ltd

ISBN (10 digit): 1-84677-071-8 (hardcover)
ISBN (13 digit): 978-1-84677-071-5 (hardcover)

ISBN (10 digit): 1-84677-061-0 (softcover)
ISBN (13 digit): 978-1-84677-061-6 (softcover)

http://www.leonaur.com

Publishers Notes

In the interests of authenticity, the spellings, grammar and place
names used in this book have been retained from the original edition.

The opinions of the author represent a view of events in which he was
a participant related from his own perspective;
as such the text is relevant as an historical document.

The views expressed in this book are not necessarily those of the publisher.

Contents

Introduction by the Leonaur Editors

Several biographies have been written of the life of James Skinner. However, the book you are now holding is the original 'autobiography', with the exception of Skinner's own work (in his own hand) which was written in Persian. This book was originally published in two volumes. This version combines both volumes into one book.

This first translation of Skinner's account reveals him to be an engaging author who carries his story in a direct, readable style which seems quite contemporary to the modern reader. Skinner's book was brought to the public with the assistance of J. Bailley Fraser – the brother of Skinner's friend and subordinate officer William Fraser.

Fraser's style is perhaps more typical of the early Victorian period than Skinner's. It is difficult to know now what motivated Fraser to provide so much additional material for this book, or to divide the Skinner narrative with his contribution. The Leonaur Editors have made some attempt to minimise the effect of Fraser's florid style and plethora of information which does little to illuminate Skinner's story whilst retaining that which relevantly enhances it.

In its original presentation, this book, as was common in 19th Century printing styles, often had the voice of Fraser blending into Skinner's narrative and out again to the degree that on occasion, the reader finds he is with another writer some time after the transition has taken place.

To minimise this confusion, the Fraser passages are produced here in smaller type on a narrower measure. Skinner's words are in larger type and to the full measure. The Leonaur editors have reduced the volume of the Fraser material by removing irrelevances and have curtailed to a degree his tendency to wax lyrical. Skinner's narrative is, of course, retained in its full and unedited form. Most importantly, it has been brought to the fore to what we believe is its proper place.

We trust we will be excused these liberties in the interests of a more immediate, accessible and enjoyable book for our readers.

The Leonaur Editors
2006

Chapter One
An Introduction To Skinner's World

India has in all ages been the birthplace of military adventure. From the time of Mahmood Ghiznavee, from Alexander himself, down to the days of Nadir and Ahmed Shah Abdallee, her cities and rich plains have been the prey of foreign conquerors or spoilers; and still, as each successive dynasty began to wane, there has arisen, amidst the disorders that preceded its fall, a crowd of lesser robbers who have sought to build their fortunes out of the fragments of the crumbling empire, or to snatch at power in the troubled waters of its ebbing fortunes. Amongst those of native origin, in later days, are the Mahrattas and the Pindarrees; the former of whom, springing forth in the feeble age of the Moghul empire, arose, almost unchecked, to a very formidable height of power; while the latter, arrested by the arms of the British government, before they had advanced beyond the stage of banditti, have been crushed for ever.

The Mahrattas, were inhabitants of Maharashta. Its people consisted of many tribes and nations, but all of the Hindoo religion, and divided into the four principal castes of Brahmins, Chettries, Byse, and Sooders, – the priests, the military, the commercial, and the cultivators.

In common with all other provinces of India, this country was overrun by the Mahomedans, in their various invasions; but its chiefs and inhabitants cherished an unceasing spirit of hatred and aversion to their conquerors, which invariably broke out into open revolt. The first of their chiefs, however, who appears to have maintained a hostilities for any considerable time, was Shahjee, father of the celebrated Sivajee, regarded as the founder of the Mahratta power.

Sivajee, before the death of his father, had taken an active part against the Moghuls, and become their terror. His career is one series of extraordinary exploits. When he assumed the title of Rajah, he successfully opposed the great Aurungzebe, the last powerful monarch of the line of Timour. Sivajee died in 1680, and was succeeded by Sumbajee, who, after an active reign of eight or nine years, was seized and put to death by Aurungzebe; an act which earned the implacable hatred of the Mahrattas; while the death of that monarch himself, in 1707, removed the only support of the falling empire, and left the weakened Moghuls to the fury of their now very powerful enemies.

In the reign of his weak successor, Ferokhshere, their power rapidly augmented; and in the years 1719 and 1720 Ballajee Wishwanaut, the Peishwa (as the first minister of the Rajah of Satarah was called), and his Mahrattas, dictated terms to the emperor concerning Chord, the Sirdesmookee, and Sewraje, amounting to many crores of rupees; and equivalent, in fact, to a surrender of nearly the whole revenue derived from these countries, to the Mahratta powers.

These followed a period of intrigues, battles, and murders among the Mahrattas for the next eight or nine years. Events were then in progress which forced all the Mahratta chiefs to suspend their private feuds, and unite for the general interest in repelling a foe who threatened their existence as a nation; nor could all their efforts succeed in averting a disaster from which it was long of recovering.

The invasion of India by the Affgan, Ahmed Shah Abdallee* is well known. His first expedition was in 1747. He returned home next year; but finding his officers driven from his acquisitions in the Punjab, he came back again in 1756, and overran both the Punjab and Moultaun, placing his son, Timour, as viceroy in these provinces; and rapidly proceeding eastward, reached and plundered both Dehlee and Muttra. His conquest would have been completed, and the Moghul dynasty destroyed before its time, had not a pestilence broken out amongst his troops, which forced him to return to the more healthy regions of his own country. The Mahrattas, taking advantage of this absence, sent Rugonaut Rao to recover their lost ground; and that chief succeeded in driving the Affghan viceroy from the conquered provinces, and placing an officer of his own nation in charge of them at Lahore.

* He is indifferently called Abdallee, or Doorannee, by historians: the latter name is derived from the word Dur, or Door, a "pearl," which was given him by a celebrated Fakeer, in compliment to his valour, and his followers thence are called Doorannees; they were all Affghans.

In the end of 1760, Ahmed Shah, furious at this affront, marched from Affghanistan with a very formidable army; and before Duttojee Sindea, and Holcar, who had been sent to reinforce the Mahratta force, could reach Lahore, the governor was driven from it, the whole Punjab re-occupied by the Doorannees, and the Shah, with a vast army, crossed the Jumna, defeating and cutting to pieces Duttojee and his party. For some time skirmishing went on, the Mahrattas being generally driven backwards and losing many men, till about the 1st of November both armies took up their positions and fortified their camps. The Mahratta encampment, which was surrounded by a deep ditch and ramparts, included the town of Paneeput, while the Shah encamped at four cós distant in their front, defending his camp by an enclosure or stockade of felled trees.

For more than two months the armies continued thus shut up, exhausting the country round of its provisions; but the Abdallee monarch was even a greater master of the foraging system of warfare than his opponents. The Mahrattas kept close in camp, until want produced insubordination. Skirmishes occurred daily, and some severe actions took place, with loss on both sides, but generally much to the disadvantage of the Mahrattas. Each day, too, the dearth increased in camp, till at length their distress became insufferable.

"The cup," wrote the Bhow to Cassee Rao, Pundit, "is full to the brim - it will not hold a drop more." to fight or to starve was the alternative, and to fight the Mahratta chiefs resolved.

The result of this determination was the memorable battle of Paneeput.

The Mahratta army consisted of 55,000 horse and 15,000 foot, with 200 pieces of cannon, besides a host of Pindarrees and followers, camel artillery, &c. amounting to at least 200,000 souls of all sorts. They formed two divisions, one under Sewdasheo Rao Bhow, cousin of the Peishwah, with whom was Wiswas Rao, that prince's son, and many of the chiefs of old families in the Dekhan. It numbered 22,000 chosen horse, besides 10,000 infantry, under Ibrahim Khan Gardee.

The other division was composed of the troops of Mulhar Rao Holcar, Dummajee Gaekwar, Junkajee, and Madhajee Sindea, and many other chiefs of note. There were also many

13

parties of Rajepoot horse, and numerous Pindarrees; and the well-known Surrije Mull, Rajah of the Jhats, had come with 30,000 of his troops. Holcar strongly advised that Bhow's families and heavy equipments be sent to Gwalior, so as to leave the fighting men less encumbered but this was rejected.

The Affghan army numbered 41,000 horse, 38,000 foot, and 70 pieces of cannon. These were chiefly Affghans, men of great bodily strength mounted on powerful horses. These were accompanied numerous irregulars, whose horses and arms were but little inferior to those of the Doorannees. Their leader, Ahmed Shah was a tried and experienced soldier, bred in the camp of the great Nadir, who saw everything himself, went daily the rounds of the camp, and who had his whole army in such discipline, that, "his orders were obeyed like destiny—no man dared hesitate a moment in executing them."

Absolute want forced the Bhow to fight though, he tried negociation to the last. On the 6th of January 1761, orders were given to prepare for battle, and all the grain in the camp was distributed. On the following morning, they marched out of their entrenchment in order of battle, and made straight for the Abdallee camp. But their aspect was one of hopeless despair rather than of steady resolution. The ends of their turbans were loosened, and their hands and their faces stained with turmeric – a token that they went forth to die. Some of the chiefs consigned their wives and families to the care of friends who they hoped might survive the day.

When word was brought to the king that the Mahrattas were moving, he rode forward to reconnoitre. Just then a general discharge of cannon from the Mahratta line was heard so he ordered up his army, with the artillery in the front.

The battle began as usual among Asiatics with a general cannonade, during which the lines drew near each other. Ibrahim Khan Gardee, who was on the left Mahratta flank, advanced with Dummajee Gaekwar against the Rohillas on the right of the Doorannee line, covering his own left by throwing back two battalions obliquely, while Junkojee Sindea on the right opposed Shah Pussund Khan and Nujeeb-u-dowlut. The Bhow, with Jesswunt Rao Powar, fronted the Grand Vizier, and the great Bhugwa Jenda, or Mahratta national standard, was raised in front.

14

When the two lines had outmarched their artillery, there arose the Mahratta war-cry —"Hur-hurree! hur-hurree!" and the battle became general, commencing with a furious charge from their centre upon the Grand Vizier's horse, which, not advancing to meet it, was broken through by the Mahrattas, but not without many riders on both sides being dashed to the ground. A great dust arose, in the midst of which the combatants grappled for life or death, distinguishing each other only in the melee by the cries of their faith –"Deen! deen!" from the Mahomedans, and - "Hur! hur! mahdeo!" from the Mahratta host.

Ibrahim Khan, on the left, led his men with fixed bayonets against the Rohillas, who received him firmly, and fought hand to hand, but so steady was the charge of Ibrahim, that near eight thousand of the Rohillas lay dead or wounded, while he himself was wounded in several places, and six of his battalions were almost entirely ruined. Still he fought on, scattering his opponents, though Shah Verdee Khan, throwing himself from his horse, strove to rally his men, calling out –"Whither do you fly, my friends? our country is far off!" But the left wing of the Doorannee army was still unbroken, and the steady coolness of the Shah retrieved the day, which seemed for some time to be going against him. Gathering a body of Nassakchees* together, he ordered them to stop all the flyers, and kill those who would not turn back, and to drive out all skulkers from the camp; then ordering the Grand Vizier with ten thousand men to make repeated charges on the Mahratta centre, he caused simultaneous charges to be made by the rallied troops on either flank. In these repeated attacks the physical weight and vigour of the Affghans had their effect; still, the Mahrattas fought valiantly, and the struggle, which had endured for seven hours, was continued for another hour, hand to hand, with spears, swords, battle-axes, and daggers. About two in the afternoon, Wiswas Rao was mortally wounded; and the Bhow, descending from his elephant in order that the wounded youth should be placed there, sent a message to Holcar, "to do as he had been directed;" and then, mounting a horse, he disappeared, and never was seen again. Holcar, on receiving this message, went off, immediately,

* *Personal guards and executioners.*

followed by Dummajee Gaekwar; and all resistance on the part of the Mahrattas ceased, – they fled, all became confusion and slaughter. No quarter was given. Thousands were cut down in resisting, and more perished by suffocation in the ditch of the encampment. Men, women, and children, crowded into the town of Paneeput, where next day they were all butchered in cold blood. Even Junkojee Sindea and Ibrahim Khan Gardee,* wounded as they were, and high as was their rank, received no mercy.

The body of Wiswas Rao was found on the field, and brought to be seen by Ahmed Shah. A headless trunk, supposed to be that of the Bhow, was also found some fifteen miles from the field. If in any way he had been the cause of this disaster, he paid for his fault with his life. Many chiefs fell, and few either of chiefs or men ever returned to their own country. Of the fighting men, it is thought that scarce a fourth survived the action; and not less than 200,000 Mahrattas perished in this campaign.

Amongst the few chiefs who escaped from this disastrous field was the afterwards celebrated Madhajee, the founder of the short-lived greatness of his family. When the rout took place, being well-mounted he cleared the crowd, and rode southward; but looking back, he saw that he was followed by one of the enemy – a huge Affghan. Spurring, he soon left the Affghan behind, but upon pulling up he saw his fierce enemy coming up at a long lumbering canter, and again he pushed on, but there was the fierce, persevering Affghan, at his heels. He now pushed on in earnest, and the chase is said to have lasted for an incredible time and space – to the vicinity of Bhurtpore, when his horse, worn out, tumbled with its rider into a ditch; and the Affghan coming up, cut down the rider by a heavy stroke of his battle-axe upon the knee. He then stripped his prey of his ornaments, his clothes, and his mare, and riding off, left him where he fell. A water-carrier, passing by with his bullock, found Madhajee in this state, and, ignorant of his rank, took him back to Bhurtpore, and attended him till he was recovered.

* By Cassee Raja's account, it would appear that Junkojee was murdered, partly to conceal his having been taken, and partly to gratify the private hatred of Nuzeeb-u-dowlut. Ibrahim Khan is said also to have died from ill treatment, or from having had poison put into his wounds while they were being dressed.

16

Madhajee was one of the four principal chiefs who rallied round the Peishwah after these disasters, and formed the heads of the Mahratta confederation. The others were Mulhar Rao Holcar, the Gaekwar, and Ragojee Bhouneslah. These chiefs, when a common danger made it their interest to act together, would, for so long, put aside their personal enmities, but no sooner was the danger removed, than their union was at an end, and each began to act for himself, - overrunning each district unable to resist their arms.

On the south, their encroachments were for a while arrested by the formidable power of the Mahomedan sovereigns of Hydrabad and Mysore; while the progress of the English to the east rendered advance there uncertain and dangerous. It was only on the north they could extend their sway. They had already crossed the Chumbul as conquerors - their officers in command at Lahore and Moultan. But misfortunes drove them from the plains and it was the great object of all the Mahratta powers to regain their lost ground.

That portion called Hindostan, and to which the business of this memoir especially refers, includes all the country to the north of the Nerbudda river, and to the south of the Sutlege. The Sewalic mountains confine it on the north-east and east, while on the west its boundary is the great desert which stretches from Meywar to the Indus. It embraces Rajahstan or Rajepootanah on the west, the provinces of Seharunpore, Dehlee, Agra, and Allahabad on the right side or western bank of the Jumna; the Doab, Rohilcund, and Oude on the east, with Bundelcund and Malwah on its southern line, though these are not generally regarded as included in Hindostan Proper.

Of these vast countries, Malwah was already the undisputed territory of the Mahrattas. It was here that Sindea had fixed his southern capital of Oojein; and Holcar, that of Indore. A portion of Bundelcund was held by Sindea, but the tenure was a loose one; for the numerous petty and warlike chiefs of that difficult country were ever rebelling against his authority, and it required the constant presence of an armed force to collect the tribute nominally assessed upon it. Even Gwalior, and the neighbouring territory in the province of Agra, though afterwards the seat of Dowlut Rao Sindea's residence was, in 1778, in the possession of the Rana of Gohud. In time, as the power of Madhajee augmented from the services of his regular brigades, the Doab fell principally into his hands. But, though his light troops and Pindarrees might make an occasional dash across the Ganges, they could make no serious impression in that quarter; and a remnant of habitual respect for the fallen and blind Shah Allum, rescued by his own efforts from his savage enemies, withheld his nominal prime minister* from seizing the few districts which now represented the once vast empire of the Moghuls.

But to appropriate Rajepootanah - this was the great object of the Mahrattas.

The Rajepoot princes retained their ancient bravery, but they appear to have lost much of that habit of active vigilance, which is as necessary to the protection of a country. The Rajepoot states defended against the invasions of the Moghul emperors. But the day of constant and active military activity had gone by, and though able to meet and drive back a formidable enemy, their modes of fighting were ill-calculated to withstand the attacks of a light-armed foe, who seemed to be everywhere at once, striking without warning, then vanishing. So the Mahrattas often overran the country, destroying it gradually, till finding their people ruined, and their resources diminishing, these chiefs became constrained to pay a tribute, to purchase security from incursions.

The Rajepoots, are all of the military caste, which, though spread over all India, have their stronghold, in the region of Rajahstan, and form the military aristocracy of the country. They are subdivided into various tribes, each laying claim to very ancient and noble descent, of which the four principal are the Seesodias, the Rhattores, the Cuchwahas, and the Chohans; the Bhattees and Powars, or Puars, are also regarded highly. And Rajepootanah is divided into several extensive principalities, of which the chiefs of these tribes are the rulers.

Of these principalities, the central one, Meywar, is regarded as the first in rank. Its ruler has the title of Rana, is the chief of the Seesodia tribe, and has been regarded by the Rajepoots as the head of them all, - the prince round whom the whole military array of the country gathers, in case of emergency. The dwelling of the former Ranas was at Chitore, a hill

*Madhajee Sindea

18

fortress of great strength. Another mountain stronghold, Combhere, is not less so. But in later times the sovereigns have made their abode in the city of Oodipore, where the Rana has a magnificent palace, situated on the brink of a large and beautiful lake.

The military force of Meywar, in former days, was great, but depending, upon the goodwill of powerful lords - called Thakoors - who were more or less ready as their prince was powerful and the cause popular. George Thomas, stated it could muster during the latter years of the eighteenth century to amount to 12,000 cavalry and 6,000 infantry. The Seesodias, are brave and trustworthy, but in neither of these respects are they to be compared to the Rhattores.

Marwar, the next state in rank, and exceeding Meywar in power and extent, lies to the west of this latter, and stretches far to the north of it.

Marwar possesses several strongholds, of which the city of Joudpore, the residence of the Rajah, and from which he is called the Rajah of Joudpore, reminded one of the castle of Edinburgh, with its high and battlemented keep rising over the city at its feet. Nagore, Mairtha, and Palee are also cities of note. The first is a more ancient place than Joudpore, though now much neglected, and on the very verge of the desert; and Mairtha has been rendered famous, being the site of many desperate engagements, and in later years by a most bloody battle with De Boigne's brigades, which will be noticed hereafter.

The Rajah is chief of the Rhattores, who are the bravest troops of the Rajepoot tribes. The Rhattore horse are celebrated over all Hindostan for their courage. Nor has the power of this state decayed to the same extent as that of Meywar; as being further removed from the Dekhan, and affording less temptation in the shape of plunder. Besides which, the habits of the Marwarees have been more formed for resisting predatory attacks.

The military power of Marwar is uncertain, from the same cause as that of Meywar, being dependent on the contingents of feudal chiefs —we hear of vast armies, —of Beejah Sing being at the head of 100,000 men, which must have included the general muster, or khere, of the state, and the contingents of his tributaries, - and of troops of 10,000 and 15,000 horse being sent to aid an ally. Thomas sets down the military force of Marwar at 27,000 cavalry, and 3,000 infantry.

Jessulmere, which lies north-west of Marwar, is a much smaller and less important state, which encroaches still farther on the western desert - in which, in fact, it forms an oasis of rocky ridges and sandy wastes, scarcely more fertile than the desert itself. It scarcely possesses a stream of running water, and its poverty and insignificance may be inferred from the number of its inhabitants, which do not exceed 75,000 souls. The ruling tribe is the Bhattee Rajepoots, and they can turn out some excellent soldiers.

Bikanere, originally an offset from Marwar, wrested from the Bhattees by the Rhattores, is a barren sandy tract in the great western desert, to the north-east of Jessulmere, and north of Marwar, but of greater importance than the former, for its inhabitants are estimated at upwards of 500,000, of whom three-fourths are Jits (Jhats?), the aboriginal race of the country; and the princes of Bikanere are said to have taken the field with 10,000 excellent soldiers, who fight well, though they are rather impatient of control and discipline. Thomas sets its force down at only 2,000 cavalry and 3,000 infantry. The country is very barren, water being exceedingly scarce.

Jeypore, or more properly Dhoondar, is the richest, if not the first or the largest of the Rajepoot states. The ruling tribe is that of the Cuchwaha Rajepoots, of whom the reigning Rajah, Pertaub Sing, a weak and some what pusillanimous personage, was then chief. Its military force consisted at this time of a foreign army of 13,000 regular infantry, with guns; 4,000 Nagas, or Ghosseins, and some cavalry. In addition to these, the feudal levies of horse amounted to 4,000; and when the khere, or leve-en-masse, was called out, it numbered 20,000 men of horse and foot. Thomas sets down the Jeypore cavalry at 30,000, and the infantry at 10,000 men.

Dhoondar is the most eastern of the Rajepoot states, bounding on that side with the provinces of Dehlee and Agra, and having, on the west, portions of Meywar, Marwar, and Bikanere. Besides the famous city of Jeypore, there are several others well deserving notice, and among them, the ancient fortified stronghold of Ambere.

Harawtee, or Boondee Kotah, which lies to the south of Dhoondar, is but a small state in point of superficial extent, the Rajah of which is chief of the Hara Rajepoots, but its soil is so rich, and its position on the river Chumbul so important, and its chief or regent at this time, Zalim Sing, so sagacious and enterprising, and its soldiers so good and so brave, that we cannot pass it without some notice. He is remarkable for having been among the first of the native powers in this quarter who appreciated the value of regular infantry, trained and commanded by Europeans. Kotah and Boondee possess another, though melancholy claim, as it was the country through which the disastrous retreat of Monson was conducted when he fled from Holcar in 1803–4, and where, little as it seems to be known, the Hara chief of Coela sacrificed himself and his men in protecting, along with the gallant Luccan, the rear of the retreating detachment.

Of the remaining smaller states, – as Kishenghur, Machery, Ooneara, Karowlee, and many more petty lordships, offsets from the greater states, it is unnecessary to say more than that they of necessity followed the fortunes of the strongest, and at the time in question paid tribute to Sindea or to Holcar, the habitual depredators of Rajepootanah, as the fortunes of either predominated in the quarters where they were situated.

Such was the country, and such the people, which it was the object of Mahratta ambition – perhaps it might rather be said cupidity – to appropriate and subdue; and of the four chieftains whom we have named above as the champions of the Mahratta confederation, Madhajee Sindea was at once the ablest and the boldest, as well as nearest to the scene of action at the proper juncture. Madhajee was the illegitimate son of Ranojee Sindea, who was a distinguished commander under the great Bajee Rao Peishwah. After the death, or rather murder, of his legitimate brother, Junkojee, at Paneeput, he succeeded to the family jaghire, in Malwah, and, for many years after, his life continued to be one course of active military enterprise and shrewd political intrigue, by which he contrived gradually to increase his power, and substantially to effect his complete independence, although in name he professed himself still the devoted feudatory of the Peishwah.

This affected humility was in fact one great mean of effecting his elevation. When at Poonah he assumed an air of the greatest respect for the Peishwah, and insisted on his right to carry that prince's slippers, as he said his father had done.

But there was another measure to which he was far more indebted for his military success and subsequent greatness, than even to his consummate political address. This was the adoption into his service of a body of regular infantry, disciplined and commanded by European officers; and this leads us to the notice of another class of adventurers, which the stirring and unsettled spirit of the times had called into being.

Every one knows that the English first made their appearance in India as merchants, and this character they maintained for a century and a half; and though they had built a fort at Madras, and another called Fort St. David on the same coast, and though during that time they had been frequently forced to defend themselves by sea against their European rivals, they never were at variance with the natives until the war which broke out with France in 1744. This war soon extended to India, and the native powers were not long of becoming parties to the struggle between the rival European nations in the south. The tyranny of Suraje-u-dowlut, at Calcutta, led also to hostilities in that quarter. Soldiers and warlike talents rose into demand, and the men who had left their homes to follow the peaceful occupation of the merchant, became soldiers themselves.

In doing this, many discovered their true bent, and became first-rate officers and leaders.

The desperate struggle between the French and English troops in the Carnatic, gave birth to a class of adventurers who flocked to either army, hoping to carve out their way to fame or fortune by the sword. Of these many fell; and others, failing, and disgusted with the ill success of their countrymen, left them to try their luck in the service of native princes. These chiefs, convinced by painful experience of the great value of military organization and discipline, and believing that if they could but introduce such discipline amongst their own troops, they should secure the advantages which had given success to the Europeans, willingly entertained such adventurers, or even deserters, from the French or English troops; and placing under them bodies of native soldiers, expected them to be disciplined, and rendered equal to the Sepoys of European Armies.

In this way, even from an early period of the eighteenth century, many native princes - as the Nizam, the Nawabs of Bengal and Oude, and several of the Rajepoot Rajahs, as well as the more newly-risen Mahratta powers - employed European officers in their service. Of these, many were highly respectable by birth, as well as education and character, and well deserved the rank and fortune to which several of them attained; while others, of originally low origin, and deficient in those qualities which are requisite for success, sank unheard of, or became degraded and despised for their vices.

In the first class of these soldiers of fortune we may mention, amongst others, the names of De Boigne, Raymond, Martine, Perron, Dudernaig, Hessing, Thomas, and, though last, certainly not the least worthy, the subject of these memoirs - James Skinner. But as the first of these gentlemen played a part which materially influenced the fortunes of the chief who became our hero's master, and was himself a very remarkable person - Benoit De Boigne.

Chapter Two
Enter Benoit De Boigne

Benoit De Boigne was a native of Savoy, who, having made choice of the military profession, commenced his career as ensign in the regiment of Lord Clare, which formed par of the Irish brigade in the service of France. In this regiment, during a period of five years' service in various countries, he acquired that knowledge of military affairs which afterwards ensured his advancement. Promotion, came too slow for his ambition so he quitted the service of France, and, entered that of Russia, under Admiral Orloff, then at war with the Turks.

In the Archipelago he saw some service, but was taken prisoner at the siege of Tenedos, and remained so until the end of the war. Being at Smyrna, he heard from some Englishmen, so dazzling a description of India, that he resolved to try his fortune there.

After some difficulties, he made his way to Madras, where he arrived in the beginning of 1778. There, he was recommended to Mr. Rumbold, the governor, and by him was appointed to the 6th Native Battalion of that presidency. While serving with that, he narrowly escaped sharing the fate of Colonel Baillie's detachment, having been sent with two companies to escort a convoy of grain from Madras.

Soon afterwards, conceiving himself unjustly treated by Lord Macartney, then the governor, in some affair of military promotion, he threw up his commission, and resolved to proceed to Calcutta, and thence overland to Russia; a design which Lord Macartney, aided, by giving him letters of introduction to Warren Hastings, then Governor-General of India.

That gentleman received De Boigne with kindness, and furnished him with letters, not only to the British authorities in the upper provinces, but to the native princes in alliance with the British Government; thus insuring him not only civility and protection, but considerable pecuniary advantage in the presents which an individual so recommended was sure to receive. This he particularly experienced at Lucknow, where the Nawab made him valuable presents, and gave him letters of credit on Cabool and Candahar for 12,000 rupees.

From Lucknow, De Boigne proceeded towards Dehlee, in company with Major Browne, an English officer, at that time deputed on a mission to the emperor. But that gentleman's progress being impeded by the jealousy of the emperor's minister, De Boigne, being taken for one of his suite, was also detained; so he embraced that opportunity of visiting the camp of Madhajee Sindea, at the invitation of the British Resident, Mr. Anderson. On his way there, he became an object of suspicion, to Sindea as to the Moghuls. Sindea, desirous of ascertaining his true character, and the motives of his journey, employed thieves to steal his baggage, that he might learn the truth from his papers. These, including his letters of credit, he never recovered. This loss De Boigne regarded as fatal both to his purposed journey and to his fortune.

It was under these circumstances, that De Boigne appears first to have entertained the idea of seeking employment in the service of some native prince; and Gwalior, then in possession of the Rana of Gohud, being besieged by Sindea, he conceived a plan for its relief, which he communicated to the Rana, through a Scottish officer in his service, named Sangster, who was in command of 1,000 well-disciplined Sepoys, with a very respectable train of artillery.

His proposition was, that, on receiving an advance of 100,000 rupees, he would raise two battalions of Sepoys within the emperor's territories east of the Jumna, in such a manner as to awaken no suspicion, and, in conjunction with Sangster and his corps from Gohud, would fall on Sindea's camp by surprise. This scheme was frustrated by the suspicion of the Rana, who was afraid to trust De Boigne with the money, and who had hopes of interesting the English in his favour; but he turned it to some advantage, by letting the plan be known as if really contemplated, in order to intimidate Sindea. And Sindea, though it increased the ill-will he had conceived against De Boigne, gave that officer full credit for the merit of the suggestion.

De Boigne, disappointed, tendered his services next to Pertaub Sing, the Rajah of Jeypore, who, with the other

Rajepoot states, was jealously watching Sindea's movements, and ready to oppose him. It is singular enough that he should thus have continued to irritate that prince, whose service he was ultimately destined to enter, and whose power he was to be the instrument of extending so greatly; and twice to have offered his aid to the very powers whom he was so soon to vanquish and humiliate. His offer was entertained by Pertaub Sing, and negotiations were entered into for the raising of two battalions; but having considered it proper to acquaint Mr. Hastings with the step he was going to take, and having addressed him in too official a form, as "Governor-General," that gentleman felt it his duty to order him back to Calcutta, a summons with which, however inconvenient, De Boigne thought proper immediately to comply. Mr. Hastings, pleased with this prompt obedience, permitted him to return; but before he could reach Jeypore, events had occurred which induced the Rajah to alter his mind, and he dismissed Mr. De Boigne with a present of 10,000 rupees.

Thus again and more seriously disappointed, De Boigne was at a loss how to proceed; but just at this time he heard that Sindea was meditating an expedition into Bundelcund; and he sent to that chief proposals to raise, for this service, two battalions of 850 men each. To this, after some negotiation, Sindea agreed, making no present advance, but settling on De Boigne himself a monthly pay of a thousand rupees, and for each man, including officers, a wage of eight rupees per month. These battalions were to be formed, as nearly as possible, on the model of those in the English service, in respect to arms, clothes and discipline. He allowed the men five rupees per month, and out of the overplus of the eight rupees paid his officers, whom he gradually collected, Europeans of all different nations; and Sangster, having joined him, became superintendent of his cannon-foundry. In spite of every obstacle, he succeeded in completing his two battalions, and reporting them as ready to march, within five months; when he was ordered to join the army in Bundelcund, under Appa Khunde Rao.

This chieftain, one of Sindea's principal officers, had under his command a large force of cavalry, but scarcely any infantry; so that De Boigne's two battalions, with their artillery, were never off duty; and they greatly distinguished themselves on all occasions, especially at the siege of the strong hill-fortress of Kalinjer. But the state of affairs in the north did not permit Sindea to leave so efficient a part of his force long at such a distance; and Appa Khunde Rao received orders to march, with all expedition, to assist his master in his operations in Hindostan.

For some time previous to these events, the intrigues of the nobles of the court of Dehlee had occasioned so much confusion in the Moghul empire, that Madhajee, ever ready to avail himself of an opportunity, thought the time had come for him to advance to the northward. Mahomed Beg Hamadanee, governor of Agra, and Ismael Beg, his nephew; led the Moghul forces after a period of feud and assassination but were unable, amid the ensuing anarchy, to take any steps towards maintaining their authority, or opposing the powerful army with which Sindea now crossed the Chumbul. Indeed, so well pleased was the emperor to see an end to these outrages, that he welcomed the Mahratta prince's arrival at Dehlee (January 1785), and bestowed upon him the dignity of prime minister of the empire, – a measure which even Hamadanee Beg acquiesced in; and marched, at his orders, to reduce the fortress of Rajoghur.

This success was, however, too rapid, and owed its attainment to circumstances too fortuitous to be permanent. The Moghul nobles, by degrees, recovered their energies; and, indignant at the obtrusion of a Mahratta chief into the highest dignity of the empire, not only ceased for the time from their own intrigues, but negociated with the Rajepoot princes of Jeypore and Marwar for their aid in humbling the hated upstart. Sindea was by no means unaware of this conspiracy, nor slow to prepare for meeting the danger. The imperial army was now under his command; and as the rebellion had not as yet broken out, nor had the disaffected declared themselves, it consisted of both Mahrattas and Moghuls; and its first movements were directed against the refractory Rajepoots.

Scarcely had they reached the vicinity of Jeypore, towards which place they first marched, than Mahomed Beg Hamadanee and Ismael Beg went over, with their followers, to the enemy. In order to arrest this spirit of disaffection, which, not unknown to Sindea, was spreading among the troops, but which he trusted to extinguish by a decisive success, he resolved on giving battle immediately. Accordingly, he placed his right under the command of a French officer, Lestineau, and his left under De Boigne; and posting twenty-five battalions of the imperial troops in the centre, he took charge of the cavalry himself, as a reserve, and began the battle by a heavy cannonade. Mahomed Beg himself was killed by a cannon shot, early in the day, while attacking the Mahratta right. But Ismael Beg rallied his wavering troops, and drove the right back upon the baggage until they were supported by the reserve. On the other side, 10,000 Rhattore cavalry came furiously upon De Boigne, charging up to the very guns, and cutting down the artillerists, in spite of immense carnage made in their own ranks. But the steadiness of the regular troops prevailed; the Rhattores, broken and greatly thinned, gave way, and the battalions advanced in their turn; but when they called on the Moghul centre to aid them, the traitors refused to stir a foot: thus was victory snatched from the Mahratta prince, and a bloody day ended without result.

Sindea, nothing disheartened, resolved to try a second battle. But, next morning, the whole Moghul infantry, with colours flying and drums beating, went bodily over to join Ismael Beg, taking with them eighty pieces of cannon. De Boigne proposed to charge them, but Sindea thought it more prudent to let them alone.

This sweeping desertion, which so powerfully swelled the enemy's ranks, rendered it impossible to show face to them for the time, so the army retired upon Alwar, followed closely by Ismael Beg; and De Boigne, who had charge of the rearguard, had for eight days to sustain his repeated attacks; but at length, by great exertions, they gained the banks of the Chumbul, and Sindea put it once more between him and his enemies.

Agra alone, of all his conquests in Hindostan, held out; defended by Lukwa-Dada, a Mahratta Brahmin of the and a favourite officer of Sindea's, against Ismael Beg, and the infamous Gholaumkawdir, chief of Seharunpore; and so well and so long did that brave soldier hold out, that Sindea, assisted by the Jhats (a Hindoo tribe of low caste, originally from the banks of the Indus), who hated the Moghuls, was enabled to muster his forces once more, in order to attempt its relief. He brought up all the troops within reach, recalled all detachments, and sent a large force forward under the command of Rannee Khan, the Bhaee, and Appa Khundoorao, to which were added the regular battalions of De Boigne. Joined by the Jhats, under Sew Sing Foujedar, and M. Lestineau, together with two Mahomedan officers, they marched straight to Agra, but were met on the way, sixteen miles from Bhurtpore, by Ismael Beg and Gholaum Kawdir, who had raised the siege to give them battle.

The action took place on the 24th of April 1788, commencing by a cannonade from the guns of Ismael Beg. The Jhats took the right, the Mahrattas the left, of Sindea's line. The former were all put to flight by a fierce attack by Gholaum Kawdir, except the corps under Lestineau, which for some time maintained their ground. Jehangeer Khan, one of the Mahomedan officers of the Jhats, deserted to Ismael Beg without firing a shot. This latter chief charged furiously the infantry of De Boigne, who received him with the most perfect firmness and intrepidity; and had he been suitably supported by the cavalry, the issue of the day would have been different from what it proved; but after sustaining heavy loss, the regular troops were forced to give way and retire upon Bhurtpore.

The triumph of the Moghul chiefs was, however, of short duration. Sindea, reinforced and nowise discouraged, returned to the charge. Luckwa Dada gallantly held out in Agra. Jealousies took place among the Moghul chiefs; and Ranny Khan, hearing of an incursion of the Sikhs, sent a body of Mahrattas and Jhats to join and encourage them to fall upon the Jagheer of Gholaum Kawdir. That chief was forced by this diversion to leave Ismael Beg's army in order to repel this invasion; while the Mahratta army, joined by the Jhats, once more gave battle to Ismael Beg near Agra. The Moghuls were utterly routed and dispersed. Ismael Beg himself, severely wounded, escaped by the swiftness of his horse, and swam the Jumna; after which, making for the camp of Gholaum Kawdir, both took refuge in Dehlee. Then getting access by treachery to the palace, he committed attrocities including digging out the eyes of the Shah Allum.

It is not easy to account for the apparent remissness of Sindea, or his general, in not following up their victory and relieving the capital. If it was occasioned by his policy in giving the robbers time to quarrel over their prey, it was at least a fatal proceeding for the wretched emperor and his family. When Sindea did come in person, he did all he could to alleviate their melancholy condition, and himself replaced the unfortunate emperor upon the throne. That these services should be rewarded by a confirmation of the former grant of the prime ministership to the chief who performed them, was a natural consequence; and to this title was added that of commander-in-chief of the imperial forces.

It is satisfactory to learn that punishment, even in this world, awaited the principal actors in this series of crimes. At the approach of the Mahratta army, Gholaum Kawdir fled, carrying with him the nazir of the Shah's household, who had been his treacherous coadjutor in his crimes, and pursued by a large body to Meerut, about six miles from Dehlee, where for a considerable time he defended himself against them. But supplies running short, and the garrison becoming mutinous, he made a rush from the fort with 500 horsemen. And gallantly cut his way through the enemy. But his troops, disheartened, began to drop away, until he found himself alone, when his horse, exhausted, fell, and he was unable to proceed. The zemindar of a neighbouring village took him prisioner, and carried him to the Mahratta camp, where, first, he was suspended in a cage made for the occasion, like a wild beast, in front of the army; then, after every possible indignity, his nose, ears, hands, and feet being cut off, he was, thus mutilated, sent off to Dehlee, but he died miserably on the way. The nazir, his treacherous associate, after being stripped and imprisoned by himself, and carried off with him to Meerut, was taken there, and being sent back to Dehlee, was trampled to death by an elephant, by Sindea's command.

For three years did De Boigne continue in the service of the Mahratta chief, who fully appreciated his talents and his zeal. But he was sensible that he was still in a false position – that with the command of so limited a force he could effect nothing of importance; and animated with a sincere desire to increase his master's power, he made proposals to Sindea to augment his regular force to a brigade of 10,000 men, formed upon the same model as the two original battalions. But though that prince was fully convinced of the value of his regular troops, and quite alive to the merits of their commander, his Mahratta prejudices were too strong in favour of cavalry, and the jealousies of his own chiefs and officers too firmly rooted against the employment of Europeans, to render it politic in him to assent to a proposal which would give to them so much encouragement. The time, in fact, was not ripe for adopting so bold a measure, added to which the expense of forming such a corps presented in itself a serious difficulty. All these considerations weighed with Sindea, who replied to the proposal in terms which Mr. De Boigne could construe into nothing less than a courteous refusal, and on this he tendered his resignation. It was accepted by the Mahratta prince: but they parted with such expressions of consideration and esteem, as portended that their separation would not be permanent.

For the present, Mr. De Boigne, free to go where he pleased, retired to Lucknow, where, he entered into commercial speculations, which promised a return more lucrative at least than the profession of arms, which he had so long been engaged in.

But he was not permitted long to pursue these peaceful avocations. Sindea, though generally successful, and conqueror of the provinces of Agra, Dehlee, and Seharunpore, must have long-felt that his power wanted stability. His shrewd intellect no doubt led him to perceive that cavalry was a force more suited to predatory warfare than for the maintenance of a fixed and permanent empire. It is said, too, that his illegitimate birth had tended somewhat to diminish his influence amongst his countrymen, and he resolved to compensate for this disadvantage by creating a force which should be more under his own command, and more available for all services than his Mahratta troops. It was, no doubt, in pursuance of this system that he enlisted a large proportion of Rajepoots and Mahomedans, and entertained large bodies of Ghosseins,*

* *Ghosseins are one of the four principal classes of Hindoo devotees, and are understood to be followers of Mahadeo. Those who affect great sanctity often go naked, and subject themselves to most severe tortures and self-privations: others follow secular pursuits, becoming merchants, soldiers, &c. They often used to congregate in bands, and range the country, committing great excesses and outrages, on pretence of seeking for alms: sometimes they assemble in large bodies, under a leader, who is at once their ghostly instructor and captain, and hire themselves out as mercenaries; and Sindea entertained a body of these men, under a leader named Himmut Bahadru, who afterwards attained to considerable celebrity. These military Ghosseins were often called Nagas, and generally fought with desperate resolution; they affected the colour of orange in their garments.*

who, until employed by Madhajee, had seldom appeared as soldiers in the Mahratta armies. It was this motive, also, which at last induced him to resolve on increasing his regular troops, and placing them under the command of European officers. He was aware, too, that the Moghul power, though scattered and dispersed, had not been so completely destroyed as to be harmless, and that the Rajepoot chiefs were hostile in their hearts, while the Affghans were even then threatening another descent from the north.

Impressed by these considerations, it is not surprising that Sindea remembered the propositions of De Boigne, and resolved to secure, if possible, the return of that gentleman to his service. His vakeel found De Boigne immersed in his new employment; but he could not resist an appeal which spoke equally to his inclinations, his pride, and his interest—for Sindea made liberal offers. After a few days spent in regulating his affairs, he repaired to Muttra, at that time the head-quarters of the Mahratta prince. A single audience, where both parties were willing, sufficed to bring them to an understanding, and an arrangement was concluded with every mark of confidence and esteem on both sides. De Boigne was empowered to raise immediately a brigade of 10,000 men, disciplined in the European style, and at a rate of pay higher than that of any other corps in the service, and the General's own appointments were fixed at 4,000 rupees per month. His two original battalions formed the nucleus of this force, and the battalion of Lestineau, which had been abandoned by their commander, and then mutinied for want of pay, after being broken up as a corps, were pardoned by Sindea, at De Boigne's request, and admitted individually into the new brigade. Thus, three of the thirteen battalions were already complete, and, by deputing steady officers into Rohilcund, the Doab, and Oude, the rest were soon raised, so potent was the name of Sindea, and the assurance of good and regular pay.

In a few months the corps was complete. Ten of the battalions were dressed like the Sepoys, and armed, as they were, with musket and bayonet. The other three, composed of Affghans, wore a Persian uniform, and were armed with matchlocks, to which the General added a bayonet. 500 Mewattees, irregular soldiers, intended for camp duty, and 500 cavalry, with sixty pieces of cannon, completed the brigade, which formed in itself a little army of 12,000 men, under the colours of him who had created it—the White Cross of Savoy.

The officers of this body were principally Europeans, of all nations, many of them British, and men very respectable by birth, education, and character; and all lent their General their willing-aid in his arduous duty of bringing under and preserving discipline amongst the new levies. The non-commissioned officers were selected from the elite of the old battalions. The object of all was to create and keep up a high esprit du corps; and in a short time the brigade was fit for duty.

Their services were soon required. Ismael Beg, with his Moghuls, supported by the Rajahs of Jeypore and Jhoudpore, appeared in arms at the town of Patun, in the province of Ajmeer; and Sindea, after some characteristic intriguing to corrupt the regular troops of Ismael, ordered Gopaul Kao Bhow, Luckwa Dada, and De Boigne, to attack his camp. The battle took place on the 20th June 1790, and was a very severe one; for Holcar, who had promised his assistance to Sindea, stood aloof during the engagement; and Ismael Beg fought with his usual courage and determination. The line had been formed at nine in the morning, but the brunt of the battle was not until the afternoon, when Ismael Beg made a furious attack upon De Boigne's infantry, penetrating even to the guns, and cutting down the gunners at their pieces. But again the resolute energy of that officer saved the corps, and repelled the desperate charge. The brigade then advanced upon the enemy's batteries, which he carried one after another; and Ismael Beg, completely routed, fled to the gates of Jeypore, leaving behind him 100 guns, fifty elephants, two hundred standards, and all his baggage. Next day, too, seven of his battalions and 10,000 irregular troops came over and submitted to the conqueror. The day was a bloody one on both sides; some assert that 11,000 or 12,000 of the Mahrattas were killed, but Ismael Beg's army was completely destroyed: all this was entirely owing to De Boigne and his regular brigade, for the cavalry did very little. The town of Patun, and its strong citadel, surrendered to the conqueror in three days after; and its commander declared himself the vassal of the Mahratta prince.

Sindea, who received accounts of the battle at Muttra, where his head-quarters still remained, now sent De Boigne to invade the territory of Jhoudpore, the Rajah of which state had so powerfully assisted his late enemy, Ismael Beg. On the route, that officer undertook the siege of the fort of Ajmeer, which had been taken by the Marwarees by a coup de main; but learning that Beeja Sing, the Rajah, had advanced to Mairtha, a town some twenty miles west of that city, he left a corps of 2,000 irregular cavalry to maintain the blockade, and advanced with the rest of his force to meet the enemy. At Mairtha, then the home of the bravest clans of Marwar,—on the plains of which the crown of that kingdom had been fought for in many a memorable battle, — whence, but a few years before, the bravest of the Rhattores, with their Prince Beeja Sing and 200,000 men, had been driven from a murderous field, by these same Mahrattas,*—on this same ground, covered with the innumerable tombs of those who had fallen in former days, was the same prince, and 30,000 of his best Rhattores, with 20,000 foot to boot, destined to sustain a no less disastrous defeat. The Mahratta cavalry, nearly equal in numbers to that of the Rajepoots, preceded by one day De Boigne, whose infantry, with its eighty pieces of cannon, was embarrassed in the muddy bed of the Loonee river; and they encamped five miles distant from the Rhattore cavalry, who were drawn out upon the plain of Mairtha, with one flank resting on the village of Dangiwas. De Boigne came up in the grey of the next morning, and completely surprised the unguarded Rajepoots by sending among them showers of grape from his. All became panic and confusion in a moment; the position was forced,—the guns and the irregular infantry put to flight.

An error on the part of De Boigne's commander, Rohan on the left seemed at this time to open a glimpse of hope to the Rajepoots, for, pressing on with three battalions, he was nearly cut off from the main body, by a party of Rhattore horse who had rallied and kept together. Some of their chiefs, it appears, awaking from the deep sleep of opium, found their camp deserted or in confusion, and calling around them their immediate followers, they collected about 4,000 of their best horsemen, with which they attacked the imprudent commander

* *In 1753, when Ram Sing endeavoured to dispute the throne with Beeja Sing, and called in the Mahrattas and Jeypooreans to his assistance.*

on the right. De Boigne saw the danger, and flew to the rescue, and forming part of his infantry into a hollow square, resisted the repeated and furious charges of the Rhattores, who, as usual, galloped up to the muzzles of the guns, in spite of the murderous showers of grape, which told fearfully in their dense mass, and cut down the gunners, but could not penetrate the square; they broke the line, however, and passed on to engage the Mahratta horse, which scattered at their approach. But they had no support, and the guns, wheeled round, continued their murderous discharge; the troops re-formed to receive them as they came back; their ranks were thinned by grape and musketry: and though they continued to charge up to the very bayonet points, it was each time with weaker effect,—until, falling in detail before the immoveable square, scarce one of the 4,000 left the field. By nine of the morning the battle was over; by ten, the camp, cannon, and baggage were in possession of the Mahrattas; by three in the afternoon the city had been taken by assault, and had become the headquarters of the Mahratta commanders.

The consequence of this victory, which, beyond the smallest question, was won entirely by De Boigne and his regular brigade, was the submission to Sindea of the Rajahs of Joudpore and Oodeypore; and by this and other successes, unquestionably owing to the same cause, the superiority of regular troops had become so firmly established, that Sindea now resolved to triple the number of those under De Boigne, and he accordingly directed that officer to raise two more brigades upon the same model as the first. He fixed his headquarters at Coel, in the Doab, where he occupied himself in bringing to perfection the material and discipline of this force, which, by the sanction of the emperor, was to bear the title of the Imperial army. The administration of Hindostan was committed to Gopaul Rao Bhow, but its defence was intrusted to De Boigne.

The next important occasion for the employment of the regular brigades, was against a Mahratta enemy. Tookojee Holcar,★ at all times a treacherous ally and jealous rival of Sindea, after betraying him at Patun, and on other occasions, took

★ *The general of Ahalia Bhye, then the head of the Holcar family, and father of Jesswunt Rao Holcar, though himself no relation of the family.*

advantage of his absence in the Dekhan to cross the Chumbul into Rajepootanah. Sindea, though successful and victorious in the north, did not feel himself by any means so independent in the Dekhan as to neglect his interest there,—especially as the celebrated Nana Furnavese, the Peishwah's minister, was known to be his enemy at that prince's court, he therefore contrived a special mission to Poonah,— namely, that of conveying to the Peishwah the khilut of investiture of the office of Wukeel-e-Mootluq, or chief minister of the Moghul empire, from the Imperial court; and so well did he succeed in his object, that, in spite of Furnavese's enmity, he gained the friendship and confidence of the young Peishwah. It was while thus employed, that Holcar, trusting not only to the absence of his rival, but to the influence of Nana Furna-vese, believed that he had a golden opportunity to deal Sindea a severe blow in the north; so picking a quarrel with Gopaul Rao Bhow, the general of his rival in that quarter, a series of petty hostilities began, which soon increased to open war.

The widow of Nujuff Khan,* formerly prime minister of the empire, having refused to surrender the fortress of Kanounde to Sindea's officers, De Boigne detached a brigade, under command of Colonel Perron, a French officer, to reduce the place. It was opposed by the indefatigable Ismael Beg, who, coming to the lady's assistance with his Moghuls, got beaten, and fled into the fort. But foreseeing its fall, and doubtful of the fidelity of the garrison, he gave himself up to M. Perron, on condition of his life being spared. By the firm remonstrances of De Boigne and Perron, his life was saved, but he was sent to the fort of Agra, where, some years afterwards, he died in prison; and thus fell the last of the Moghul nobles of that party.

Soon after the surrender of Kanounde, Gopaul Rao Bhow summoned both Luckwa Dada and De Boigne to join him in opposing the progress of Holcar, who mustered, as was understood, 30,000 horse, with four regular battalions of foot

---

* *This nobleman was well aware of the power of De Boigne and his brigades. He told his Begum—the same in question in the text—that if Sindea sent to demand the surrender of the place—to hold out; but if De Boigne or Perron came, to surrender at once; she was persuaded, to his own loss, by Ismael Beg to resist.*

and numerous artillery, under command of the Chevalier Dudernaig.* The combined forces of Sindea amounted to 9,000 of the regular brigades, and 20,000 horse, with a suitable proportion of cannon. Holcar at first seemed desirous to avoid a pitched battle: but after several marches and countermarches, De Boigne having ascertained that the enemy was encamped near a forest, resolved to attack them. The conflict, which took place in September 1792, was very bloody, and the most obstinate ever witnessed by the general. Early in the day, an unlucky accident had nearly turned the chances against him,— for a shot having struck and caused the blowing up of an open tumbril of ammunition, it was followed by the explosion of twelve more, while the enemy took advantage of the confusion to charge. But the unfailing steadiness and presence of mind of De Boigne, and the perfect discipline of his troops, averted the evil consequences of this mishap. The enemy were checked by a murderous fire, and as they retreated were charged by his own chosen cavalry, and the route became general. Dudernaig's four battalions were all but annihilated; their 38 guns, all taken; and almost all their European officers were killed. The broken remains of Holcar's army quickly crossed the Chumbul.

The submission of the Rajah Pertaub Sing, of Jeypore, followed this victory; and after consenting to pay seventy lakhs of rupees, by way of expenses, he received the victorious general at his capital in style.

The term of De Boigne's service under the great Madhajee was, however, drawing to a close. That able prince died at Wunoulee, near Poonah, in the month of February 1794, at the age of sixty-four, leaving to his grand-nephew, Dowlut Rao Sindea (for he had no male heirs), an extent of territory, and an amount of power, which none of his family could ever have

---

* *The Chevalier Dudernaig was the son of a French naval captain, and is represented as being a man of highly-finished education and agreeable manners. He took service with Holcar, with whom he continued for some time, and afterwards in that of Kassee Eao. But finding the service or the cause a bad one, he left his battalion, and returned to Kotah, under protection of Zalim Sing. Holcar endeavoured to induce Zalim Sing to give him up; but that chief refused to stain his name with infamy by such an act: and the chevalier was permitted, on payment of a small sum, to retire to Hindostan, with all his property, which he did, escorted by a party of Zalim Sing's troops; and he soon after took service in the brigades of Sindea.*

hoped to attain. His possessions in the Dekhan and Malwah were tolerably secure and well managed, but across the Chumbul there was no power to contend with his. Rajepootanah was humbled—Hindostan was his own; and the young Dowlut Rao, whose independence even the British Government acknowledged, and to whom the high title of Maharaje was freely conceded, succeeded to an empire which might well take rank with the most powerful native states in India.

In spite of many brilliant offers made to him from others General De Boigne had resolved to continue in the service of his employers Dowlut Rao, who set less value upon his possessions in Hindostan than on those to the southward, was contented to confirm De Boigne in the government and protection of all to the north of the Chumbul.

But the constantly sustained efforts which De Boigne had kept up for so many years began to tell upon his constitution, and he longed to renew his exhausted health. Sindea, fully sensible of his value, sought to retain him but De Boigne feeling his indisposition increase, persevered, and at length received permission to retire, upon the understanding that he should resume his post if health should permit.

In February 1796, he proceeded to Calcutta, accompanied by his personal guard of 600 Persian chosen cavalry, the horses and equipments of which were all his own property. These were purchased at once of him by the Governor-General, who also entertained the men. In the month of September he finally quitted India, carrying with him to his native land a vast fortune.

There is one other fact which, to Britains at least, must be interesting. When he first enlisted with Sindea, one of the principal articles of agreement he made with him, and that in writing, was, that he should never be ordered to bear arms against the English; and this, independent of what related to himself, was ever his advice to that prince.

Such was the commander under whom young Skinner was destined to make his debut in arms; but he was not destined long to enjoy this privilege, for he had only entered the service a few mouths when De Boigne quitted it, and the command of the regular brigades, now largely increased, fell to Colonel Perron. Perron came to India as a petty officer of a French man-of-war, but, desirous of mending his fortune, he left the navy, and, travelling up the country, first entered the service of the Pvana of Gohud, under the orders of Sangster. After the fall of the Rana, he entered into a corps commanded by Lestineau, then in the service of Sindea, as quartermaster-serjeant, on an allowance of sixty rupees per month. Lestineau was supposed to have got possession of Gholaum Ivawdir's saddle when he was taken near Meerut, and to have obtained in it the valuable jewels -which that miscreant had plundered from the palace at Dehlee; and with this booty, and some money which had been given him to pay his troops, he made his escape to Europe. On this occurrence, Perron received from Rana Khan the command of a battalion; but the troops being reduced soon after, he lost this employment. When De Boigne began to form his brigade, having had experience of Perron's talents, he gave him command of a battalion called the Boorhanpoor Battalion; and he conducted himself so much to the General's satisfaction, especially at the battle of Patun and at Kanounde, that De Boigne gave him the command of one of his brigades. He subsequently accompanied Sindea into the Dekhan, and was with him when he died. He then was attached to the young Dowlut Rao Sindea, whose confidence he won. Of Perron, De Boigne always entertained a high opinion, and spoke of him with great respect. But, in several matters of politics, his opinions differed widely from De Boigne's, for he entertained as strong a dislike to the British as the General did a partiality; and, instead of following up the sentiment of De Boigne, of "never to quarrel with the English," Perron made no secret of his disposition to thwart and oppose them in every possible way—a policy which in the end proved fatal to his master as well as to himself.

We shall now turn to the more immediate subject of this narrative, Colonel James Skinner.

Chapter Three
Skinner & the Irregular Cavalry

The name of James Skinner is known to almost every one at all acquainted with India, as that of a gallant and successful soldier, a distinguished leader of irregular horse. Thrown in early youth amongst scenes of high excitement,—of daring adventure and bloody rencontres,—of military pomp and Eastern magnificence; at one time struggling with danger, and privation, and fatigue, —at others, revelling in the short-lived profusion and reckless enjoyment purchased by victory and success, he became the creature of the times and circumstances in which his precarious life was passed; and even when the changes in his eventful career brought him back into contact with his countrymen, there still hung around him an air of barbaric splendour, acquired by his Asiatic habits, which invested him with an interest that few failed to sympathize with as striking and attractive. No one, indeed, especially those possessed of any military enthusiasm, could look upon James Skinner—or, as they called him, "Old Secunder"*—at the head of his fine corps of horsemen—his "yellow boys," as they were named, from their yellow uniform—and witness their martial air, as they careered about in their wild and rapid manoeuvres, without admitting that they were a gallant band,—that, as irregulars, they were unequalled in India, and that the leader and the men were worthy of each other.

In truth, the real character and worth of the more respectable bodies of Indian irregular horse is scarcely comprehended by those who have had no opportunity of becoming acquainted with them, and distinguishing between their various classes;

---

* *This appellation—half name, half sobriquet—was given him by the natives, from the similarity of sound between Skinner, pronounced "Iskinner" by them, and Iskunder, which is the name for Alexander; they cannot pronounce the sk without prefixing the vowel i; and as the idea of Skinner's valour was something extraordinary, they fairly changed his name into Secunder, which is that used for the great Alexander; and by that he became familiarly known throughout the country.*

for many classes there are, differing from each other as widely as the purposes they are meant for, and the stuff from which they are formed. In the days of Moghul power and greatness, both cavalry and infantry were raised, maintained, and paid upon a regulated system, which secured the services of good and faithful soldiers. And in the commencement of Mahratta power,—in the days of Sivajee and his immediate successors, when foot soldiers were made use of as well as horse, a similar arrangement was adopted. As the Mahratta tactics assumed their peculiar and predatory character, and the objects of their rapid expeditions were more distant, infantry fell more into disuse, and cavalry, in time, almost entirely superseded it. They thus became a nation of horsemen; and though their chiefs had their villages and jagheers to retire to when the rains prevented them from keeping the field, yet their boast used to be, that "their house was the back of their horse." When the celebrated Nizam-ool-moolk was opposed to the no less famous Bajee Rao Peishwa, in the first campaign between them, the former sent a famous painter in his service to the army of Bajee Rao, with orders to take his picture in whatever act or attitude he might first find him. The painter, on his return, exhibited a likeness of the Peishwa mounted, with the head and heelropes of his horse in his feeding-bag, like that of a common Mahratta, his spear resting on his shoulder, whilst he was rubbing, with both hands, some ears of ripened joowaree (a species of grain), which he had plucked from the field, and was eating as he rode.

In later times a change came on, and instead of tying up their horses under the wall of a fort during the rains, and pasturing them in the country round, a regular camp was formed, as Sindea did at Gwalior; and for which, with other departures from the customs of his forefathers, he underwent the grave rebuke of some of the chieftains of the former time, who had seen the growth of power under the old Mahratta system, and augured little good from the change. In these early times, when the Moghuls of the empire were driven from the field by the swarms of Mahratta cavalry, that cavalry was regularly paid, and held under a species of discipline by its own officers; but as the ancient dynasties crumbled to pieces, and spread disorganization over the length and breadth of the land, quarrels and jealousies arose amongst the victors; the robbers fell out about the spoil,

41

and each tried to grasp what he could. Plunder, rather than pay, became the soldiers' object; and the character of the Mahratta troops degenerated accordingly. There continued, no doubt, to be large standing armies, on the old footing, under such chiefs as a Sumboojee, a Bajee Rao, or a Ballajee, though these were often left largely in arrears; but these armies could not absorb the floating multitudes of lawless troopers which this system of robbery and plunder had called into existence; so that they shifted their services from one chief to another, as each was able to pay or lead his followers to plunder: or, in default of a leader whom they liked, they would plunder in small bands on their own account. And such continued the practice until the whole of Central India became a ruined waste, nursing few besides the robbers who destroyed it. The ordinary army of Madhoo Rao Peishwah is said to have numbered 50,000 good horse, without including the troops of the Bhounslah, the Gaekwar, of Sindea, or Holcar. These consisted either of his own regularly paid troops, or those of the chieftains and Jagheerdars of his own family and clan; his infantry was inconsiderable, and consisted chiefly of mercenaries, who were often discharged at the end of a campaign. The contingents which the four above-named chiefs were bound to furnish has been estimated at between 40,000 and 50,000 more; so that the Mahratta empire, if working together, a case that rarely ever occurred, might furnish in all about 100,000 good horse. But to these there were always added clouds of Pindarrees and plunderers,

Contrasted with the splendour of the Moghul camp, we may view the horde accompanying one of these freebooters. Differing from the organized bands of Sivajee, but still more destructive to a country,— an irregular assembly of several thousand horsemen, united, by preconcerted agreement, in some unfrequented part of the country. They set off with little provision; no baggage, except the blanket on their saddles; and no animals but led horses, with bags prepared for the reception of their plunder. If they halted during a part of the night, like the Pindarrees of modern times, they slept with their bridles in their hands: if in the day, whilst the horses were fed and refreshed, the men reposed with little or no shelter from the scorching heat, excepting such as might occasionally be found under a bush or tree; and during that time their swords were laid by their sides, and their spears generally stuck in the ground at their horses' heads. When halted on a plain, groups of four or five might be seen stretched on the bare earth fast asleep, their bodies exposed to the noonday sun, and their heads, in a cluster, under the precarious shade of a black blanket, or tattered horse-cloth, extended on the points of their spears. The great object of this class was plunder; and the leaders and their troops, though they sometimes rendered a partial account to the head of the state, dissipated, or embezzled the greater part of their collections.

Thus the army of a Mahratta chief or prince was always a motley body, and but little qualified to resist a resolute foe; for beyond the Pagah, or household troops, mounted and armed by the prince and his nobles, and the small number of truly gallant retainers, who went into action resolved to defend their chieftain and his cause, the materials it was formed of were not of a nature to command much confidence. The Sillahdars, a respectable class who furnished their own horses, were not likely to be very forward in exposing their property to danger; and still less was the mere mercenary, whose object was gain from plunder, to risk either life or property where the attainment of his object was doubtful or hazardous. But as, until the introduction of regularly disciplined troops into the service, numbers were always imposing if not effective, the quantity of the troops entertained was frequently more studied than the quality, although it often interfered with the efficiency of the actual fighting men. It was this that induced the leaders to permit those clouds of Pindarrees who came in swarms, like vultures, to the battle-field, to encamp on the skirts of the army; and they paid for this sufferance by contributing to these leaders a portion of any plunder they might obtain.

Such bands of marauders were not confined to the Mahratta country—they swarmed over all Hindostan. Every chief who claimed independence, however ephemeral, had, indeed, his body of horsemen, whom he kept in regular pay, and on whose services he therefore could more or less rely. But when called to defend himself, or wishing to attack others, he enlisted all who came to his standard; and these mercenaries, when they saw but little prospect of pay or plunder, or regarded the cause of their leader as desperate, made no scruple of leaving him, and probably going over to the enemy. Even at the best, they acted rather as foragers for the army, and cutting off supplies from the enemy, than as actual combatants; and the unscrupulous manner in which they first supplied their own wants, rendered them often more formidable to their friends than to their foes.

Even amongst the Mahrattas, though professedly and emphatically a nation of plunderers, who seek and have achieved conquest not so much by hard-fighting in pitched battles, as by wearing out their prey by incessant desultory and harassing attacks, we find on record instances of the most devoted gallantry exhibited by these large bodies of cavalry; and, to prove this, we need go no further than the disastrous field of Paneeput, where their light-armed horse stood in obstinate and unyielding conflict for hours against the gigantic and well-trained Doorannees.

But if we seek for a picture of chivalrous gallantry, unswerving fidelity, and fearless self-devotion, we have only to turn to the cavalry of the Rajepoot states; and particularly to that of the Rhattores. We shall there find acts of resolute heroism that have not been surpassed by the troops of any age or country. In the history of their own wars we find repeated instances of bodies of their horsemen dashing themselves against lines of spears and bayonets in the field, and against batteries bristling with cannon, regardless of the havoc in their own ranks made by grape and steel; while, in defence of their fortresses, we find them dying to the last man, rather than accept quarter from their assailants on any terms but such as they deem consistent with military honour,—for it is the izzut, the abroo, of the Rajepoot, which is dearer to him than life, which instigates him to peril that in its defence; while his devotion to his chief and clan, like that of the Highlanders of yore, makes all sacrifices easy when these are in peril.

A striking instance of this unyielding sense of military honour was given to the writer, by Skinner himself, who had been not only an eyewitness, but personally engaged in the business. A detachment of the British army, marching down the Doab from Anoopsheher, observed at some distance on their flank a small half-ruinous mud fort, called in India a gurhee; and which being occupied, though offering no molestation, it was thought fit to empty of its garrison; and, accordingly, a halt was called to reduce it. Skinner, who was present, observed that it was not worth the trouble of stopping for, and that, if authorized, he would go and bring in the garrison, who probably were Rajepoots, and would evacuate it quietly if civilly treated; but if otherwise, might give some annoyance. The younger officers smiled scornfully at this idea; but the commander told Skinner he might go and tell the garrison to give themselves up as prisoners and thus save their lives. Skinner accordingly rode up to the place, alone, and soon brought the garrison to a parley. It consisted of thirteen Rajepoots, who at once agreed to give up the place, provided they were permitted to go free, and carry off their arms. To these terms Skinner agreed, never imagining that any objection could be made to their miserable matchlocks and swords; and they followed him out to the place of halt. But there were young and inexperienced heads there, who scouted the notion that a dozen of miserable wretches should think of terms at all; and the Rajepoots were told they might go about their business, but their arms they must leave. To this the men objected, urging not only the promise given by Skinner, but their own customs, which made it impossible for them to give up their arms consistently with Rajepoot honour. But their remonstrances were derided, and they were told to "go to the devil," lest worse might befall them. The poor fellows begged hard. They declared they would rather die—that they could not return dishonoured to their families; and that giving up their arms did in fact dishonour them. They even took grass, and, putting it in their mouths,* prostrated themselves, and entreated the British commander to adhere to his agreement. Unhappily, all was in vain; the commander's councillors grew indignant, and again ordered them to be gone, and their arms to be taken from them. But Skinner, who had heard all this with deep mortification, knowing the people well, now stepped forward,—"No," he said; "these people have come in on the faith of my pledge, and you have no right to dishonour me. If you don't like the terms, put them where they were—send them back to their fort, and make better if you can."

"Well, then," said the thoughtless young men, "do so; let them go back, and see if they will gain by it—what can they do?" "You will soon see that," replied Skinner; "there will be blood before long." Unfortunately, the commander permitted

* A Hindoo custom, expressive of the most humble submission.

45

them to return; and the men, their faces instantly brightening up, went back to the fort, exclaiming contemptuously, when they entered it— "Khoob! toomhara lushker lao!" "It is well! Now bring on your army!"

A party of twenty men was accordingly told off, and, headed by one of the young men, went on at quick time to the storm. The Rajepoots made not a movement until the party was close to the wall, when every one taking deliberate aim brought down just as many men killed or wounded as they themselves numbered—and amongst the rest lay the young officer. The party, thus disabled, retreated; and, being reinforced, advanced again. Again the Rajepoots gave their fire with equal effect, and then, throwing down their matchlocks and drawing their swords, quietly awaited the assault. They neither barricaded the gateway, nor attempted to defend it; but, the moment the party entered, they fell furiously upon them, careless of themselves, and, cutting to right and left, killed and wounded numbers,— nor did they desist until all of them lay dead upon the place. The commander, alarmed or curious, now brought up more troops, who, on entering, found the inside of the little fort thickly strewed with their own people, among whom lay the thirteen Rajepoots, all dead and covered with wounds. Thus a piece of headstrong and cruel folly cost not only the life of these brave fellows, but to their own people a loss of three or four times that number.

Such gallantry and self-devotion is not confined to Rajepootanah. There is no more faithful servant or brave soldier than a respectable Mussulman. The annals of the empire afford proof of this; and it is to Oude, Rohilcund, the Doab, and the Mahomedan provinces east of the Jumna, that we look for a great portion of our Sepoys. Many efficient body of horse have these provinces furnished, and so convinced were the European officers who were intrusted with raising brigades of regular troops, and who well knew that quality, not numbers, gave efficiency to an army, that we find every one, from Sangster down to Perron, including De Boigne, George Thomas, all attaching to their regular brigade a corps of Hindostan and Rohilla horse.

At the battle of Lukhairee, against Holcar, De Boigne, when the fate of the day was endangered by the blowing up of his tumbrils, restored it, not more by the murderous file-firing of his infantry, than the close and irresistible charge of his small troop of cavalry. In like manner, Thomas, when forced to abandon George-Ghur, by the desertion of many of his other troops, found his chosen band of cavalry stick to him to the last. They cut their way with him through Bourguoin's regulars, and the thousands of Sikh and Mahratta horse, and brought him safe to Hansee; and when at length Thomas was forced to yield, they rejected all Perron's offers of service, and some of them, swore they never would serve any other master.

Nor have the British Government found such men less efficient, for many a good corps of irregular horse has been raised and borne their part in lightening the duty of the regular troops. The deficiency, if any, has arisen from such corps being seldom kept long enough embodied, or receiving sufficient encouragement to give them that consistency, and security of service which is essential to the morale of a corps. Without hope of permanent service, the soldier has no stimulus to exertion or self-elevation. Nor is it less essential that the men should know and have confidence in their commander, as well as one another—which can only be the result of long service. It is this, in no small measure, which has made Skinner's horse, the first in India. They were the very men whom Skinner himself had commanded while in Perron's army—his old companions in many a hard-fought day and weary march. Cast adrift by the sudden breaking up of that General's force, they flocked in with delight at the summons of their former and well-loved commander. It was but a return to former habits, former confidence, and dependence; not a man of them but would have risked his life at the least word of his officer; and the result proved the sound judgment of the able general, Lord Lake, who called the corps into being.

They soon were in active service; and during that busy and exciting time, from Lord Lake's first appearance in the Doab to the day when, after annihilating the power of Sindea and Holcar, and reducing every chief in Upper India to such terms as the British Government imposed, the grand army was broken up, and peace was proclaimed throughout the land, never did that most useful corps enjoy a day's repose. First in the advance, it was ever sent ahead to dog the flying enemy, to tell of his whereabouts, to cut off his supplies, or secure provisions for the army; and last in the retreat, its charge was again to watch and check the flying parties that might be hanging on flanks or rear to plunder or intercept supplies.

In the pursuit of Holcar to the centre of the Punjab, in dogging and baffling Ameer Khan and his Pindarees in their daring inroad on Rohilcund, in bringing up convoys, or foraging for supplies, Skinner's horse were always hazir—always indefatigable, no murmuring, no grumbling, not an instance of insubordination ever harassed their officers, or cast a shade upon the corps, and never turned their backs upon an enemy.

It is true that the nature of their service in the British army forbade their being engaged in those desperate and bloody conflicts which many of them had witnessed in the Mahratta service, where large bodies of men were engaged on either side, and the carnage was often dreadful; but on all occasions, when called on to act against the enemy, they acquitted themselves in a manner that called forth the high commendations of their commanders. To those who have seen Colonel Skinner and his 3,000 "yellow boys" exercising on the plains of Hansee, it is unnecessary to enlarge on their fine and soldierlike appearance; we need only mention, generally, that the men were picked from amongst thousands of applicants—for Skinner, at any time, had but to beat his drum, and hang out his colours, to bring a host of old soldiers around him. They were chosen with reference to character as well as to physical qualifications, and a bad man never was long retained. Their horses were all well sized and serviceable animals, fully trained to their work; and there was always a considerable number of bargeers, or household horse, belonging to the officers and the commander, who were picked and confidential men. All were well trained to the exercise of the spear, the matchlock, and the sword, in each of which their leader and his brother excelled; and to see, as the writer has often done, this large body of bold and active men, in their handsome uniforms of yellow tunics, with red turbans, and girdles edged with silver, their black shields and long spears, charging in line, or breaking into divisions, and wheeling and careering in their various evolutions, with equal rapidity and precision—firing and loading, and firing again, all at speed, and seldom missing their mark,—to see all this was truly a spirit stirring sight. And if they wanted something of that exquisite uniformity which is the characteristic of a well-drilled line of regular troops, a candid observer might confess that there was no deficiency of steadiness, or of that sober business-like aspect which vouches for readiness and efficiency. Such was the corps which Skinner was destined hereafter to raise and command.

But at the period when this Memoir commences, the times were as different as his circumstances. India in those days—before the victories of Wellesley and Lake had shed their lustre on the British arms—though broken, as we hare said, into fragments, still retained a gleam of that ancient and peculiar splendour which distinguished it from all other lands, as the court of Dehlee transcended all other courts in riches and magnificence. The Moghul power had fallen, and the glory of its throne had become dim; but it still retained a tone of glowing interest. The long succession of military enterprises which marked the wars between the native princes, and which were only terminated by the British conquests in the north-western provinces, were still fresh in the minds of men; the names of the celebrated actors in these scenes were still, "like household words, familiar in their mouths"; and their actions and history formed the great and most captivating subject of social converse. In all these subjects, Skinner, who in the course of his military career had borne no inconsiderable part in them, was of course well skilled, and his friends may well remember, as the writer does, how admirably, yet unassumingly, he fought over his many fields, and what a fund of anecdote he would pour forth, both of those who had fallen and those who yet survived. It was his joy to assemble a knot of friends at his hospitable home at Dehlee, or at Hansee, the headquarters of his corps, where, for many years after the more active part of his career was past, he lived in a style more suited to his warmth of heart than to his moderate means; and many a pleasant day, and week, and month was spent with "old Secunder," in the pastimes or pursuits which then made India so delightful, and which he so well knew how to promote. The joyous excursions that were made amongst the interesting environs of Dehlee, when pitching our tents amidst ruins that extend for twenty miles around it—now at the noble mausoleum of Hoomayoon, now at the gigantic pillar of the Coutub, or again, amongst the

Cyclopean walls and speaking silence of the old grey city of Toghlucabad, we used to wander and explore day after day, till the evening saw us all gaily seated round our well-spread table, and, hookahs in mouth, enjoying the comforts of excellent fare, and no less pleasant converse,—these were enjoyments which none who partook of them will ever forget. It was at these happy times that the rare and attractive qualities of our host would come freely forth—that his warm-hearted kindness, his devoted friendship, his boundless liberality, and unaffected simplicity, appeared in their full force. In truth, it was singular to see that childlike simplicity united with so sound a judgment and so feeling a heart, with so firm and resolute a mind. Often would the tears start into his eyes, and his voice falter, when listening to some touching story, or some brave or generous act; yet at the call of duty he could be as stern as the occasion required. Few, indeed, on a casual glance at Skinner, would have detected in his round good-humoured countenance the bold soldier of so many fights—the daring leader of the far-famed "yellow boys." In truth, his outward man had but little to attract, beyond the excellent expression of his face, its bright dark eye and beaming smile, for his complexion was very dark, and his figure, though active and athletic, scarcely exceeded in height the middle size. It was at the head of his corps that both face and figure became lighted up with the military ardour which glowed in his heart; at other times his manners were plain and simple, though ever courteous and gentle. Kind and affable to his dependants, he won their attachment and fidelity. Strict, as well as liberal, with his men, they dreaded his displeasure, while they were devoted to his person. Benevolent and charitable to all who required his aid—his left hand, in scripture phrase, often not knowing what his right hand did—he was universally loved and esteemed; and let who will come after him, there is none in the wide countries through which he was known, native or European, who will be longer remembered, and more regretted, than "Old Secunder Sahib." We now commence his history, and in his own words.

Chapter Four
James Skinner in his Own Words

I was born in 1778. My father was a native of Scotland, in the Company's service; my mother was a Rajepootnee, the daughter of a zemindar of the Bojepoor country, who was taken prisoner at the age of fourteen, in a war with Rajah Cheit Sing, I believe near Bejaghur in the Benares district. My father, then an ensign, into whose hands she fell, treated her with great kindness, and she bore him six children—three girls and three boys. The former were all married to gentlemen in the Company's service; my elder brother, David, went to sea; I myself became a soldier; and my younger brother, Robert, followed my example.

In the year 1790, my poor mother died. She could not endure that her two daughters should be forced from her and sent to school. She conceived that by their being taken from her protection, the sanctity of the Purdeh★ was violated, and the Rajepoot honour destroyed; and, apprehensive of their disgracing themselves, from being removed from the care of all their female relatives, contrary to the custom of the Rajepoots, she put herself to death.

After this event, Robert and myself were sent to a charity-school, as my father, being still but a lieutenant, could not afford to pay board for us. In 1794, my father having obtained the rank of captain, we were removed to a boarding-school, and I believe he could then afford to pay thirty rupees a month for each of us. In the beginning of 1796, I was bound apprentice for seven years to a printer, and was sent to the office to learn the business.

★ *That is, the purdeh, or curtain of the harem, which shuts out the females of the family from view of all but their husbands or children. To violate this is to dishonour a female.*

On the first night of my entrance I was kept up till two next morning, daubing the printing blocks with ink, along with several other boys. Next day I was set to learn the alphabet, and the art of putting the letters together in a brass plate. At night I was again sent to the same work as on the previous one. This disgusted me, and I determined to run away and go to sea. On the third night, accordingly, I clambered over the walls of the house, and off I set, with only four annas (eightpence) in my pocket. For six days I made these four annas support me, wandering about the bazars; and at length, when I had no more, I worked with any one who would hire me well. For several days I got my living by carrying loads, or pulling the driller for the native carpenters, at the rate of two annas a day. But while thus supporting myself, I was surprised by a servant of my eldest sister's husband, who laid hands on me and took me to his master. From him I got a great scolding, and was sent to his office and put to copy law papers, for which work I received my daily food. In this way I remained three months, when Colonel Burn,★ who was my godfather, arrived in Calcutta. He called on Mr. T., and, on asking how I was getting on, received from that gentleman a very sorry report,—in fact, he declared I was a good-for-nothing fellow, and not worth my salt. The colonel, after reprimanding me for my idle conduct, asked me what line of life I wished to follow? My answer was,— "That of a soldier or sailor." On this he gave me 300 rupees, and bade me get into a small boat and go up the river to my father at Cawnpore, whither he would soon follow, and get me employment.

Accordingly, a few days afterwards, I started, and arrived at Cawnpore in April 1796, where I found my father. He was glad to see me; and Colonel Burn, who arrived about fifteen days after me, gave me a letter to General De Boigne, who

★ *An officer in the Company's service, who afterwards distinguished himself in the Mahratta war, the siege of Dehlee, &c.; and who always continued to be Skinner's friend.*

commanded the Mahratta army at Coel. I arrived there early
in June, and, having presented my letter of recommendation,
was very kindly received by the General, who gave me an
ensign's appointment on 150 rupees per month, and sent me
to the 2nd brigade at Muttra, then commanded by Colonel
Sutherland, a Scotchman. By him I was posted to a Nujeeb
battalion of matchlocks, under command of Captain Pholman.
At this time Juggoo Bappoo was the Mahratta commander-
in-chief; De Boigne had thirteen battalions under him. I
remained at Muttra several months, during which time
General De Boigne left the Mahratta service, and retiring to
the Company's territory, went home. The command of the
regular troops, at that time in Hindostan, thus devolved upon
Colonel Sutherland; while that of the first brigade, then in the
Dekhan, fell to Captain Perron.

The change which thus took place occasioned the march
of the whole troops at Muttra towards Bundelcund, where
Lukwa Dada, with 20,000 Mahratta horse, and the second
brigade, composed of eight battalions, 300 regular Sowars
(cavalry), 1,000 Rohillas, 600 Mewattees, and fifty pieces of
cannon, had taken the field. We continued six months out
in Bundelcund, reducing several refractory petty Rajahs; and
during this time I saw my first service, being present at two field
battles, and at the taking of five or six forts. This increased my
shouq* (earnest taste) for soldiering; and I made it my study to
become a proficient in all the Hindostanee modes of warfare-
I gave all my time to learning to play the Mahratta spear, to
archery, and the sword exercise on foot: and in a few months
I found the value of these arts. I also laid myself out for getting
acquainted with the native chiefs, and they soon began to take
a liking for me. At this time Captain Perron was promoted
to the rank of a colonel; and received the appointment, from
Dowlut Rao Sindea, of commander of all the regular forces in

* *A very common and very expressive Hindostanee word for "a strong ruling
passion."*

Hindostan. He therefore set off for Muttra, where he arrived on the 1st of February 1797, and was very kindly received by Juggoo Bappoo, the Mahratta commander.

Chapter Five
The Affair of the Bhyes

The next portion of Colonel Skinner's narrative relates to an event which, without some explanation, might be unintelligible to those unacquainted with Mahratta history; and which raised a storm against Dowlut Rao Sindea that threatened to ruin him.

When Madhajee Sindea died, he left three widows; one of whom, Bhagirthee Bhye, was young and beautiful. Dowlut Rao, at that time the acknowledged heir and adopted son of his uncle, promised to make ample provision for these ladies. They accordingly continued to reside in his camp: but no steps were taken to ensure them a permanent establishment, and soon they found some of their ordinary comforts circumscribed.

Still no complaint appears to have escaped them: when suddenly it was discovered, or alleged at least, by the elder widows, that a criminal intercourse subsisted between Sindea and the youngest,—an atrocity which they denounced with the utmost abhorrence; and declared that they could no longer regard as a son a person whom they deemed guilty of an incestuous crime. An officer, lately entered into Sindea's service, named Shirzee Rao Ghatkey*—an active and bold intriguer— attempted to interfere; but the ladies denied him admittance into their presence: upon which the miscreant, having forced the enclosure of their tents, seized, flogged, and barbarously degraded them. The Shenwee Brahmins,—who held the principal offices under the government of Madhajee, and many of whom were connected by relationship, as well as by caste, with the ladies,—indignant and disgusted, espoused the cause of the two Bhyes; and after much dissension it was agreed that

---

This man, whose character and name is held in utter detestation, had a daughter very handsome, for whom Sineda convinced a passion so strong that he made her his wife, greatly to the disgust of his family and court, as Shirzee, or Surjee Rao, was neither respectable by birth nor character. This however, gave hime a great influence over Sindea, which he made use of for the worst purposes.

they should proceed to take up their abode at Boorhanpoor, where they were to be provided with a suitable establishment, and funds for its support.

They accordingly departed from Poona; but, instead of taking them to Boorhanpoor, their escort was directed to place them in confinement at Admednuggur. This treachery being immediately discovered by their adherents in camp, they had scarcely reached Korygaom, on the Beema, when Moozuffur Khan, a Patan officer, in the interest of the Shenwee Brahmins, who commanded a choice body of Hindostanee horse in Sindea's service, suddenly assailed the escort, rescued the ladies, and brought them back to the neighbourhood of Sindea's camp. Sindea did not dare attempt to punish this daring act, from dread of the possible consequences, which might have subjected him to disgrace and odium throughout the whole Mahratta country. But, yielding at length to the evil counsels of Ghatkey, that officer received permission to act against them. Moozuffur Khan, being informed of this, withdrew the ladies to the camp of the Peishwah's brother, Amrut Rao, who instantly afforded them his protection: and the Khan no sooner had deposited his charge in safety than he turned upon Ghatkey, who had pursued them, routed his party, and returned in triumph to the camp of Amrut Rao.

On the 7th of June, Sindea sent five battalions of regular infantry, under a French officer, Du Prat, to surprise the camp of Amrut Rao, and carry off the Bhyes; but he failed, and was driven back with loss. Negotiations ensued: a suitable provision and place of residence were again promised to the Bhyes; and Amrut Rao, not doubting Sindea's sincerity, took up his ground at the Kirkee bridge, near Poonah. No sooner, however, had he thus been thrown off his guard, than Ghatkey, taking with him Mr. Drugeon, a French officer, with two brigades of infantry, came, on pretence of preserving order, during the Mahomedan festival of the Mohumum, and suddenly opening a fire from twenty-five guns on the unsuspecting troops of Amrut Rao, advanced, charged, and dispersed them, and totally pillaged their camp.

This insulting outrage threatened an open war between the Peishwah and Dowlut Rao Sindea. Kassee Rao Holcar, glad of the opportunity of dealing a blow to his rival, took part with the Peishwah; who immediately concluded an offensive and defensive alliance with the Nizam, with whom he had previously been at war. Sindea, now seriously alarmed, requested the mediation of the British Government, which had previously been rejected. Colonel Palmer accordingly endeavoured to bring round an accommodation; but the Bhyes, supported by their party, now strengthened by the Peishwah himself, became so extravagant in their demands that nothing-could be done. Both princes now endeavoured to enter into negotiations with Tippoo, the Sultan of Mysore; but the events which now came thickly on tended, of themselves, to bring about a reconciliation between these two important chieftains of the Mahratta nation. The English, having resolved on war with Tippoo, concluded a treaty with the Nizam, and endeavoured to do the same with the Mahrattas. But the Peishwah, especially, was of too jealous a disposition, and too narrow a mind, to take any such decided step; and even the fall of Tippoo, which so soon took place, tended but to give birth to a deeper scheme of deception on their part,—a system which terminated in their own disgrace and ultimate ruin. Another circumstance contributed, for the time at least, towards an apparent reconciliation between the Peishwah and Sindea. Ghatkey, the person whose insolence had been the cause of the rupture, having continued his excesses to a height which looks like madness, and evinced a decided contempt for his master's authority, was seized and disgraced.★ This was regarded as a concession to the wounded honour of the Peishwah's family. But the effect of the treatment of the Bhyes upon the affairs of Sindea himself continued to be seriously damaging. After the treacherous attack upon Amrut Rao's camp, they had fled to the Rajah of Kolapore, who then was at variance with the Peishwah; and there they were joined by Narrain Rao Bukhshee and the principal Shenwee Brahmins from Sindea's camp, of whom Lukwa Dada, a favourite and able officer of that prince's, was one of the most important. Large bodies of horse

---

★ *Even this act of justice and policy was only effected by a surprise—in fact by a stratagem; a proof of the power of the minister, and the weakness of his master. It was not till more than ten years afterwards, that, in resisting a second attempt to arrest him, he was speared by one of the officers sent on that duty,—an act, probably, very grateful to Sindea, who felt great remorse for the crimes he had been led to commit by the counsels of this monster.*

flocked to them, and soon there was not a village of Sindea's—from the Kishtna to the Godavery—which was not plundered or attacked; and himself insulted, even in his lines.

Sindea attempted in vain to oppose them; his horse were inferior; and no sooner had the regular battalions, sent to repress their attacks, returned to their camp, than the insurgents faced about and followed them. The whole of the Peishwah's territory was swarming with predatory horsemen, and exhibited a scene of utter anarchy. The flame spread to Hindostan: Luckwa Dada, being deprived of power and dismissed from office, was driven to the ranks of the insurgents; where, raising a powerful army, he repeatedly defeated the troops sent against him, and reduced all the country from Oojein to Seronje. It is at this juncture that Skinner, then, by his own good conduct, having been entrusted with the charge of a battalion, takes up the story of this insurrection.

Skinner's memoir continues:

The Bhyes, had come to Kotah, with several respectable chieftains of his uncle's, the Old 'Pateill'* (Madhajee Sindea). They mustered 20,000 horse, and about fifteen Mahratta battalions, and twenty pieces of cannon. Luckwa Dada, who was at Karoulee, near Agra, with about 5,000 horse, left Juggo Bappo, and joined the Bhyes. A large force was ordered to assemble at Gwalior, to oppose this army of the Bhyes, under command of Ambajee Engliah. Captain Butterfield was ordered from our brigade with two battalions, one of which was under my command, and ten pieces of cannon. We joined Ambajee at Parie, twenty côs west of Gwalior, and found there a brigade, under command of a native in that chief's service, named Colonel Kaleb allee; four battalions, under Kootub Khan, in the same service, and about 15,000 Mahratta horse, under Ambajee's son, called Bhow.

One force thus consisted of about 15,000 horse, fourteen

* Madhajee, who was too politic to publish his aspirations after empire, would never allow himself to be called anything than Pateil, or Poteel, which signifies the chief of a village or district.

58

battalions of infantry, and thirty pieces of cannon. We marched to Kotah under the command of Bhow, and overtook the Bhyes army at a place called Chaundkhoree, south-west of Kotah. "We came up with the enemy in the morning. Luckwah, my old master, was made commander of all the Bhyes forces, and the whole of our line was commanded by Bhow. The troops faced each other at three p.m.; and, soon after, a tremendous cannonade began. About five, our whole line was ordered to advance, but we soon found that the whole brunt of the battle was to fall on our two battalions, and that both Kaleb allee and Kootub Khan had an understanding with the enemy.

After fighting for two hours, we learned that both these traitors had joined; and, as soon as Bhow perceived it, he galloped up to Captain Butterfield, and directed him to retire and throw himself on the bank of a small river, about a mile in our rear. We commenced retiring by wings, in carrying which point we lost a great many men, but succeeded in effecting our object. Captain Butterfield then directed us to get the men under cover, for the whole of the enemy's guns were now directed on us, and several charges were made by the Bhyes troops, all of which we managed to repulse, our men being staunch, and our cavalry behaving well.

At seven p.m. Bhow came to us, and a council of war was held, when all agreed to retreat to a fort called Shairghur, about eight côs in our rear. Our loss in the two battalions was about 500 men killed and wounded, out of 1,600. What our cavalry had suffered we could not learn, but report said that their loss must have amounted to 2,000 or 3,000 men; three chiefs of note were killed among them, and one or two more wounded.

We commenced retreating about ten p.m., leaving all our wounded and nearly all our baggage behind us. We had to go through the pass of Shairghur, a côs and a half in length; and this we did not reach till twelve at night, as our gun-carriages were so much shattered that we could move but very slowly. On coming to the pass, I was ordered to remain behind, with two companies and a six-pounder, until the line had cleared the pass. This I accordingly did; and, about two in the morning began to hear the enemy's drums. By this time the line had got well on through the pass, and I commenced retreating. But I had scarcely gone a mile, when one of the wheels of our gun, which had been much shattered by the enemy's shot, broke down, and it took us an hour to determine what was to be done with the gun. We at length resolved to leave the tumbrils, and with their bullocks to drag on the gun. With this view we threw away the other wheel also, and resumed our retreat.

By this time the enemy's van had come up, and there was nothing left but to abandon the gun, or stand like good soldiers and die defending it. The cry was "not to leave the gun," so I immediately ordered it to be charged with grape, and then for all to remain quiet until the enemy should come to the charge. The pass was narrow, being not above 200 yards broad, and very steep on both sides. The enemy thinking we had retired, their van, composed I think of about 500 men, came up within a hundred yards of us, when we gave them the round of grape and a volley of small arms. We then rushed out upon them, sword in hand, took three stand of colours, and destroyed a great number. They retired in great confusion, and we came back to our gun; then blowing up our tumbril, we made good our retreat, and joined our detachment under the fort of Shairghur.

Next morning I received great commendation from Captain Butterfield, as well as from Bhow, who likewise gave me a grand khilut (dress of honour); and both made a favourable report of my conduct to Perron. The enemy then began to make their appearance, but we were snug under the walls of our fort, our left flank supported by a fine river called the Goorah Pachor, and our right by the hills.

On the third day the whole of the enemy's army arrived,

and we remained thus for a month looking at each other. Skirmishing took place every day, but never anything of consequence. No sooner had the report of our retreat, and of the treachery of the two infantry officers, reached head-quarters, than Juggoo Bappoo and Ambajee in person resolved to come to our assistance with a large army; but whenever Luckwa Dada heard of the approach of this force, he advised the Bhyes to take shelter at Oodeypore. They wrote to the Rana accordingly, who immediately agreed to give them protection, and advised Luckwa to bring the Bhyes and his army to Chitoorghur, where he would join him with all his Rajepoots. With this advice Luckwa immediately complied, and we were freed from our imprisonment.

Both battalions had suffered so much from casualties, sickness, and desertion, that we had only a thousand men left; so we immediately began to recruit and put our guns in order. Captain Butterfield received a very flattering letter, while I was promoted to the rank of lieutenant, with 200 rupees per month, and we were permitted to refresh ourselves for a month after our fatigues at Shairghur, before recommencing our march against Luckwa.

Ambajee then ordered us to join him at Kotah, which place we reached in fifteen days, and found collected there a large army of every sort of troops. There were about 10,000 horse, and 15,000 infantry, with forty pieces of cannon. Captain Butterfield and I both waited upon Ambajee in our grand khiluts, and the infantry commanders with the natives were put under Captain Butterfield's command. I was made commander of our own two battalions. Colonel Sutherland also with the second brigade, from Muttra, was ordered to join Ambajee at Chittoor, and there we all assembled in the beginning of May.

Luckwa Dada, who was the best Mahratta general of his time, threw himself under the fort of Chittoor Ghur,* having two rivers in his front, and his flanks well defended by hills, which gave him the command of all the country in rear of the fort. His army, with that of the Rajepoots, amounted to about 30,000 horse, of different tribes and castes, besides 20,000 foot and fifty pieces of cannon. Ours now numbered about 20,000 horse, and a regular brigade of infantry, about 8,000 men strong, added to what was with Ambajee.

We encamped in front of Chittoor Ghur, about four côs on the Oodeypore side; and skirmishing and cannonading took place every day, but no attempt was made to cross, as most of the Mahrattas had taken a dislike to Sindea, and had no wish to destroy each other, while at the same time they affected great zeal for his service, and in obeying his orders.

We remained thus for a month; troops pouring in on either side from various quarters: amongst them, George Thomas, a soldier of fortune, who at this time had six battalions and twenty guns, hired himself to Ambajee for a salary of 30,000 or 40,000 rupees per month. As we continued thus harassed day after day, supplies became scarce, and the difficulty of getting forage became inconceivable. Cash also failed, and all fell into arrears. To our brigade five or six months pay was now due; to the Mahrattas, I believe, some years' arrears. Plundering became general, insomuch that, instead of fighting, parties from both sides were daily sent out to plunder the Rajepoot country; and the consequence was, that, in the course of a month, every village for fifty côs around was burned and deserted, the Rajepoots or Ryots taking shelter in their large forts.

One morning, as I was exercising my horse, in full armour, I met Hurjee Sindea, with about 500 chosen horsemen, proceeding towards the river, and, riding up, I asked him where he was going. He replied that he had been ordered to find out a ford, and that as soon as he should have done this

* *The celebrated family stronghold of the Rana of Oodeypore; a hill fortress, said to be impregnable.*

the army would be ordered to attack the enemy. He then asked me if I would go with him, to which I replied that I should be too happy to do so. I asked him in turn whether he had any guides, to which he replied that Ambajee had sent two with him.

Now, Hurjee Sindea was a relative of Dowlut Rao Sindea, and both Ambajee and Luckwa Dada were his enemies, and sought his destruction. And it turned out afterwards that the present expedition was a snare laid for that purpose by these two persons. Luckwa had agreed with Ambajee that if he would send Hurjee out with a small party, on pretence of discovering a ford, or to reconnoitre the enemy's grounds, he, Luckwa, would place a large body of cavalry in ambush to destroy him. The guides who were sent with Hurjee were, in reality, spies, who had been sent by Luckwa to Ambajee to arrange the ambush, and lead their victims into it.

These rascals led us towards the bank of the river under Chittoor, on the left flank of Luckwa's army. When we had come within a thousand yards of the river I espied a single horseman on the bank, who immediately, on seeing us, went down and disappeared. I mentioned this circumstance to Hurjee, next whom I was riding, but he replied that he must be a Pindaree. Scarcely, however, had he said this, when we perceived several horsemen appearing from various parts of the ravines, and in a few minutes they assembled to the number of 1,000 good horsemen, with Balaram, a native chieftain of Luckwa's, at their head.

They instantly charged us, but were repulsed with great loss. This check had an excellent effect, and our men continued quite staunch. Hurjee, who was a noble soldier, called aloud that this was a snare laid for him, but that he put his trust in God, who would assuredly defend him from all his enemies. The men cried out that they were all ready to die for him. He then gave the word for a deliberate and orderly retreat; and we fell back skirmishing for about a côs, when Balaram, heading his men, brought them again to the charge. We repulsed this attack also, but my mare was wounded by a sabre cut, and I received two or three sword blows on the body, from which I was only saved by my armour, Hurjee, who was also in armour, received a spear wound in his right arm. I happened to be close by when this occurred, and cut down the man who speared him. But in this attack we lost some of our best sowars, and one or two Indians of note and courage. We still had two côs between us and our camp, and Balaram had become furious—charging us still on all sides. Our party now began to lose ground, the retreat began to be a flight, the soldiers to be disobedient to orders, and poor Hurjee Sindea to get confused. Balaram himself appeared in our rear, pressing us close, with about seventy or eighty sowars. On seeing this, Hurjee Sindea called aloud to the few who remained close to him, amongst whom I had the good fortune to be, telling them not to run like cowards, but to die like Rajepoots; that he well knew that Balaram, who was leading the party in his rear, and that he never would fly from him. About fifty men turned with him, and with this handful of heroes he made a desperate push, and cut down Balaram himself, while others levelled several of his sowars with the ground; the rest fled on all sides, and we began once more to retreat with coolness. As soon as the rest of our pursuers knew that their chieftain had fallen, they began to draw up, and soon gave over following us. We now had not more than 200 men left, with whom we pursued our way to camp, and reached it unmolested. Had it not been for my armour I should have been cut to pieces this day, but my mare, less fortunate, received several cuts.

When close to camp I made my salaam, and a movement to retire; but Hurjee said, "No, you must come to my tent." I followed accordingly, and we all sat down in the Durbar tent. Hurjee then rose, and embracing me, said, "All those men who fought with me this day were my servants, and did but their duty; but you are my friend, and fought for me as a friend."

He then took a pair of golden bangles, set with diamonds, and put them round my wrists, and presented me with a sword, a shield, and a very fine Dekhinee horse—all of which gratified me very much. I thanked him for his kindness, and declared that, though but a poor soldier, I was as much his servant as I was of Dowlut Rao's. He then gave me betel, as is the custom of the Mahrattas when they permit a soldier to retire, and assured me he never would forget me.

Colonel Sutherland, who had heard the whole circumstance, and also that I had been with Hurjee, now sent for me, and I related to him all that had happened, explained how I had chanced to accompany him, and showed him the present I had received. He blamed me for what had passed, and told me he should report to Perron the circumstance of my accompanying the Mahratta chief without orders. On returning to my tent, it was intimated to me that if I would give the horse I had got, and which was a noble animal, to the colonel, he would say nothing of what had happened, to Perron. To this I replied, that I might give the bangles, but with the sword, the shield, and the horse, I would not part; and though several schemes were had recourse to by Colonel Sutherland, in order to obtain the animal, he did not succeed in depriving me of him. On the other hand, Hurjee himself had written to Perron describing my conduct, and I received direct from that gentleman, in consequence, a letter of thanks—a circumstance which greatly annoyed Colonel Sutherland. But, ere long, the colonel himself was discovered intriguing with the Mahratta chiefs, and Perron discharged him, bestowing his command upon Captain Pholman, who was promoted to be major. About the same time Captain Butterfield also quitted the service.

Whilst we were thus amusing ourselves at Bhittoor, accounts were received that Zemaun Shah, the Affghan, had arrived with a large army to invade Hindostan. This news made the Mahrattas all friends in a few days. Visits passed between Luckwa and Ambajee; and the whole army, combined, marched forth into a fine plain near Nauthdewarra, north of Chittoor. Sindea sent orders for having the Bhyes* conducted to Gwalior by Ambajee, with an escort of 5,000 horse; and, as soon as he was gone, Luckwa Dada was proclaimed commander-in-chief, a measure which pleased all the troops, both Mahrattas and Europeans, for they all knew him to be an able, generous, and excellent soldier.

Luckwa gave orders that the different chiefs should march and join Juggoo Bappoo at Muttra, where all the troops were ordered to assemble. We remained in the rear with the second brigade and 20,000 horse. George Thomas marched towards Hansee, his capital, which had been given him by Appa Kundoo Rao. After all the various parties had left us, we commenced our march towards Muttra, at the rate of five or six côs a day.

When we arrived at Shahpoorah, Zalim Sing, the Kotah Rajah's karinda,† who had accompanied us with two of his battalions, offered Luckwa Dada a large sum if he would take a fort called Jhajeghur, eight côs east of Shahpoorah, and belonging to a Rajepoot chieftain named Kasree Sing, who was always giving annoyance to the Kotah chief. This fort was situated on an immense hill, having under it a large town also well fortified, and with some 5,000 good Rajepoot defenders.

Kasree Sing was related to the Shahpoorah Man, who interested himself much in his behalf,— but not being able to pay more than the Kotah Rajah, we marched against Jhajeghur, and on the second day sat down before it, and encamped about four miles from the town. Kasree Sing was summoned to give up the fort, which being refused, preparations were

---

* Frequent negotiations were entered into with these ladies, but were as often broken off; either by suspicion of treachery on their part, or their own overweening pretension. The affairs of Sindea in Malwah remained in a very uncertain state.

† Agent, factor.

made for attacking the town. Six battalions of our brigade, and 10,000 from the Mahratta and Kotah troops, were ordered to march with a large battering train. Next morning we arrived within a thousand yards of the town, and opened our trenches, without a shot being fired by the enemy.

In the course of twenty-four hours, the batteries of our brigade, consisting of six 18-pounders, four 12-pounders, and two mortars, were reported to Captain Donnelly (an Irishman) as ready. The battalions also had got into cover, and Donnelly reported the same to Luckwa, who was present with the troops. He told us that we must wait a day, as there was some hopes that Kasree Sing would give up the fort. At daybreak, however, next morning, orders were issued to commence the attack; and our batteries opened, as well as the guns of the Mahrattas.

For six hours the enemy let us have it all our own way, without returning a shot, when a ghole* of Rohillas of 800 men, belonging to the Mahrattas, imagining that it was fear that prevented the Rajepoots from firing, pushed on and took possession of a height about a hundred yards distant from the walls of the town. On this, about 100 Rajepoots sallied out, and drove them from the height like so many sheep, with the loss of fifty or sixty men; and the fort opened all its cannon on us, keeping up a very smart fire for about two hours, when they ceased.

Next morning at nine o'clock, the breaches were reported practicable, and a general storm was ordered to take place immediately. The signal, a discharge of five guns from Luckwa's tent, was given about an hour after the orders reached us, and the whole of the troops moved out in six columns. The different points of attack were indicated, and every commanding officer led on his column, Luckwa Dada himself being present, and giving his orders in person; but the Rajepoots only gave us a few rounds from their matchlocks

*Means a body, a troop,—from keeping together.

as soon as we got near the walls, and then retired into the fort. Thus, the taking of the town did not cost much bloodshed, our loss in killed and wounded being only from the matchlock fire, and did not exceed 200 men.

We now commenced regular approaches against the fort. The Mahrattas took the east side, leaving the west to us. It took us fifteen days to get within two hundred yards of the fort, and during that time there were many desperate sallies made by the Rajepoots. They sometimes succeeded in these, at other times got well beaten. The breach having been effected, a general storm was ordered to be made, by about 10,000 men, in four different columns. Our six battalions were formed into two columns, of which one was commanded by Major Pholman, and the other by Captain Donnelly. The Mahrattas were formed, I believe, into four columns, under native commanders. The signal of advance was to be the lighting of a port-fire. This was seen a little before dawn, and we moved out immediately on all sides, under a tremendous fire from the Rajepoots, kept well up from small arms and cannon. When we reached the walls, the breaches were found to be impracticable. We persevered, nevertheless, though at infinite disadvantage. They first rolled large stones down upon us, and then powder-pots, on which were thrown grass and chuppers (large pieces of thatch from houses), which caused much havoc. For two hours we stood this and a heavy fire, and then were forced to retreat, with, great loss. I was wounded in the hand early in the business, while standing under the wall, and protecting myself with my shield against the powder-pots. A matchlock ball passed through the shield and the palm of my right hand, which held it. Captain Donnelly and Lieutenant Exshaw were killed, and Lieutenant Turnbull wounded. Our six battalions lost 1,000 men in killed and wounded, besides our two officers killed, and two wounded. The Mahrattas suffered still more than we did, for the Rajepoots sallied out upon them sword in hand, and drove them back to their trenches, and several chiefs of note were killed. The Rajepoots were believed to have lost only from 300 to 400 men, but we could not ascertain the truth.

For four days after this we remained quiet, just amusing the Rajepoots from our trenches. But, on the evening of the fourth day, a body of 2,000 of them, in two parties, made a sally on the trenches, from which one of the parties succeeded in driving us. But Lieutenant Tickers,* who commanded in one of our trenches, beat them back, and followed them into the fort. When the Mahrattas saw this, a general storm from all quarters took place. The Rajepoots defended themselves like heroes, but they were utterly beaten and cut to pieces, all except Kasree Sing, who, with about 1,000 that remained, took refuge in a small ghuree, or keep, with four bastions, that was in the centre of the large fort. When Luckwa Dada, who was a brave man, came in and saw the carnage, he praised the Rajepoots as noble fellows who ought to be saved, and he ordered Pholman to make any terms he liked with them. Lieutenant Tickers was accordingly sent to treat with them, and the Rajepoots at once said that if Colonel Pholman would give them his word that they should be allowed to march out with their arms, they would give up the ghuree; otherwise, they would blow it up, with all their wives and children, and die, sword in hand, like good Rajepoots.

On this, Pholman ordered a cessation of all hostilities, and, going up to the gate, gave them his word that he would see them and their wives and families, with their arms, safe to Shahpoorah, and promised to leave with them Lieutenant Tickers, as a hostage for the performance of this capitulation. This being accepted by them, Colonel Pholman, next morning, procured hackerees, camels, and bearers, for their baggage and families, and Lieutenant Tickers received orders to escort them, with his battalion, to Shahpoorah; all of which was duly performed.

*Afterwards in Holcar's service, and put to death by him, wishing to quit it on the approach of war with the English.

In this place Luckwa Dada made prize of powder and lead, grain and cannon, to the value of five lakhs of rupees, besides what he received from Zalim Sing for reducing the fortress. It was then given up to him; and we, after a few days' rest, marched for Muttra, assaulting and taking on our way several other Rajepoot forts, and making the owners pay large sums to get them back. The only one among them of consequence, and which gave us trouble, was a fortress called Bujgarrah, in assaulting which we lost 1,000 men.

In July 1797, we arrived at Muttra, where we were very kindly received by both Juggoo Bappoo and Colonel Perron,—both native and European officers of our brigade receiving khiluts, as well as the Mahrattas.

In September, we marched towards Dehlee, to oppose the progress of Zeemaun Shah, who was still at Lahore; and Mahrattas and troops of every description began to pour in from all quarters. We halted at a place called Shairghur, near Horall, half-way to Dehlee, where I believe there were collected of Mahratta horse at least a lakh, with 200 pieces of cannon. Sindea also marched from the Dekhan with an immense army. Colonel Perron directed Major Pedron, at Coel, to raise another brigade with all possible expedition. And the English collected a large army at Anoopsheher, under General Craig.* Had Zeemaun Shah advanced, we had orders to join the English. But after a stay of two months at this place (Horall), news came, that, in consequence of some disturbances in Cabool, the Shah had marched back to his own territories: so we returned to Muttra, and the different armies went to their homes.

The new brigade, raised by Major Pedron, was, however, completed, and the command of it was bestowed on that officer.

* *Afterwards Sir James Craig.*

Chapter Six
Mahrattas & Rajepoots

In January 1798, the Jeypore Rajah, Pertaub Sing, haying refused to pay the tribute he owed to Sindea, Luckwa Dada marched to compel him to return to his allegiance. Luckwa Dada had 20,000 Mahratta horse; our second brigade was ordered from Muttra; General Dudernaig, who had left the service of Mulhar Rao Holcar, and entered that of Sindea, was ordered with his brigade from Rampoorah; four battalions with their guns were sent from Kotah; some infantry and horse from Gwalior; and troops were sent by certain other small Rajahs, tributary to Sindea, according to their ability. The whole met at Mallpoorah, to the south-west of Jeypore, and amounted, at the lowest calculation, to 60,000 horse, 40,000 infantry, and about 150 pieces of cannon, besides 10,000 Ghosains, called Nagas, armed with rockets.

Rajah Pertaub Sing also began to collect his troops to oppose us, and sent his tents, artillery, and brigades, out to Sanganeir. Here we remained a month in camp, vakeels passing backward and forwards continually; and here I was gratified by meeting a number of my old Mahratta friends,—and, amongst the rest, Hurjee Sindea, who gave me every morning regularly a lesson at the Mahratta spear-exercise; in fact, perfecting myself in soldiering was my only pleasure. Luckwa Dada had taken a great liking to me; and I made myself well-known amongst the Mahratta chieftains, whom I found a good, generous-hearted race of men. The Hindostanee officers, and chieftains in their service, on the other hand—such as Moghuls, Pathans, and others of the Mahomedan castes—seemed to me proud, cunning flatterers, and great bullies too. A few Seyeds of note, and some Bopal Pathans, who were respectable, formed the only exceptions to this description in this immense army. But the most abominable race I ever saw were the Rohillas, from Rampore. Arrant cowards, they would rush onwards where they met with no opposition; but whenever checked, they would run like jackalls. The Rajepoots were far the first for cool courage; but they were not active. As for the officers in our regular infantry, we had them of all nations—French, English, Germans, Portuguese, and country born, of English fathers.

Towards the end of March, we heard that the Jeypore Rajah had arrived at his camp at Sanganeir, and his troops assembling daily. The spies reported that there were 50,000 Rajepoot horse— 10,000 of which were Rhattores, commanded by Sewan Sing, the Chela* of the Jhoudpore Rajah, who would not himself join Pertaub Sing, on account of what was regarded by the high caste Rajepoots his disgraceful conduct in giving up Vizier Allee to the English, after promising him protection.† The rest of this cavalry were Kutchawutees, Hurrowtees, and Shekawuttees. The other principal Rajahs followed the Jhoudpore man's example, except the Ooneara Rajah, who was a near relation. There were, besides, about 50,000 regular infantry, and 20,000 irregulars on foot—Rajepoots, Meenas, and Bheels; so there was no saying on which side the victory might light.

In the Rajah's camp a great display was made. He mounted his elephant carriage, and went out to review his troops, and there was a vast firing of small arms, cannon, and rockets, with abundance of salutes; and after his return to camp, great sacrifices were performed, and he distributed some lakhs of rupees in presents to the Brahmins and alms to the poor.

---

* *"Chela" - to be a person who is adopted or admitted into a family on the terms of a dependant relation—a confidential dependant. It sometimes means a disciple.*

† *Vizier Allee, after the rebellion, in which he was defeated, fled to Pertaub Sing, Rajah of Jeypore. And the Rajah, after promising him protection, had him treacherously seized, and delivered up to Colonel Collins, British resident at Sindea's court, in December 1799. This transaction was viewed by all the Rajepoots as a foul stain on his name and nation.*

Next morning he commenced his march towards us, and approached to within twenty côs.

When Luckwa heard of the Rajah's approach he moved the whole army forwards to the bank of a deep but narrow river, near Mallpoorah, and took up a good position, with the river in our front; our army covering an extent of several miles. Next day we were all drawn up, and Luckwa inspected the whole of the troops, and addressed to them the following short speech: — "To regain the old Pateil's turban,* I am resolved to conquer or to die,—hear this, O, ye sons of the brave!" And to this they all replied, with three loud shouts, "May God assist us!"

On the following day a council of war was held; at which all officers in command of brigades, and all chieftains of note, were called to assist. They assembled in Luckwa's tent; and it was there decided on that the army should change ground, and take up a stronger position. This was accordingly done next morning, and our position was as follows:—keeping the river about a mile in our front, we had on our right the range of hills that rise above Mallpoorah; and on our left a strong mud fort: in our rear were several small hills, and also some deserted villages.

The cavalry of both armies now began to see each other, for the Rajah's camp was only ten côs distant. Cattle were carried off and brought in by both parties; and there was plundering on all sides. After many clays of this sort of suspense, the Rajah again made a move, and encamped at five côs distance in our front; and now skirmishing and distant cannonading took place every clay, and Luckwa formed his plan of battle. The attack was to be made in two lines; the first consisting of infantry, the second, a thousand paces in their rear, of cavalry. Each flank was to be supported by 5,000 horse, and chieftains of great trust were appointed to this duty.

* *In a battle with the Rajepoots, on a former occasion, Madhajee Sindea, "being beaten, was forced to fly, and in his flight lost his turban.*

The Rajah's troops now moved, and took up their position in rear of the river, which, by this means, was all we had between us. Next day we advanced, and came within cannon reach. A smart fire was kept up almost all clay by the great guns, and both lines slept for two nights under arms. Luckwa then resolved to strike the first blow, and gave the different commanders of our army their signals of attack. The post these signals were to be given from was a hill in our rear. The first port-fire shown from thence was to be the signal for advancing, with our guns limbered; the second, was to unlimber; and the third, to commence firing.

At four o'clock in the morning we saw the first light, when the army moved off in high order. In half an hour after, the second was seen, and we unlimbered, the lights of the enemy's fires along their line being in view. They had lighted these fires to keep themselves warm, in the belief that we dared not attack; and were completely surprised. Unfortunately, before we saw the third light, our right had reached the enemy's left; and our cavalry, finding them not on the alert, cut in and gave the alarm. In an instant the whole of their line was seen in a blaze, each golundaze, as he awoke, firing off his gun.

By this time we had reached the river, and every commander got his own corps over as best he could. Our brigade crossed, and formed in a column on the opposite bank. Not a single gun was fired from our line until our colonel grave us orders. The enemy's guns were, by this time, only about five hundred yards distant, and the day had dawned, when we received orders to commence firing. Our guns then opened; but after a few rounds the order to advance was given, and on we went. The guns that were before us, about forty in number, we took immediately, with the loss of about one thousand men, killed and wounded; my horse was killed under me.

We now saw Chevalier Dudernaig's brigade, which was on our left, charged by the Rhattores. He received them nobly, but was cut to pieces by them. Out of 8,000 men he had not 200 left.

The writer of this has heard Colonel Skinner describe this event, not in the curt manner in which it is given in his journal, but with all the characteristic energy and spirit which he never failed to infuse into his word-of-mouth descriptions. The Rhattores, more than ten thousand in number, were seen approaching from a distance; the tramp of their immense and compact body rising like thunder above the roar of the battle. They came on first at a slow hand-gallop, which, increased in speed as they approached: the well-served guns of the brigade showered grape upon their dense mass, cutting down hundreds at each discharge; but this had no effect in arresting their progress:—on they came, like a whirlwind, trampling over fifteen hundred of their own body, destroyed by the cannon of the brigade; neither the murderous volleys from the muskets, nor the serried hedge of bayonets, could check or shake them: they poured, like a torrent, on and over the brigade, and rode it fairly down, leaving scarce a vestige of it remaining,—as if the sheer weight of their mass had ground it to pieces. Then, as if they had but met with a slight obstacle, they looked not even behind them at the fallen; but went on, unshaken, and still in their formidable mass, to attack the cavalry of the second line. "These," as Skinner says, "ran like sheep," while the Rhattores pursued them, cutting them down, for several côs.

Skinner continues:

In this charge Captain Paish, and several other officers, were killed; and Dudernaig only escaped by throwing himself amongst the dead. Several other corps of our side, however, succeeded in capturing the enemy's guns. But we now saw the Rajah, on his ambarree* elephant, moving towards our brigade, with 5,000 or 6,000 choice horse. Colonel Pholman, in order to oppose the threatened attack, gave the word for each battalion to form close columns of companies, in rear

* *Bearing the royal pavilion.*

of the right company; which was done in great style. He next ordered columns of battalions to close upon the centre battalion; and this manoeuvre was equally well performed; with our artillery supporting the front of the columns.

The Rajah now approached us within two or three hundred yards, when we gave them a salvo, which brought his elephant down. The horse twice attempted to charge us, but were beaten off with great slaughter. On this, the Rajah mounted his horse, and retired, and was seen no more. The horse went off along with him.

We now could see something of the effect of our attacks. In the various points, some were gaining and some losing, and hundreds of loose horses were running all over the field of battle; but it was soon seen that victory was inclining towards our side. The enemy's infantry was everywhere defeated, but their cavalry seemed still disposed to make furious attacks on all sides; and we were ordered to throw ourselves into squares of brigades, to resist them. For my part having lost my horse early, I remounted myself, by catching one of the loose ones of the enemy.

About nine o'clock the field began to clear. Our brigade had taken forty guns and thirty stand of colours from their infantry. The Rajah's cavalry, not knowing what had become of him,* had retired to their camp to look for him. The field was ours; but the Rhattores had not yet returned from their chase. They had licked the whole Mahratta cavalry, and driven them several côs; and in a few hours we saw their dust, and

---

* *The Rajah, having fled from the field, never halted till he reached Jeypore, whither, however, the news of his defeat and rout had preceded him. It is said that when he reached his own zenanah, his mother, a woman of far more courage than he, and better fitted for a sovereign in troublous times, was sitting prepared to receive him, while a female attendant was preparing food for her in an adjoining apartment. It is the custom with the Rajepoots, that, of whatever substance the dishes they eat from he made, the food, while being prepared, is stirred with a spoon made of iron. As the Rajah entered, the noise of this spoon against the sides of the dish was heard, on which the lady called out, "Ai!" (such a one) "be quiet! Here is the Rajah, and you know he cannot bear the sound of steel!"*

found they were returning in a gole, nokarahs★ beating victory. When they came closer, and saw their colours flying in our lines, they took us for the Jeypoor infantry; but they soon found out their mistake, by receiving a discharge of grape from thirty pieces of cannon, which brought many of them to the ground. Twice they charged us; and, though each time repulsed, several broke into our squares, and were bayoneted there. A Rhattore sowar attacked me in the square, and shot my horse, and I only escaped him myself by getting under a tumbril. The acts of these Rhattores, and the cool intrepidity they showed in the square, surpasses all that I can say in their praise. At last they extricated themselves, and the survivors retired towards their camp.

About noon, running camels brought intelligence that the Rajah, and all the troops that had escaped from the battle, had retreated towards Jeypore. The three hundred cavalry attached to our brigade were ordered to go on, and collect information. With them I volunteered, and was permitted to go. On reaching the enemy's camp, I found the news correct,—it was utterly abandoned; and accordingly I instantly sent word of this back to Colonel Pholman. I marched into the encampment; it was the largest and best I had ever seen, but totally deserted. Here were most beautiful tents, and large bazaars, filled with everything imaginable, but not a man to be seen. My three hundred sowars dispersed, and went to plunder; and I myself, with two of them, went on, and reached the Rajah's wooden bungalow, the most beautiful thing I ever saw— all covered with embroidery and crimson velvet. I entered, and saw nothing but gold and silver. In opening one of the Rajah's poojah baskets,† I found two golden idols, with diamond eyes, which I immediately secured in my bosom, for fear they should be discovered. I found also several other trinkets, which I likewise took. But about this time our Mahratta cavalry had also returned, and in an hour or two the whole encampment was full of them. In coming

★*Kettle-drums.*

†*That is, containing the images and sacred articles for his private worship.*

77

away I found a brass fish, with two chowrees hanging to it, like moustachios. It attracted my curiosity, and I tied it to my saddle. On my way back I met numbers of Mahratta chieftains going and coming, who all looked at me, and laughed as I passed, for what reason I could not then imagine. I found our brigade had been ordered to move, and lay down our arms near the camp; when half the men were permitted to go and plunder. But meeting a trooper who had been sent by Colonel Pholman to call me, I instantly followed him to that officer's presence. I found him sitting with Luckwa Dada along with several other chiefs, under a large tree; and on my approach to Luckwa, he came up, and ordered me to dismount. I feared that he might have heard some-thing about my prize, which, however, I had secured in my charjameh;* and thinking that he wanted to examine my saddle, I began to excuse myself by saying that I was much fatigued, and would be glad to have some rest. But Luckwa told me that he wished to see me, for I had saved the "Old Pateil's" turban in this day's battle. I thought that by this he meant to say that my battalion had especially distinguished itself in the charges of the Rhattores: but he came closer to me, and Pholman, seeing me confused, perplexed me still more by his laughing. At last Luckwa asked me what it was I had hanging to my horse. I replied, "A brass fish." "Will you give it me?" said he. "By all means," said I, "provided you will demand nothing more of me." "No," said he, "I will not." "Give me your word on that," replied I, and he immediately did so; on which I loosed the fish, and presented it to him.

"Well," said he, "dismount now, and let me embrace you;" and as my orderlies and groom had now come up, I dismounted, and he embraced me. He then explained to me that the fish I had given him was the actual mahee muratib† or imperial

---

*A sort of padded saddle, used by the Mahrattas and other natives.

† The mahee muratib, literally "the fish of dignities," was a standard conferred by the Moghul emperors only on the chiefs of highest rank; and consisted of the image of a fish, as described in the text, with a golden ball: it was equivalent to the three horse-tails of the Turkish empire.

ensign of honour bestowed by the King of Dehlee upon the Rajah.

I then showed to Luckwa the few trinkets I had brought from the Rajah's bungalow, amounting in value to about 2,000 rupees, and offered them to him as a nuzzur: but I took good care to say nothing about the idols. At first he would receive nothing; but, on my pressing him, he did accept of a diamond ring, of the value of about 200 rupees. Luckwa then presented me with a fine embroidered palankeen, an aurenee (a sort of chittah or parasol), besides a grand khilut, and an allowance of forty rupees per month to maintain the bearers.

I expressed my gratitude to him for all his kindness, but observed that, being under Colonel Pholman's command, I could not accept of it without his permission. On which that gentleman immediately gave his consent, and I was dismissed from the Durbar.

Our loss in this battle was about 20,000 men killed and wounded; that of the Rajah must have been greatly more, probably double of ours, for the Mahratta cavalry followed them, killing, plundering, and burning, to the gates of Jeypore. Many chieftains of note were slain on both sides, and amongst those of ours, much to my sorrow, was my worthy friend and protector, Hurjee Sindea, who fell in the charge of the Rhattores. About 150 pieces of cannon were captured by different parties of our troops, and about 100 by the infantry commanded by Europeans.

Next day I carried the palankeen and presented it to Colonel Pholman, who graciously accepted it. My day's plunder and khilut might amount to the value of 15,000 rupees. All our soldiery were enriched by the plunder they obtained. Luckwa ordered all the dead of the enemy to be burned or buried, and gave five rupees to each of the wounded soldiers, whom he also sent to Jeypore. He gave grand khiluts to all the wounded chieftains.

After a stay of fifteen days here, general orders were received from Perron, which were read at the head of our brigade. They bestowed high commendations on the corps, and I found myself promoted to be Captain-lieutenant, with 300 rupees per month; the allowance for my bearers was confirmed; and, more than all, I received a most flattering private letter from Perron himself, with assurances that he would not forget me.

The army now moved to Chaksoo, within twelve côs of Jeypore, where Luckwa Dada reviewed the troops, and thanked them for their good conduct on the clay of the battle. Khiluts were given to all the officers, according to their ranks. In May, Colonel Perron himself joined us with five battalions and his body guard, which consisted of 500 horse, called the khassee risalah (or household horse). And the Rajah of Jeypore was forced to pay up his tribute, amounting to twenty-five lakhs of rupees.

On the 1st of June, the army dispersed to their different quarters. Perron, and the troops he brought with him, remained with our brigade. Invitations were now sent by the Jeypore Rajah to all the European officers, and we accompanied Perron to Jeypore. The Rajah met him about a côs from the city,—between it and the Motee Durgah. The Rajah's sowarree* was very grand and superb. He had twenty elephants, with richly embroidered ambarrehs,† the whole of them mounted by his Sirdars,—he himself riding upon the largest, just in the centre. A hundred golden ensigns, two hundred long-pointed spears, and about a hundred large rockets, with golden flags at the end of their bamboos, were carried running before him in three separate lines. The rear was brought up by 500 chosen Rajepoot horse, and some infantry.

Perron's sowarree consisted of five elephants, his khassee risalah, and all his European officers—about sixteen in number. The meeting took place with fear and mistrust on both sides. Perron, after shaking hands with the Rajah,

---

* *Cavalcade, procession.*
† *Canopied howdahs, generally used by princes.*

was permitted to bring his elephant on that prince's right. The sowarrees mingled together, and all moved towards the town. Two battalions were drawn up near the gate. A salute of twenty-one guns was fired on the Rajah's approach, and, whilst he passed, the troops presented arms. We entered the town, which appeared to my eyes the handsomest I had ever seen: the streets were broad, the houses regular on both sides the streets; the bazaars, with their rich red broadcloth purdahs as a canopy, looked extremely handsome; the town full of inhabitants, who seemed rich and happy. We dismounted at the Hawah Muhul (or palace of the winds*), which was most splendidly furnished and decorated. A rich guddee,† with embroidery and pearls, was placed on a marble throne, on which the Rajah took his seat. Three hundred chieftains, all dressed in yellow jamahs (robes) and large turbans, seated themselves on his right, while we took our places on his left; the people of the Rajah's household took up their stations in the Rajah's rear. The sight was very grand,—the Rajepoot chieftains all leaned on their shields, and had their tulwars (or swords) resting on their right thigh. The Rajah was covered with jewels, as were a great many of his favourite chieftains. It was one of the richest durbars I ever beheld.

The prime minister then rose with Perron, and introduced us one after another, according to our respective ranks. He accepted of our nuzzurs;** and, after a little conversation, he begged of Perron to permit us to retire into his khilut-khanat, to be robed. This being of course granted, we followed the prime minister into a large hall, where we were all handsomely

---

*There are several royal palaces at Jeypore, of which the Hawah Muhul and the Sath Muhuleh (a seven-storied structure, of great size), with fine gardens, are the chief.

† The large flat cushion on which the prince sits. It is equivalent to the word musnud, and signifies "the throne."

** The gift presented by an inferior to a superior, the acceptance of which implies favour and protection on his part, as the presenting it does subservient obedience on that of the inferior.

robed; and having returned to the Durbar, the Rajah rose to receive us. When we had made our salaam, he sat down, and we advanced one by one, according to rank, and presented our second nuzzur, which he also accepted. The Durbar was then dismissed, with the exception of a few favourite chiefs. A grand entertainment, in the true Hindoo style, was prepared for us, to which the Rajah accompanied us.* We had several sorts of liquors, besides strong Hindostanee spirits; and we spent the day very happily, After dinner, several sets of handsome Nautch girls were introduced, who sang and danced well; and, about three p.m., we were called by the Rajah to see some fights between elephants, as well as with tigers and buffaloes. This amused us highly until near sunset, when we received our dismissal, and went back to camp.

We remained at Chaksoo till the end of June, when the Jhoudpore Rajah requested Perron to punish some of his refractory thakoors (chieftains). We accordingly marched to Mairtha, a large town belonging to the Rajah; and in this vicinity we remained until July, reducing several chieftains who would not pay their tribute to the Jhoudpore man.

*To honour them with his presence, not to partake of the feast: as no Hindoo, particularly of so high a rank, would eat with Europeans.

Chapter Seven
War Against Mahrattas & Sikhs

Nothing of consequence occurred until the 15th of August, when news arrived that Sindea, by the advice of Shirzee Rao Ghatkay, his father-in-law, had seized and put to death the following chieftains, who had joined the Bhyes in their insurrection against his authority. Narrain Rao Buxshee, son of Jeea Dada, was blown up by rockets, a new mode of torture invented by Ghatkay; Manajee, Dhallojee, and two others, were blown from the mouths of cannon; and Balloba Pajanevese, Elleet Tantia, and Sewdashea Bhow, had their heads crushed with tent mallets. Jesswunt Rao Huldea, and Bharoo Buchilot, were poisoned. These were all chiefs of Dowlut Rao Sindea's uncle, the "old Pateil," men high in rank and of great ability.

Of lower ranks many more were killed, and others got off by paying every pice they had for their lives. This was the most fatal blow Sindea ever gave his army.

The remaining chiefs of note all dispersed, and flew for shelter wherever they could find it. Luckwa Dada and Juggo Bappoo fled from Muttra, and Perron was made commander-in-chief of all Hindostan. The only friends Sindea now had, were his European officers; his best protectors, the regular brigades in his service.

War broke out on all sides. The various Mahratta soobahs* in Sindea's territory revolted, and refused obedience. Jesswunt Rao Holcar, natural son of Mulhar Rao Holcar, now escaped from prison, began to collect troops, and was joined by many of Sindea's chieftains. There was nothing on every side but confusion and discord, and Perron received orders to raise as many brigades as he could.

On the 15th September, letters arrived from Colonel Pedron, at Coel, to tell that Simboonauth, soobahdar of Seharunpore, had collected about 5,000 Sikh horsemen, 10,000 infantry, and

---

* *Governments, provinces; thus the Soobah of Bengal, of Bahar, &c.*

twenty pieces of cannon, intending to invade our jaidad* for the brigades; and that he had sent Ashreff Beg, an old officer, and held in much respect by the soldiers, in command of three battalions, 1,000 horse, with ten pieces of cannon, and some Rohilla infantry, to oppose the invasion.

General Perron, on hearing this, immediately detached Captain F. L. Smith, with two battalions, to join Ashreff Beg, by forced marches; and he left us on this duty on the 20th, whilst we, with the rest of the troops, marched for Dehlee on the 1st of October, by Futtipore Jhoonjhuo, in the Shekawut country.

Ashreff Beg and his force reached Khandowlee unmolested, when information came that Simboonauth had marched, with the whole of his troops, to attack him. The Beg immediately took up a strong position near Khandowlee, and next morning the Sikhs made their appearance. They tried in vain to decoy the old soldier from his post; but, on the following morning, the whole of the enemy's army having arrived, Simboonauth summoned him to surrender. To this old Ashreff scornfully replied, that buneas (or shopkeepers, of which caste Simboonauth was) had best mind their own business, and not think of threatening soldiers, whose lives were sold as sheep were to the butcher; and that, for his own part, he had come there to die, or to teach him to sell grain.

Simboonauth, enraged at this reply, made an immediate and sharp attack, which Ashreff Beg gallantly repulsed, capturing four or five of the enemy's cannon; but this was not effected without severe loss, for out of his three battalions, which did not number more than 2,000 muskets, he lost 500 men. In the evening he retired into the town; and, on the following morning, the enemy, taking courage from his retreat, came and encamped within two côs of it.

Ashreff Beg now resolved to try the effect of a surprise; so, taking 1,000 infantry and all his horse, he moved out, about three in the morning, and reached their camp a little before dawn. He succeeded completely in surprising them, and took several pieces of cannon, which, however, he could not bring away. The day had broken, however, before he commenced his retreat, and the enemy, recovering from their fright, attacked

Jaidad means territory assigned for the support of troops.

him on all sides. Ashreff Beg then ordered the horse to set off for the town, which they reached with the loss of 100 men; while he threw his infantry into a square, and made good his retreat, with all his cannon, though the Sikhs pressed him hard, and fought nobly. His loss in this gallant affair was about 300 men, but several brave and good native officers were killed, which disheartened him so much that he remained inactive for five days. News then came that Smith had arrived at Boughput, which, had he exerted himself, he ought to have reached sooner, and that Perron, with his whole army, was not far off. These news alarmed Simboonauth, who commenced his retreat to Seharunpore; but Ashreff Beg would not let him off without another attack, and he succeeded in bringing away some guns; after which he was joined by Mahomed Auzim Khan, an officer commanding a battalion in Simboonauth's service, who brought his corps along with him. Captain Smith, having joined Ashreff Beg's force, took the command, and in a few days marched towards Seharunpore, which place Simboonauth had already reached. On Smith's approach, he set off with the Sikhs to the Punjab, but the remaining infantry and guns surrendered to Smith.

On the 1st of November, Perron and his army reached Seekur, and Skinner's brother, Robert, joined him from Berhampore. Perron immediately gave the young man an ensign's commission, and appointed him to his brother's corps. His introduction of their young officer to the men he was now to command was highly characteristic. Calling his most trusty native officers together— fine old fellows, with scarred faces and grizzled beards—steady intrepid soldiers—he drew himself up in military fashion, and pointing to young Skinner, said— "Yeh humara bhaee hye—oosketeen sumbhalo!" — "This is my brother! see that ye be his protectors!" And the veterans, stroking their beards, and carrying their hands to their foreheads, replied, with strong emphasis, "On our heads be it."

Skinner continues:

Nothing of consequence occurred during our march through the Rajepoot country eastward; but when we reached Rewarree, information was received that the killadars of Dehlee and Agra had declared against Sindea. Perron summoned the killadar of Dehlee, who was a Mahratta, but he treated the summons with contempt; on which Perron marched to Dehlee, in the vicinity of which he arrived on the 25th, and encamped at Talkatorah. On the following morning he occupied the ground between Hoomayoon's tomb and Dehlee, and again summoned the killadar to give up the fort.

This being refused, six battalions, with their guns, were next day sent to attack the town, and we marched in at the Dehlee gate without molestation. Perron then, by beat of drum, proclaimed his own authority, and appointed his own officers over the different departments. On the 29th our guns were opened against the fort, and the fire from them and from small arms lasted all day. Our trenches, too, were opened both at the Dehlee and Toorkoman gates. On the 2nd December the killadar came to terms, and was, at the Shah's request, permitted to go off with his private property. Captain Drugeon, a French officer, was then appointed killadar, and Shajee, a native, the soobahdar.

On the 15th, we marched for Kurnaul, to bring the Sikhs into order, who were assembling in a large body to overrun the Doab; and on the 1st of January 1799 we arrived there. Perron then summoned all the Sikh chieftains between the Jumna and the Sutlege, of which the chief were Sahib Sing of Pattialah, Bunjah Sing of Tanessur, Goordial Sing of Ladooah, Bhycoll Sing of Kythul, Bhaug Sing of Jheend, and many other petty ones. At first they all made a show of resistance, and for this purpose they assembled at Pattialah, and Perron began to recruit for cavalry at Kurnaul. Goolshair Khan, the nawab of Kunjepoorah, then joined us, and several other Mussulman chiefs of note raised their standards in aid of Perron against the Sikhs, so that about the 20th of February we had mustered 10,000 horse, and marched to Tanessur. Bunjah Sing retired on our approach, and joined the main body at Pattialah; but, on the 10th of March, a treaty was entered into, and ratified, with all the Sikhs, which terminated the business amicably.

By the 1st of April, till which time the army remained at Tanessur, all the Sikh chieftains had paid their visits to Perron; and on the 2nd we marched towards Dehlee. About the 10th we reached Paneeput, where the Begum Sumeroo joined us, with four battalions; and on our way to Dehlee we chastised some large villages for refusing to pay their rents to Perron's collectors. Among these was Naweltha, which lies about seven côs west of Paneeput. In the end of April we encamped at Deetaram-ka-Serai, from whence the Begum was ordered to return home to Seidhannah.

Colonel Pedron had by this time completed the third brigade, and a number of officers were taken into the service and posted to it. Captain Smith was also moved from our brigade. Perron retired with the cavalry to his head-quarters at Coel; and the fortress of Alleeghur was ordered to be put in complete repair, and garrisoned with 2,000 Bhadawar Rajepoots. Our brigade (the second) was sent, under the command of Colonel Pholman, to Muttra, where we arrived on the 1st of the month.

At this time Sindea, who lived in fear of the Mahrattas, left Poonah, on his way to Hindostan. When he reached Asseerghur he detached Colonel Hessing's brigade in advance, meaning soon to follow; but by the end of July, when Hessing had reached Oojeine, the Nerbudda rose, and Sindea was obliged to remain during the rains at Asseerghur. In the mean time, Jesswunt Rao Holcar, who had raised a large army, both infantry and horse, surrounded Hessing and his brigade, and cut it to pieces. He fought gallantly for ten or fifteen days, but no succour arriving, he and all his troops fell victims to Holcar's rage and cruelty.* In this sad affair sixteen

---

* Before attacking Hessing, Holcar had cut off a smaller detachment, under Captain MacIntyre, which laid down their arms to him at a place called Neuree. He afterwards attacked Sindea's grand park of artillery, escorted by Captain Brownrigg, with four battalions; but that officer, hearing of Holcar's approach, took up a strong position, and beat him off with great loss.

country-born officers, who were all my school-fellows, were killed at their guns. They all had entered the service within a month of each other. Among them were Captain-lieutenant MacPherson, son of Captain MacPherson of the Company's service; Lieutenant Graham, whose father was an ensign in the same; Lieutenants Montague, Davis, and Arcote. Hessing was the only European that escaped. Major Dareebdoon, a half Frenchman, was wounded and made prisoner; and old John Hessing paid 30,000 to 40,000 rupees to get him out of Holcar's hands.

On the 1st of August, Perron came to Muttra to punish Ackajee,* the Mahratta killadar, at Agra; and, on the 20th, we laid siege to the fort of that city. Ackajee defended it well for two months, and we lost a great number of men; but at length we were obliged to blow up a bastion on the river-side near the town, and when this had been levelled, and Ackajee informed that not a man should be spared if he did not give up the fort, he kabooled (acquiesced) and surrendered it, stipulating for being allowed to retire to Gwalior with his private property. Our loss in this siege was about 1,000 men in killed and wounded.

Perron returned to Alleeghur about the 10th of November, and I was sent with three battalions, a battering train, and 500 horse, to attack a fort near the Chumbul river, belonging to a Rajepoot thakoor, called Ram Paul Sing. The rest of the brigade marched back to Muttra, and Colonel Sutherland, forgiven by the interest of his father-in-law, Colonel John Hessing, was sent to command the first brigade with Sindea.

I arrived with my detachment before the fort of Ram Paul Sing on the 15th November, reconnoitred it forthwith, and next day prepared to attack it. It was a little mud fort, so level with the crest of the glacis that there was no touching the bastions with our guns. On the 20th, I opened our trenches,

* There seems a mistake in this name, probably it was Abajee.

and advanced by regular approaches to the glacis. From thence I ordered a mine to be carried on under it, because the guns could not bear upon the rounee (counterscarp). By the 5th of December the mines were loaded; and, on the morning of the 6th, the whole of the three battalions were ordered into the trenches, ready to storm, in three columns. At ten A. M., after a smart cannonading of four hours, the mines were sprung, and so well did they work that the whole of the glacis was thrown into the ditch. Immediately after, the troops moved out with scaling-ladders, and placed them, but Ram Paul, with his 300 Rajepoots, defended the walls so well that the storming party was beaten back.

I gave the men an hour's rest, and then, at noon, the parties moved again, and carried the place with great difficulty, the whole of the brave garrison being put to the sword. Only Ram Paul and a few more were taken prisoners alive, but all were severely wounded. Our loss was 200 men killed, and about 100 more wounded. My brother, who was with me, was wounded through the neck by a matchlock ball. I sent him with the wounded to Agra, but Ram Paul and his comrades were sent to Alleeghur.*

Having reported the whole affair to Major Pholman, two of the battalions, with the horse and battering guns, were ordered to join the brigade at Muttra; while I, with my battalion, was directed to join the Karowlee Rajah, to the south of Agra, which I did in the end of December. It appeared that the Karowlee Rajah had fallen out with the Ooneara Rajah, whose territory lies near Tonk-Rampoorah, and had hired several battalions belonging to native chieftains, and my battalion from Perron, to fight his battles. Our force amounted to six battalions, and about 2,000 horse, but very bad; and fifteen pieces of cannon, besides the five 6-pounders belonging to my battalion.

* This serves as another illustration of Rajepoot resolution and sense of honour, which will yield to no odds, and prefers dying sword in hand.

On the 1st January 1800, the Rajah reached the Bunas river, near Tonke. I sent my spies to the Ooneara Rajah's camp, pitched about two côs from his capital, and discovered that he had about 3,000 Rajepoot horse and 3,000 infantry, belonging to his relative, the Jeypore Rajah, with about twenty pieces of cannon. He moved to a spot five côs distant from us, and there encamped, keeping the Bunas river between us.

The business, however, began to wear a bad aspect; for not only was the Karowlee man a coward, but he had not cash to pay us regularly, and the battalions he had hired grew dissatisfied, and teased him every day for money. I now began to be uneasy about the fate of my own corps, and reported to Colonel Pholman that no dependence was to be placed on the troops which the Rajah had hired, so that he would require to reinforce me immediately, as otherwise the battalion must be cut to pieces.

The Ooneara Rajah soon became aware of the badness of our troops, and, crossing the river on the 25th of January, took up a good position about six miles in our front, from whence he began to correspond with the native commandants of the battalions with us. I informed our chieftain of this, but I could not convince him of the treachery of the native commanders. On the 31st, the Ooneara Rajah moved in battle array to attack us, and we drew out to meet him in one line, with cavalry on the flanks. About nine a.m. the armies came in sight of each other, and at eleven the cannonading commenced. After a few rounds, the whole of the infantry on our side silenced their guns. The Ooneara cavalry charged the Karowlee cavalry on the left, and immediately our infantry went over and joined the enemy.

As soon as I perceived this, I commenced retreating to a deserted village in our rear, which I gained with difficulty. Two of the enemy's battalions came up to attack me, but I charged and drove them back. I now saw the whole of his cavalry and infantry moving towards us; and, as I had no hopes of succour,

I resolved to retreat, if possible, to Tonke, which was about four côs distant, and belonged to Sindea.

I called together all my native officers, and asked them what they thought of my plan, which was to defend the village till night should come on, and then retreat to Tonke. They said that it would be impossible to stand out in the village against the force and cannon that were coming against us; and that it would be better to commence the retreat immediately, and try to gain the ravines, which were about two côs distant, before the main body should come up, and cut the Karowlee man's cavalry to pieces. I agreed to this proposition accordingly, and moved out, resolved to die or make good my retreat.

The two battalions of the enemy that were near me had been joined by the Rajah himself, with about 1,000 horse, who charged me several times as I commenced to retreat. I repulsed them, but with the loss of one gun, which broke down, and of my own horse mortally wounded, though it still kept on; but the remainder of their battalions now coming fast up, I found further progress impossible, and drew up in a fine plain to receive them. Here I made a short speech to the men: I told them we were trying to avoid a thing which none could escape—that was death; that come it would, and, as such was the case, it became us to meet it, and die like soldiers.

Thus resolved, we allowed the enemy to come within fifty yards, when we gave them a volley, and charged. Those in our front gave way, and we captured their guns. As those on the flanks, however, now galled us with their cannon, I threw myself into a square, and sought to gain the ravines, now only about half a côs from us. But fate had decided against us. They pressed us so close on all sides, that my men began to lose their coolness; we were charged too, and lost three more of our guns. Still, with the one left I kept moving on, and got clear of the enemy's infantry, who had got a little sickened, and showed less disposition to chase; but the cavalry kept on charging, and my men giving up very fast.

I still had some 300 good soldiers and my gun left, but a party of horse pressed us so hard, that I moved out with 100 men and stopped them; but when I looked back, I found only ten had followed me—the rest had turned back and joined the gun. As I was going to follow them, a horseman galloped up, matchlock in hand, and shot me through the groin, I fell, and became insensible immediately; and, after my fall, the poor remains of my brave but unfortunate fellows met the same fate. I do not believe that fifty men out of the 1,000 escaped from the field untouched.

It was about three in the afternoon when I fell, and I did not regain my senses till sunrise next morning. When I came to myself, I soon remembered what had happened, for several other wounded soldiers were lying near me. My pantaloons were the only rag that had been left me, and I crawled under a bush to shelter myself from the sun. Two more of my battalion crept near me;—the one a soobahdar, that had his leg shot off below the knee; the other, a jemadar had a spear wound through his body. We were now dying of thirst, but not a soul was to be seen; and in this state we remained the whole day, praying for death. But alas! night came on, but neither death nor assistance. The moon was full and clear, and about midnight it was very cold. So dreadful did this night appear to me, that I swore, if I survived, to have nothing more to do with soldiering,—the wounded on all sides crying out for water—the jackalls tearing the dead, and coming nearer and nearer to see if we were ready for them; we only kept them off by throwing stones, and making noises. Thus passed this long and horrible night.

Next morning we spied a man and an old woman, who came to us with a basket and a pot of water; and to every wounded man she gave a piece of joaree bread, from the basket, and a drink from her water-pot. To us she gave the same, and I thanked Heaven and her. But the soobahdar was a high caste Rajepoot; and, as this woman was a Chumar (or of the lowest caste), he would receive neither water nor bread from her. I tried to persuade him to take it, that he might live; but he said that in our state, with but a few hours more to linger, what was a little more or less suffering to us—why should he give up his faith for such an object? no, he preferred to die unpolluted.

I asked the woman where she lived, and she gave me the name of her village, which was about two côs from Tonke, and a côs and a half from where we lay. About three in the afternoon, a chieftain of the Ooneara Rajah's, with 100 horsemen, and coolees and beeldars,* arrived on the ground with orders to bury the dead, and to send the wounded into camp. The poor soobahdar now got water, of which he was in the utmost need—indeed, nearly dead for want of it. When we were brought to camp, we found a large two-poled tent pitched, in which all the wounded of my battalion were collected, and, to the best of my recollection, they amounted now to 300 men. No sooner was I brought in, than they all called out, "Ah, here is our dear captain!" and some offered me bread, and some water, or what they had. The chieftain had wrapped me in a large chudder (sheet) when he took me up; and right glad was I to find so many of my brave fellows near me.

My wound was now dressed by the native doctors, and the ball taken out. They soon sent the Rajah word of my arrival, and he sent for me immediately. His tent was close by, and they carried me thither upon my charpaee (low bedstead). The Rajah got up when I entered and made my salaam, and sending for a morah (stool), he sat down by me, asked my name, who I was, and what rank I held. I replied that I was a soldier, and now his prisoner. He then sent me back to my tent, saying that I required rest, and gave me much praise for my conduct in the day of battle.

No sooner had I reached my tent, than a chobedar came, on the Rajah's part, and presented me with 500 rupees, and

* *Porters and pioneers.*

a tray of cooked meats for dinner. Of the first I gave the chobedar 100 rupees as a present; the other 400, with the victual, 'I divided amongst my men. As for myself, the surgeon gave me a good dose of opium, which procured me a fine night's rest. Next morning the Rajah pitched a small tent for me, and wanted to remove me from the men, but I begged he would permit me to stay with them; on which he came himself, and sat talking to me for an hour of different things, and sent me food from his own kitchen, and was kind and generous to all the wounded.

We remained ten days with him in camp, after which he sent us all into his capital of Oonearah, where we were lodged in a large pucka house (that is, built of stone and lime). In a few days he followed, and visited us every day, and allowed me to write to Perron, stipulating for my letter being in Persian. We remained with him a month, when he sent us all to Bhurtpore, presenting me with a grand khilut, including a horse, a shield, and a sword; and giving ten rupees to each of the men, with more in proportion to the native officers. I am glad to say that my friend the soobahdar was also fast recovering.*

"We reached Bhurtpore on the 15th of March, and after remaining there five days, we went to Muttra, and joined our brigade there. Perron, who was there, came immediately to see me: he gave us all high commendation for our conduct, and promoted every man that was able to do duty; on the rest he settled pensions. To me he gave the command of his own body-guard, which consisted of two battalions, the 1st and 2nd, called by his own name. Here, too, I met my brother, who had perfectly recovered of his wound, and who had been promoted to the rank of lieutenant, with the command of a battalion in the 2nd brigade under Colonel Pholman, at

* The generous conduct of the Oonearah Rajah, one of the least of the Rajepoot princes, cannot fail of striking the reader, especially as contrasted with that of Holcar. and some of the native chiefs: it breathes of, and illustrates that generous and chivalrous spirit which of old was the toast and the attribute of the Rajepoot tribes.

94

that time in the Jeypore country. By him I sent a thousand rupees to the good and humane Chumar woman who had first assisted us, and who I called my mother.

I had now almost recovered, and went to join the body-guard at Alleeghur. Perron's conduct to me continued most kind and generous; but the two battalions of his body-guard were soon after drafted into the 3rd brigade, under Colonel Pedron, as all his force was now required for another service. In the beginning of August, this brigade was ordered to Gwalior, to join Ambajee, who had received orders to assemble all his troops to attack my poor old master, Luckwa Dada. Luckwa, after the slaughter of so many chieftains, who had taken part with the Bhyes, was convinced that Sindea would work his destruction also; so, in junction with Juggoo Bappoo, and others of that party (the Shenwee Brahmins), he raised troops, and resolved to resist. He had now collected a large army at Duttea, in Bundelcund, and was joined by the Rajah of that place, a man of note in that country.

Ambajee (Inglia) had collected at Gwalior about 20,000 horse, and three brigades of regular infantry; one being commanded by Colonel Sheppard, one by a native, Colonel Caleb allee, and ours by Colonel Pedron, But not liking to proceed against Luckwa, with whom he had been on friendly terms, he was delaying from day to day to march, in spite of repeated orders to that effect from Sindea: at length, however, being threatened by that prince with sequestration of his whole country, in case of further demurring, he placed the whole army under the command of his brother Bala-rao, and we marched on the 15th of October.

We arrived, at length, at a large town, called Baja Ghur, fifteen côs east of Soundah, a strong fortress on the banks of the Sone river, belonging to the Rajah of Duttea; under the walls of which Luckwa and the Rajah, with their combined forces, were encamped. It was reported that these amounted to 10,000 Bundelah troops, infantry and cavalry, with two regular brigades, one of which was commanded by Colonel Toone,* an Irishman, the other by a native Rajah, Buroor Sing; and 15,000 Mahratta horse. Here we remained encamped for a month; our chief not being inclined to move till Perron himself marched from Alleeghur, with five battalions of the fourth brigade, and 5,000 regular Hindostanee horse. He reached us about the 20th of December, by which time we had crossed the river, and encamped about ten côs distant from Luckwa's position.

Skirmishing now took place every day, but nothing of consequence occurred; till, at last, Perron determined upon making an attack. Luckwa's position was a strong one, having Soundah and the river in his rear, ravines extending for five côs in his front, and his flanks supported by ravines and two strong forts. Through these ravines there were but three passages, all well defended by Luckwa's infantry and guns.

Perron formed his infantry into three columns. The right consisted of our brigade, under command of Colonel Pedron; the second, or centre, of Sheppard's brigade, commanded by Colonel Sheppard; and the left, of the five battalions of the fourth brigade and the regular horse, under Captain Syme. We moved on the morning of the 5th of January 1801, and took up our ground in front of the enemy; each column severally having to attack one of the three passages so well defended by Luckwa. At dawn on the 6th, we were ordered to attack. Colonel Toone's brigade happened to be opposed to our column, and he defended his pass with great bravery: we carried it, however, though with great difficulty, making prisoners of Colonel Toone himself, Captain Evans, and several other officers.

Colonel Sheppard attacked Rajah Burar Sing, and succeeded also, with difficulty; but Captain Syme, who had to deal with the Duttea troops, was beaten back, with great slaughter.

* *Probably Tone, who published an account of the Mahrattas, and was brother of the well-known Wolfe Tone.*

Perron, on hearing this, galloped up, and placing himself at the head of the column, led them on with great bravery and coolness, and beat back the Duttea troops in their turn. Our brigade (third) took sixteen suns belonging to Colonel Toone's force; our loss on the occasion being two officers killed, one wounded, and about 1,000 men killed and wounded. Captain Sheppard had three European officers killed and one wounded, and about 1,500 men killed and wounded. The third column lost Captain Syme and Lieutenant Arnold, killed, and Lieutenant Paish wounded. The fifth battalion lost half their men, and had it not been for General Perron's prompt and gallant assistance, the whole would have been cut up. Perron himself was slightly wounded by a spear.

Poor Luckwa Dada's fate was more severe. Both the Duttea Rajah and Rajah Burar Sing were killed, himself severely wounded, every gun he had taken, in number thirty-five, his whole army destroyed and dispersed, and both his and the Rajah's camp totally plundered. He himself took shelter in the fort, while we returned in triumph to camp with Colonel Toone and his officers. On the 7th, in the evening, General Perron visited Colonel Toone, and behaved very kindly both to him and to his officers, supplying them with handsome camp equipage, such as tents, camels, and horses. To the Colonel he offered service, but that gentleman declined it; and Perron permitted him and his officers to retire to Mundoosore, the capital of Holcar, furnishing him, as I understood, with 10,000 rupees for their expenses. Luckwa, with a few horsemen, fled to Bettoor, where he soon died of his wounds. On the 15th of March we arrived again at Alleeghur, and went into cantonments.

Chapter Eight
Holcar & Thomas

General Perron had now succeeded in bringing all Hindostan under subjection; and every rajah and soobah, from the Nerbudda to the Sutlej, regarded him as lord and master. He had now under his command four regular brigades, of 8,000 effective men each, and 10,000 regular Hindostanee horse, besides the command of all the troops of every Rajah and chief in that wide territory. He now began to feel his power and to change his manner. Instead of being, as formerly, a good, plain, honest soldier, beloved by the soldiery and esteemed by all about him, he. began to turn his ear to flattery, and to neglect merit, while his favourites got all the good appointments, and he himself thought only of amassing money. All the Mahratta chiefs began to hate him, and to lay plots for his ruin. They even entered into correspondence with the English authorities for this purpose, for they had all taken a great aversion to the regular troops, who they thought had much supplanted them in the favour of their master. Yet even the interests of this generous master began to be neglected by Perron, in spite of all he owed to him. His allowances were indeed enormous. Besides his stated pay of 15,000 rupees a month, as commander-in-chief, his table expenses were allowed him; and for his khassa risaleh, or household troop of 800 horse, he drew pay at the rate of forty rupees each per month. Then from the Jaidad collection he had five per cent; and on every mamleh, or settlement he made with the independent Rajahs, he exacted twenty-five per cent; so that, upon the lowest calculation, of the natives he drew about 50,000 to 60,000 rupees per month: and so puffed up was he with his riches and power, that he allowed himself to be persuaded by his flatterers to send an ambassador to Buonaparte. Monsieur Desoutee was the person despatched, but the purport or result of his embassy was never known.

It became, at all events, his policy or his pleasure to give the preference in his choice of officers to his own countrymen over all others, and this to such an extent as not only to disgust the

Mahrattas, but to excite the jealousy of the English and country-borns against them. But this was not the only error committed by Perron about this period. Besides his own brigades, Sindea had several others in his employ, of whose commanders Perron became extremely jealous. Of these, the first was commanded by Major Brownrigg; an Irishman, a very brave and able commander, who was much liked by the soldiery, and high in Sindea's favour at Oojeine, in consequence of his successes against Holcar. Another was commanded by Colonel Hessing, Feloze,* Mecule, and Babtiste†, had each of them another, besides two or three more commanded by natives. Most of these commanders returned this jealousy, and the Europeans, in this respect, had become as bad as the Mahrattas. To add to the critical situation of Perron, he was hated by Surjee Rao Ghattkey, Sindea's father-in-law, who ruled all his son-in-law's councils, and who sought the General's ruin. All these jealousies and intrigues had a lamentable effect upon the interests of Sindea. The Mahrattas became quite disunited and changed. No longer held in dread of the Moghuls and Patans in Hindostan, they began to fall like them. Gopaul Rao Bhow, a chief of great name, of sixty years of age—a Mahratta of the old school —and who had been made commander-in-chief with Sindea at Oojeine, made a striking remark as to this degeneracy in open durbar, on the occasion of Sindea's desiring him to build cantonments at Oojeine:— "Our fathers," said he, "the first founders of the Mahratta power, made their houses on the backs of their horses; gradually the house came to be made of cloth; and now you are making it of mud; take care— and mark my words—take care that in a very short time it don't all turn to mud, and is never rebuilt." The flatterers called him a fool for this, and Sindea laughed at him, and said, "Who is there that dare oppose me, as long as I have my infantry and my guns?" On which Gopaul and Jadoo Rao both replied, — "Beware, it is those very infantry and these guns which will be your ruin."

Sindea, indeed, seemed as mad as the rest, for he now took to kite-flying, nautching, and drinking, with all the other worst native vices; and Perron, feeling himself master of Hindostan,

*Fidele Filoze was an Italian, well known for his treacherous seizure of Nana Furnavese.

†This is probably Jean or Gian Battiste Filoze, son of the former, called by the natives John Butteejs.

99

paid little regard to his master's orders. The Peishwah, at Poonah, was quite as bad as Sindea. The Nagpore Rajah did not seem much inclined to move in any way; and of all the Mahratta chiefs, Holcar was the only man of enterprise remaining in the Dekhan; nor did he lose the opportunity afforded him by circumstances of laying a good foundation for future power. But as this chief played so considerable a part in the struggles of this eventful period, it may tend to elucidate the narrative to the general reader if we describe, in a few words, the history of his rise, and the position he held at this time in Central India.

Mulhar Rao Holcar, the founder of the family greatness, was descended from a tribe of shepherds, and was born about the year 1693. He was the rival of the great Madhajee Sindea, with whom he for several years disputed the ascendency in Hindostan. He had but one son, Khundee Rao, who fell in the great battle of Paneeput, and who married that Ahalia Bhye, afterwards so well known in Malwah. This prince had also but one son, who succeeded his grandfather, Mulhar Rao, but who, fortunately, lived a very short time, as he proved not only wicked and cruel, but deficient in intellect. On his death, Ahalia Bhye claimed and maintained the right of succession to the government in her own person; and she proved so wise, so amiable, and benevolent a princess, that all her subjects rejoiced under her rule, and adored her as an avatar of the Deity when she died.

On her accession, she raised a sillahdar, Tookojee Holcar, of the same tribe, but no relation of the family, to the station of commander-in-chief to the forces,—a duty she could not herself discharge. She even acknowledged him as son and successor to her dignity; and that chief very ably executed his trust, and played a conspicuous part in the contests which continually agitated the Dekhan, particularly with the family of Sindea. He left two legitimate and two illegitimate sons. Cassee Rao, the elder of the former, was weak in intellect and deformed in body: Mulhar Rao, the younger, was brave and aspiring. A contest took place between them for the supremacy; and the elder applied to Sindea's minister, Sirjee Rao Ghatkia, for assistance,—a fatal measure, which, after some insidious negotiations, terminated in the treacherous murder of Mulhar Rao, and the plunder and dispersion of both the camps by Sindea's troops.

Jesswunt Rao, the elder of the illegitimate sons, fled from the place, and, after being for some time a fugitive, found refuge at Dhar, a small Rajepoot state, where he was joined by some old adherents of the family. He now became a professed freebooter, directing his enter-prizes as much as possible against the country of Sindea, the hereditary enemy of his house, and in whose hands the imbecile Cassee Rao had remained a passive instrument against its interests. His younger brother, Ettojee, had worse luck in his lawless career; for, having been taken by the Peishwah in arms, that prince had him relentlessly trampled to death by elephants, looking on from a balcony all the time,—an outrage which Jesswunt Rao never forgot or forgave.

About the year 1798 he made overtures to Ameer Khan, another freebooter, who afterwards became but too well known throughout Hindostan, and who at that time was at Bopal with 1,500 followers on foot. The negotiation led to an alliance, which continued till Jesswunt's death. His enterprizes now became more important, and we soon find him plundering many towns and districts on the Nerbudda, belonging to Sindea; and even destroying a strong detachment of the brigade commanded by the Chevalier Dudernaig, at that time in the service of Cassee Rao. These successes, combined with the utter inefficiency of Cassee Rao himself, induced not only Dudernaig and his battalions, but other parties of troops in the same service, to come over and join the more energetic commander; so that before the year was well out in which he had fled from Poona, Jesswunt found himself at the head of a powerful force, and the recognised guardian of Khundee Rao, son of the murdered Mulhar Rao, in the eyes of all the adherents of the family, in Central India.

In conjunction with Ameer Khan, his predatory enterprizes continued, and Saugor, Bersiah, Seronje, Shujahalpore, and many other towns and districts, belonging both to the Peishwah and to Sindea, were sacked and destroyed with the most relentless barbarity, before the latter could well look about him or collect an army to protect his country. That prince did, however, now exert himself, and advanced his brigades to meet his enemy: but Holcar, who had now collected from 60,000 to 70,000 men, including Ameer Khan's force and that of other Pindarree chiefs, attacked a detachment of eight battalions and twenty guns, under Hessing and MacIntyre, and (as we have already learned), notwithstanding the obstinate and gallant resistance of these officers, and the unmanageable description of his own force, he almost utterly annihilated them.

But this success was far more than balanced by his subsequent defeat at Indore, where he lost all his cannon (ninety-eight pieces), with his camp and stores, and saw his whole army destroyed and dispersed. Had Sindea followed up this blow, Holcar must have been annihilated; but believing his ancient rival quite humbled, he left him quietly at the fortress of Sarem, whither he had fled for refuge; and even entered into negotiations, having for their object the recognition of Holcar as guardian of the family interest, upon certain conditions. But into these, whether sincere or otherwise, Jesswunt Rao would not enter; and time having been given him to recover and recruit, he resumed his life of plunder and aggression, and his camp soon became filled with the rude freebooters and reckless adventurers with which Hindostan and Central India at that time swarmed, afterwards so well known as Pindarrees. He told them plainly that he now had no means of paying them regularly, but he would, at all events, lead them to abundant plunder—and this was all they required.

In 1801 he appears to have been again joined by his infantry brigades, though Dudernaig had quitted his service for that of Sindea; raid thus strengthened, he continued to levy his contributions,—sometimes in Rajepootanah and on the banks of the Chumbul, at others in Malwah and the banks of the Nerbudda,—sometimes checked, and forced to retreat, at others gathering strength. and vigorously pursuing his predatory course, but always marking his track with blood, and cruelty, and desolation.

At length he attacked Candeish, and proceeded towards Poona, with the usual exercise of atrocities and outrage. But the alarm occasioned by his progress aroused Sindea once more, and he detached a force, under Sewdasheo Bhow Bhaskur, to aid the Peishwah. Their combined forces, after some negotiation and a minor affair or two, gave battle to Holcar, on the 25th of October 1802, Holcar had succeeded in mustering fourteen battalions of regular infantry, six being under command of Colonel Vickers, four under that of Major Harding, and four under Major Armstrong. Besides these, he had 5,000 irregular infantry, and 25,000 horse. Sindea had ten battalions, six being commanded by native officers, with no Europeans, and four, though of De Boigne's old troops, had only four Europeans to lead them.

A momentary success at the beginning of the engagement seemed to incline the fortunes of the day in favour of the combined army: but the energy of Holcar, and the steady gallantry of Vickers, Harding, and Armstrong, which the inferiorly commanded battalions of Sindea could not resist, turned the tide, and secured to Holcar a complete victory;— guns, baggage, and stores all fell into his hands, and the army of his rival was utterly driven from the field. The conqueror behaved on this occasion—no doubt from motives of policy— with unwonted moderation. Poona, was left unplundered, entirely by his exertions in controlling his unruly troops; and he affected to desire an amicable arrangement with the Peishwah,—a disposition which certainly was by no means sincere, for, as we have already observed, he never could forgive that prince the savage murder of his brother, Ettojee. The mask was soon thrown aside, and Bajee Rao, the Peishwah, having fled from Poona, and ultimately to Bassein, Holcar took up Amrut Rao, the adopted son of the former Peishwah, and put him in charge of the government of Poona. Enormities of all kinds were committed by these confederates, in order to obtain the funds required for paying their armies and retaining their adherents: and so miserable was the condition of all Malwah and Rajepootanah at this time, and indeed from the year 1800 to 1818 inclusive, from the excesses of the numerous bands of robbers, called Pindarrees, who ranged over these countries as if they were their common prey, and of the no-less ferocious chiefs and princes who disputed for power upon their soil, that the greater portion of them was utterly ruined and depopulated;* and the natives have given to that period the expressive appellation of the "gurdee-ka-wukht," that is, "the time of troubles."

---

* So reduced was the actual number of human beings, and so utterly cowed their spirit, that the few villages that did continue to exist at great intervals, had scarcely any communication with one another; and so great was the increase of beasts of prey, and so great the terror they inspired, that the little communication that remained was often actually cut off by a single tiger known to haunt the road.

But at this time the Treaty of Bassein took place; and the interference of the British authorities in favour of the oppressed and more peaceable parties gave a new turn to affairs, the results of which are well known, and which terminated in the gradual re-establishment of quiet and comparative prosperity in this long-vexed portion of India.

But there is another personage,—one of the many European adventurers born of the disjointed and troublesome times,—who at this period had risen into considerable importance, and who makes a prominent figure in the immediately-succeeding portion of the Memoir, — this was George Thomas.

George Thomas was a native of Tipperary, in Ireland, and came first to India as a quartermaster, or, as some say, a common sailor in a British man-of-war, in 1781-2. But, tired of the sea, and, like many other adventurers, tempted by the prospect held out to soldiers of fortune in India, he left his ship, and took service amongst the Polygars in southern India, Here lie remained some years; but probably finding little temptation to continue among such a people, he turned his steps to the north, and actually travelled through the centre of India to Dehlee. At that place he received from the Begum Sumroo a commission in her army, and soon obtained great influence over her, by successfully opposing the incursions of the Sikhs, insomuch that he became her principal adviser, and married a slave-girl whom she had adopted.

His influence, however, did not last, for in the course of six or seven years he found himself supplanted by the intrigues of a rival; and about the year 1792 he quitted the service of the Begum, and betook himself to Anoopsheher, then the frontier station of the British army. But it was to the native powers, and not to the British authorities, that he looked for employment; and after a while overtures were made to him by Appa Khunde Rao, a Mahratta chief of distinction, but at that time in disgrace with Sindea, and who was raising troops upon his own account. Thomas joined this chief with 250 tried and chosen horsemen,—an accession of force which, at the time, was very valuable to the Mahratta.

Appa Khunde Rao, who appears to have aimed at independence, directed Thomas to raise a battalion of 1,000 foot and 100 cavalry, for which he assigned him certain pergunnahs in Jaedad, situated in the county of Mewatt, south-west of Dehlee, but at that time in a state of total insubordination; so that Thomas, as soon as he could raise troops, had to go and reduce his Jaedad to order. He reached Thajara, a principal village in the centre of the country, on a dark and rainy night, after a weary march, and the inhabitants gave him a characteristic welcome, in the shape of a specimen of their skill as thieves: for they stole a horse and some things from the very centre of his camp.

This led to an attack upon the village next day, which proved rather disastrous, as his troops, seized with a panic, ran away, leaving their wounded to be cut in pieces by the enemy. The energetic courage of Thomas, in recovering a nine-pounder which had stuck in a nullah, and then using it with admirable effect upon the advancing villagers, saved his remaining troops, 300 in number; and with this small party he still offered battle to the enemy, who, however, declined it; nay, such was the effect of the gallantry displayed by Thomas in this action upon them, that an amicable adjustment was come to, by which they not only restored the stolen articles, but agreed to pay him a year's rent. The impression, thus made rendered the general settlement of the country a far more easy matter; and the burning of one or two refractory villages convinced the rest that opposition to such a power was vain, so that they agreed to pay up all arrears.

But, from the reduction of Mewatt, Thomas was shortly after summoned to the assistance of Appa Khunde Rao himself, whose troops, having mutinied, held him a sort of prisoner in the fort of Kotepootelee. Marching instantly, in spite of the heavy rain, he reached that place, and encamped under its walls, from whence he held communication with his master. The result was that Appa, with his family and effects, quietly leaving the place, were received by Thomas, who escorted them safely to the fortress of Kanounde. For this service Appa adopted his deliverer as his son, made him handsome presents, authorized him to increase his troops by 200 foot and the same of horse, and added to his Jaedad the four pergunnahs of Jygur, Byree, Mandote, and Phatoda, worth 150,000 rupees a year.

It would be tedious to detail the strange and unaccountable system of intrigue which Appa practised against Thomas, in spite of the unwearied course of good service in which the latter persevered, with a constancy almost as unintelligible as the persecution of his capricious master, and which he maintained till the death of that chief. Frequently did he find his liberty or his life treacherously attempted; and yet still did he adhere to the fortunes of his first employer, and even transferred his allegiance to his son and successor, Wamun Rao, a person of less talent, and even less principle, than his father: and thus did Thomas's life become one series of petty contests and escapes from open or secret attempts to destroy him. But his military fame increased, and the name he had acquired enabled him to gather so much head as to give rise to the extraordinary project which he appears about this time (1798) to have first entertained—namely, that of establishing for himself an independent principality in the country.

As a singular proof of the estimation in which Thomas was held, we may mention that the Begum Soomroo, his first mistress, who had often joined in intrigues against him, having been made prisoner in her own palace, knowing his valour and generosity, wrote entreating him to come to her assistance,— nor did she plead in vain. Thomas, receiving permission from Ambajee Englia, in whose employ he was, and bribing Bappoojee Sindea to march to her assistance, came upon and made the usurper prisoner, and sent him bound to Dehlee, and replaced the Begum in her own place,—and very ungratefully did she requite the obligation.

Pursuing his object of establishing an independent principality, he fixed upon the country or district of Humana, which from its peculiar position and nature, as well as the disturbed character of the times, had hitherto fallen a presto every invader or adventurer of the age, yet could hardly be said to belong to any, and which therefore appeared best suited to his purpose.

In accordance with these views, having recruited his army and replenished his stores, he marched and commenced the enterprize by attacking the town and fort of Kanhoree, whose inhabitants were notorious thieves. His first attack was unsuccessful, being repulsed with the loss of 300 men; and the rains having come on and put an end to active operations, he turned the siege into a blockade, in which he suffered much from sallies of the enemy. On one of these occasions he had a very narrow escape, being deserted by his men in a redoubt that was the object of the enemy's attack. The weather improving, however, his batteries were erected and worked with such effect that the garrison evacuated the place in the night. This being the stronghold of the country, he soon gained possession of the southern part of it; but it was much longer ere he was enabled to establish his authority so far north as the river Caggur.

Here, then, Mr. Thomas fixed himself, selecting for his capital the town of Hansi, ninety miles west of Dehlee, it being nearly in the centre of his newly-acquired domain. He rebuilt the walls and repaired the fortifications,—encouraged inhabitants to come and fill its depopulated streets,—established a mint, and coined his own money, —collected workmen and artificers of all sorts,— cast his own artillery, made matchlocks and muskets, gunpowder, and all the munitions of war: and made every effort possible for fixing himself permanently in his possessions, and for succeeding in what had for some time become his favourite, though unproclaimed object, namely, attempting the conquest of the Punjab, and, as he himself expresses it, "having the honour of planting the British Standard on the banks of the Attock."

The comparative smallness and uncertainty of Mr. Thomas's resources, however, forced him to have recourse to measures which he would gladly have avoided, but which were quite in the spirit of the times and country. He subsisted his troops upon the pillage of other countries; and though generally successful, he was occasionally involved in situations of difficulty and danger, from which it required all his ability and constitutional intrepidity to extricate himself. Once, in particular, he permitted himself against his own judgment to join with Wamun Rao in an expedition against the Jeypore territory, when the Rajah came upon their party with a large army; and, though defeated by the astonishing bravery and address of Mr. Thomas, he forced the invaders to retreat with severe loss. By a better regulated system of predatory warfare, however, the Rajah was at length forced into the payment of a regular "black mail," to purchase immunity and quiet for his country.

After a series of successful expeditions against Bikanere, and the Sikhs to the south of the Sutlege, Thomas joined his troops to those of Ambajee Englia, and was employed against Luckwa Dada, who at this time was in arms against Sindea. On the march he gave a striking proof of his intrepid coolness and presence of mind, in quelling a mutiny among his troops, by personally seizing the leaders, and having one of them blown from a gun. But his engagement with Ambajee was soon brought to a close by a series of the same sort of unaccountable intrigue as had disgusted him with his first Mahratta employers; and he therefore left their army, and retired to his own territories about the end of 1799.

Of the subsequent enterprises of Thomas against Bikanere, Bhutnere, and the Sikhs of Pattialah, and other desert states, we shall only remark that they were constantly recurring, generally with success upon his part; and that he returned some time in 1800 to his own country, after a very various, active, and severe campaign, which he thus himself describes: —

"Thus ended a campaign of seven months, in which I had been more successful than I could possibly have expected when I first took the field with a force consisting of 5,000 men, and thirty-six pieces of cannon. I lost—in killed, wounded, and disabled—nearly one-third of my force; but the enemy lost 5,000 persons of all descriptions. I realized nearly 200,000 rupees, exclusive of the pay of my army, and was to receive an additional lakh for the hostages which were delivered up. I explored the country, formed alliances, and was, in short, dictator in all the countries belonging to the Sikhs south of the river Sutlege."

However he was overshadowed by the displeasure of Sindea, and his commander-in-chief, Perron, who saw with uneasiness the progress of a stranger and adventurer, in the midst of their territories, towards independent power. They had repeatedly offered him service, and invited him to act as commander of his private forces against their common enemies. But this Mr. Thomas had as constantly refused to do,—averring, that, as to serving with Perron, the natural enmity existing between an Englishman and a Frenchman would always prevent that cordiality of co-operation so necessary to insure success. But he added, that if Sindea should choose to bestow upon him a separate command in the Dekhan, Hindostan, or the Punjab, he would willingly undertake it as soon as arrangements for payment of the troops should be completed.

Such offers and replies led at length to a more definite correspondence, and a negotiation, which, as it was conducted by Perron, was not likely to be favourable to Thomas's interests. But Sindea, with Holcar still in the field, was unwilling to engage in another contest, and therefore sought to temporize. An interview was at length agreed upon between Perron and Thomas, to take place at Bahadurghur. They met accordingly in September 1801, but with something of mutual distrust. Captain Felix Smith, of Perron's brigades, was sent to conduct Mr. Thomas to the Mahratta camp; and he came accompanied by two choice battalions and 300 cavalry.

But Perron's conditions soon brought matters to an issue. He proposed that Thomas should give up entirely his jaedad of Jyjur, and receive in lieu of it 50,000 rupees per month for payment of his battalions, and consider himself from thenceforth as the servant of Sindea. This, which was but a repetition of offers which he had repeatedly declined before, excited Mr. Thomas's indignation; and, in order to avert further and more hostile discussion — perhaps even some attempt at treachery— he broke up the conference at once, and withdrew in disgust.

It appears extraordinary that the usually clear judgment of Mr. Thomas should not perceive that by such conduct he was throwing away the only rational chance remaining to him of realizing with greater certainty a high station as a soldier, than he could ever rationally hope to do by his own unaided resources, against the jealous enmity of the most potent princes in Hindostan—for it had been his fortune to be opposed to them all, and to have incurred their implacable displeasure. But visions of glory and supreme power appear to have blinded him, and possibly he may still have calculated something on the fickleness of purpose and strong international jealousies of the native powers. However that might be, all hopes of peace had vanished for the present, and Mr. Thomas returned to his own country to make preparations for resisting the storm which was about to burst upon him; while Perron, on his side, made arrangements for securing his destruction—with what result, Skinner's narrative, to which, after this somewhat long digression, we now return, will show.

Chapter Nine
Fighting George Thomas

Skinner continues:

George Thomas, to whom Appa Khundoo Rao had given Humana,* had repaired the fort of Hansee; and having raised eight battalions of infantry, with forty pieces of cannon, 1,000 Rohillas, and about 500 Sowars, he began to dart out with these troops, sometimes into the Bikanere country, sometimes into Jeypore, till, having accumulated some lakhs, he determined to attack the Sikhs and take their country from them. He marched as far as the Sutlege river, beat them wherever he met them, and made collections from their country; but he could make good no footing, nor could he take any of their large forts. He returned to Hansee, by the way of Sirhind, Kurnaul, and Paneeput. The Sikhs had assembled at Thanessur, and were very near cutting him to pieces; but he made his retreat good by some manoeuvre and false promise. These chieftains then came to Perron, and solicited his assistance in destroying Thomas; and Sindea being referred to on the occasion, issued his orders for Perron to do so, they having agreed to become subsidiary, and having paid him five lakhs of rupees.

Perron, upon this, ordered the 3rd brigade, under Major Louis Bourquoin, and 5,000 regular horse, to proceed to Dehlee; and George Thomas was summoned to that place, to reply to the following proposals:—That he should enter into Sindea's service, with a brigade of the same strength as those of ours—namely, eight battalions, 300 regular horse, 1,000 Rohillas, and 500 Mewattees, with forty pieces of cannon, for which he was to be allowed 60,000 rupees per month, either

* *In this way of putting it, Skinner appears to be in a mistake, as may be seen by the sketch above given of Thomas's history.*

in money or jaedad. He was also to be permitted to keep Hurriana, provided he furnished other five battalions for the service. Should these proposals be rejected, he might prepare himself to fight.

Thomas agreed, and marched from Hansee on the 1st August 1801. Our brigade had arrived at Seetaramka-Serai, four côs west of Dehlee, and there encamped. Perron joined us by dak, and Thomas arrived on the 19th August, and encamped two miles distance in front of us. Several meetings took place between him and Perron, and he dined with us repeatedly, and all seemed to be going on well. We saw his troops, who looked well, but were not over-disciplined: his artillery was very fine, and the bullocks particularly good and strong. The only European officers he had, were Captains Hearsey, Hopkins, and Birch; and there were some Europeans acting as serjeants in his artillery.

About the 25th the treaty was broken off, as Thomas would not agree to send four battalions of his brigade to Oojeine; so he was allowed to march back to his capital at Hansee, and both parties prepared to fight. Perron now sent the 3rd brigade, under Bourquoin, with a large battering train, and two thousand regular Hindostanee horse, to Bahadoorghur, where we encamped; and several Sikh chiefs received orders to assemble there. We remained here till the 10th September, during which time 6,000 Sikh horsemen came and joined us; and Perron went back to Alleeghur by dak. We next marched to Jyjur, within three côs of Georgeghur, a strong fort of Thomas's, where we learned that Thomas himself had marched towards the Sikh country. Three battalions, the battering train, and 100 horse, were now ordered to lay siege to Georgeghur, under command of Captain Smith; while the rest of the army went on to Jheind in pursuit of Thomas. We found, however, that he had moved off towards Futteabad, pretending that he was going to Pattialah. On this we marched in three days from Jheind to Kythull, where, on our arrival, we heard that Thomas had made a forced march and returned to Hansee. Thither we followed, but on the way were informed that he had gone off to Georgeghur. This was 44 côs* from Hansee, and Thomas had made this distance in two days, attacked Smith, and cut up one of his battalions.

It appeared that Smith, on hearing of Thomas being within five côs of him, had raised the siege and commenced his retreat, leaving this one battalion under command of a native, Poorun Sing, a brave old soldier, as a rear-guard. Thomas, with five of his battalions, overtook this single one; and while Smith, with the battering train, gained Jyjur, a fort belonging to us, Poorun Sing drew up his men, and a fierce fight took place. The brave old fellow charged the two first of Thomas's battalions which came up, and drove them off, capturing four pieces of cannon. Thomas himself then headed his five battalions, and came on, but was again repulsed. Unfortunately Poorun Sing was wounded, and fell from his horse, which threw the battalion into confusion; and as Smith, though only two miles distant, would not turn back, they all fell victims, being cut to pieces by Thomas.

Bourquoin had detached Lieutenant Ferdinand Smith, with all the horse, to support his brother, whom he reached in eighteen hours,† though the distance was one hundred côs; and we marched without halting, except two or three hours at a time to refresh the men and cattle, so that we reached Jyjur on the third day. There we halted for one day to rest, and next morning, moved on to Baree, within two côs of Georgeghur. Bourquoin then went to reconnoitre the place, and I accompanied him. We found that Thomas had drawn up in one line, having Georgeghur on his right flank, and a large village, which he had fortified; on his left he had a small

---

* *Fully sixty-six to seventy miles.*

† *There must be some error here, as 150 miles in eighteen hours, with cavalry, is impossible; but it is given as in the original.*

fort, or ghurree, in which he had stationed 1,000 Rohillas and four pieces of cannon. His rear was likewise defended by a large village.

At three p.m. we moved to the attack, in open columns of companies, except two battalions and two eighteen-pounders, with some horse, which were sent to try his rear. Having come within gunshot we formed line, under a heavy cannonade of thirty-five pieces. The cavalry were on our flanks, but took good care to keep out of cannon reach. Our right had come into a line with Thomas's left, when the word was given to wheel into line, and thus we moved to the attack. Both parties fought well, and disputed the day with great courage. About four p.m. we came within musket range, but found that Thomas had thrown up sand-banks★ in his front, which brought our line to a halt. Both musketry and cannon now showered on us like hail, and the men began to fall by hundreds. Two of Thomas's battalions now moved out in columns of companies, under command of Captain Hopkins, a gallant officer. They formed just in front of our left wing, and gave their fire exactly as if they had been at a, review: when all had formed, they gave a volley and came to the charge, which completely succeeded in driving back our left wing. However, our golundauze kept to their guns; and the gallant Hopkins having his leg shot off by one of our six-pounders, whilst advancing at the charge, the battalion gave way as soon as he fell, and ran back, taking their leader along with them. Our left wing then rallied and resumed their position, but the fire was so murderous that our whole line was ordered to sit down; as for Thomas's men, they were sheltered by the sand hillocks in his front.

In this way we remained till night; for neither could Thomas come out to attack us, nor could we attack him. At sunrise we hung out a flag of truce; the firing ceased, and we were allowed to clear the field, which took us till twelve at noon. The flag

★ *This deadened the cannon-shot, so that it buried itself without recochetting.*

was then pulled down, and we retired out of cannon reach. But Thomas was so well sickened that he would not follow up the blow.

This was the severest battle I had ever seen; our troops were nearly equal as to infantry—we had each about 8,000 men. Thomas had thirty-five pieces of cannon, we twenty-eight; the cavalry did not come into play. Our loss in killed and wounded was between 3,000 and 4,000; out of seven European officers we had two killed, namely Lieutenants Smith and McCullough, and two wounded, Captains Oliver and Rabells. Twenty-five of our tumbrils were blown up by the enemy's shot, and fifteen of our guns dismounted. Thomas had about 2,000 killed and wounded, and Captain Hopkins, who died of his wounds. Had Thomas possessed another officer like him, he would have gained the day.

An interesting circumstance occurred after this battle which Skinner does not mention, but which many of his friends have heard him tell with great effect. His brother Robert was likewise in this action, though separated from him at a considerable distance; so that neither brother knew how the other had fared. The cannonade was so fierce and continuous, and the slaughter so great, that all was smoke and carnage, and there was little communication between the different parts of the field. When it ceased, however, a report came to Skinner that his brother had been killed; while a similar one reached Robert, as to James. Both, moved by one impulse, ran to the bloody field, without thinking of refreshment or rest, and sought all over it for the body of their brother; but in the darkness, amongst the thousands of corpses torn and mutilated by the cannon shot, none found what he sought, and after a weary and fruitless search, they each returned to the tent of their commanding officer to make their report. By a singular chance they entered from opposite sides at the same moment, and the first thing that met their eyes was the object on which their thoughts were dwelling. They saw nothing else, and the reader may conceive with what feelings they ran and embraced, calling out each other's names, before the officers that filled the tent.

Skinner here proceeds to criticize the conduct of Thomas, which in truth did not appear consistent with his general decision and gallantry.

"We had always heard, that Thomas was a brave, active, and clever soldier, and an able general; but we were surprised that he now permitted us to remain for fifteen days without attempting to attack us, or to make good his retreat to Hansee, for there was no doubt on our minds that, had he tried either plan, he would have succeeded. The state of our guns, and the spirits of our soldiery, was such, that had Thomas shown any inclination to move towards us, we should have got out of his reach; for our commander, Major Lewis Bourquoin, was not only a coward but a fool. He was one of those who had got on by flattery; and, had it not been for Captain Burnear, a Frenchman, we should certainly have lost the day, for the Major was not seen at all during the battle,—and our being saved from total destruction was entirely owing to the exertions of Captain Burnear, who was a brave and able soldier.

Thomas now gave up all the management to Captain Hearsey, who joined him a few days after the battle, and to his native officers, while he himself took to drinking. These officers, instead of inducing him to retreat to his capital, began to fortify his camp, and gave out that some refractory Mahrattas were coming to their assistance. Reinforcements now began to join us from various quarters. Colonel Pedron came with five battalions of the 4th brigade, two battalions were sent by the Begum Sumroo, and Perron sent five battalions from Hessing's brigade, at Agra; and horsemen to the amount of 5,000 also came to join the force, so that Thomas was completely surrounded.

Skirmishes now took place every day, but he was always thrashed back into his lines. Supplies and forage began to get scarce; his soldiers became dissatisfied, and began to desert. One of his chieftains, named Shitaub Khan, who commanded the fort of Georgeghur, was enticed over by Pedron, and informed us that the troops, having been for two days without grain, were living on sheep and bullocks; so that Thomas must either give in at once, or make a start with his horse to Hansee. On this, Pedron immediately hoisted a flag, and proclaimed that all soldiers taking refuge under it should get quarter. About 200 came over that day, and we were ordered to get within cannon reach, and to keep on the alert at night.

About nine at night on the 10th November, Thomas, with 300 of his brave horsemen, made a dart through the five battalions commanded by Colonel Hessing; and, although the whole of the cavalry was sent in pursuit, he made good his escape to Hansee from Georgeghur, about sixty miles, in fourteen hours. All his guns and camp were taken, and his soldiers having laid down their arms, were offered service, but they refused it with contempt. They all appeared very much attached to him, and several native officers, who had been a long time in his service, rent their clothes and turned beggars, swearing that they never would serve as soldiers again. Captains Hearsey and Birch, and two other Europeans, went along with him.

Pedron completed the 3rd brigade from the five battalions of the 4th, which he had brought with him from Alleeghur; but it was unfortunately Bourquoin under whom we were ordered to attack Hansee. The 3rd brigade, with a large battering train, 500 regular Hindostanee horse, and about 5,000 Sikhs, marched for that place, while Pedron went back to Alleeghur.

When we reached Sewannee, seven côs southeast of Hansee, we received information that Thomas had choked up all the wells within six côs round the place. Bursee, four côs in our front, had five pukha wells; and Hansee was three côs distant from Bursee. I was ordered, with two battalions and all the pioneers, to clear out one of these wells,—and this I effected in two days; after which, the troops marched, and all the rest were cleared out. We discovered, too, that the little tanks of water near Hansee had been denied with pork and beef.

Bourquoin reconnoitred the fort several times, and formed his plan of attack. Thomas had still about 5,000 foot and 200 horse, with two 24, four 12, and six 6-pounder guns; and he had fortified strongly three outworks, about a hundred yards from the town. One to the south-east, at the Bursee gate, was defended by sixty men; another at the Kootub gate, to the south, by 100 men; and one on the west, towards Hissar, with 200 men.

At three in the morning, Bourquoin ordered these three works to be attacked. Two battalions, under Lieut. Mackenzie, were directed to assault that towards the Bursee gate; two others, under my command, to that at the Kootub gate; while Captain Bunnear, with two more, was ordered to that at the Hissar gate. We arrived at our destination near daybreak, and led on our respective columns. Mackenzie and I both succeeded without much trouble, the enemy's parties running into the town. But Captain Bunnear having got between his outwork and the town, and thus cutting off their retreat, the men resisted obstinately, and beat back the party. Bunnear rallied them, but in so doing was killed in the ditch, on which his men rushed on, carried the place, and put the whole of the enemy's party to the sword. On our side the whole loss did not exceed 200 men in killed and wounded, but the death of Bunnear was much felt in all our circle, and especially by the soldiery.

These three works were fixed as points for our trenches, and between them three batteries were ordered to be erected. During the siege of the town nothing was done to interrupt us by Thomas, though the garrison kept up their fire from musketry and cannon pretty well. The battering guns then opened, and the walls of the town being breached, three parties of 1,500 men were told off for the storm. One was under command of Lieut. Mackenzie; a second under command of my brother, Lieut. Skinner; and the third under my own.

At dawn of day, on the 3rd December, the signal of attack was given. Mackenzie was opposed to Captain Hearsey: my brother to a native, Ellias Beg; and I had to contend with Captain Birch. Both Mackenzie and my brother made good their way in, after some resistance; but Birch, who defended his post well, beat me back twice with great loss. Burning choppers, powder-pots, and everything he could get hold of, were showered upon us; but our greatest loss was from the powder-pots, which greatly disheartened the men: however, after a desperate struggle, I drove them from the breach. Just as I had got up, I saw Birch about twenty yards from me taking aim at me with a double-barrelled gun, the contents of which, both barrels, he fired at me; but "the sweet little cherub" saved me from them. I immediately levelled my javelin, and, putting my shield to my breast, darted it at him, and took off his hat,—on which he set off and joined his men, who were now leaving the wall, and retreated about 200 yards behind houses.

All my storming party had now got in, and we moved towards the chowk or centre of the bazaar, where we saw our columns. The fight now became desperate. Thomas had come down from the fort with 1,000 of his chosen men, and, attacking the column commanded by Lieutenant Skinner, drove it back to the walls of the town. I immediately hastened to my brothers assistance, and beat Thomas back to the gate of the fort.

All our columns having now joined in the chowk, Thomas made another attempt, bringing up a 6-pounder, and, after great resistance, drove us out of the chowk. We were then joined by our reserve of a battalion, with a couple of 6-pounders, and, in spite of a very obstinate resistance by Thomas, drove him back to the fort. About noon we had complete possession of the town; but it cost us dear, as the slaughter on our side was very great, for several times we had come to the sword (that is, hand to hand with the sword). My brother got a cut at Thomas, but his armour had saved him. We lost, in killed and wounded, 1,600 men. Lieutenant Mackenzie was wounded, and several of our native officers were killed and wounded.

Bourquoin, soon after, arrived with 3,000 dismounted troopers and two battalions, who took up our position, and we were allowed to go to the rear to refresh ourselves. Next morning the guns moved into the town, our trenches were commenced within 200 yards of the fort, and a battery of eight 18-pounders was erected in the centre of the chowk. Thomas, on his side, made every preparation to defend the fort; but, in consequence of the losses he had sustained, his men were dispirited and little to be depended on. The siege was, however, carried on with great spirit on both sides: several sallies were made upon our trenches, and sometimes Thomas drove us out, at others we gave him a proper thrashing. But our battering guns produced no effect, for the fort of Hansee being a solid mound of earth, the balls merely buried themselves in it, without in the least shaking the rampart.

In consequence, we commenced mining, and advanced to within ten yards of the crown work called, in Hindostanee, goongas; when Bourquoin began to intrigue with Thomas's men, and wrote them letters promising them six months' pay and permanent service if they would give up the fort and Thomas. These letters were rolled upon arrows, and shot into the fort from our trenches, and they were answered in the same way by Thomas's men, who agreed to give him up, but said there was some misunderstandings among themselves; but, as soon as the parties should unite, due notice of it should be sent.

Thomas was not ignorant of these intrigues, and kept himself on his guard. He had still about 1,500 faithful and trustworthy soldiers, who were posted with himself in the inner fort. On our side, Bourquoin was the only French officer, the rest were country-borns and English, who felt indignant at this underhand treachery, and agreed that it would be disgraceful if through such intrigues Thomas should be taken prisoner and put into confinement; for Bourquoin had declared in bravado that so he would use that blackguard Englishman when he got hold of him. This was language which we did not admire; but knowing Bourquoin to be more of a talker than a doer, we managed to persuade him into offering terms, assuring him that he would himself gain a higher name by inducing Thomas to capitulate than by catching him by treachery. It was one day after tiffin, when the wine he had drunk had put him in high spirits and good humour, that we plied him thus, and at last he called out, in his broken English, "Well, gentlemen, you do as you like— I give power; he be one damn Englishman, your countryman, that treat their children very ill." He meant that the country-borns were very ill used in not being admitted into the Company's service.

We lost no time in making use of this power, but sent Captain Smith into the fort to treat with Thomas. That gentleman received him with great joy, and told him of the treachery that was brewing among his men; on which Smith said that he was sent by the whole English officers (meaning European and country-borns) to save him from dishonour, Thomas thanked him, and begged he would return and say that he would accept of any terms the officers should make for him. With this reply Smith returned; and, after some trouble, we prevailed on Bourquoin to grant the following terms,— namely: — That Thomas should be permitted to go free, with all his private property—that is, ready money, wearing apparel, shawls, jewels, and all household stuff: and that one of our battalions should escort him safe to the Company's territory. That his soldiers should be allowed to march out with their private arms, but that all arms belonging to Thomas should be left in the fort.

These conditions being signed by Bourquoin, Smith was sent next morning with them into the fort, and Thomas was glad to agree to them. It was settled that the fort should be given up in two days; and, meantime, a cessation of hostilities on both sides was proclaimed. A meeting took place between Thomas and Bourquoin, at the bungalow of the former, on the bank of the Umtee tank; and all the officers, except myself, who was left in command of the trenches, were permitted to go and see him. He received them all very courteously, and was particularly gracious to my brother, whom he embraced, and showed him the cut he had received from him on his belt. After spending two hours together, during which time Bourquoin and he became great friends, he returned to the fort.

Bourquoin then invited him to dine with us all on the 21st, which Thomas agreed to; and all the officers were permitted to come to dine in camp, the trenches being left under charge of the native officers. Hearsey and Birch spent the whole day with us, talking of our various exploits; but it was about seven in the evening when Thomas arrived with about fifty of his sowars, much affected, as it appeared, by his misfortunes. About eight we sat down; and, after dinner, did all we could to cheer Thomas, taking great care to avoid all conversation about our attacks, or anything that might give him offence. By eleven o'clock all of us had got pretty merry with drinking bumpers to such toasts as "General Perron," "George Thomas," &c, and Thomas was quite happy; when, all of a sudden, Bourquoin called out —"Let us drink to the success of Perron's arms." At this we all turned up our glasses; and Thomas, on hearing and seeing this, burst into tears, and, putting his hand to his sword, called out to Bourquoin that it was not to him but to his own ill fate that his fall was due, and (drawing his sword) — "One Irish sword," said he, "is still sufficient for a hundred Frenchmen." Bourquoin, in terror at this, jumped from his chair, and ran out of the tent, calling out for his guard. Then Thomas's sowars, hearing the hubbub, also rushed in; and we, apprehensive of a row, called out to them to keep off, as it was only the sahib that was drunk: while Thomas, in the midst of us, kept waving his sword, and calling out in Hindostanee to look how he had made the d-----d Frenchman run like a jackall! It was not without much persuasion, and no small fear of some accident, that we got Thomas at last to sheath his sword. We then got the soldiers out of the tent; and, when Thomas had sat down, we explained to him that the wine had made Bourquoin forget himself, but that he must not regard it as an insult, but agree to make it up. To this he at once consented; and, going to seek Bourquoin, we brought him in, and he immediately shook Thomas's hand, and told him he was sorry for what he had said.

A few more glasses now went round; and, perceiving that they were getting still more "jolly," being captain of the day in the trenches, I rode off to the town, and cautioned the men not to challenge Thomas's sowars, for that their master was drunk. About midnight Thomas arrived by the Bursee gate, where there was a guard of a naik and six sepoys, whom I had omitted to caution; so, when he came close, the sentinel challenged. Thomas's man replied "Sahib Bahaudoor," as he was usually called by his men. The sentinel replied that he knew of no Sahib Bahaudoor, so that he must stop until lie got permission from his officer to pass. Thomas, who was much in liquor, now turned round to his sowars, and said—" Could any one have stopped Sahib Bahaudoor at this gate but one month ago?" "No, no" replied they; on which he dismounted, drew his sword, and making a cut at the poor sentinel, smote off his right hand. Up got the guard immediately on this, and gave the alarm; but, fortunately, I was only a few yards distant from the gate, and on hearing the noise ran up. There I found Thomas walking up and down with, his naked sword in his hand, and Hearsey and several of his sowars, who had dismounted, endeavouring to lay hold of him. At length a rissaldar, named Meer Mahummudee, caught hold of him from behind, when the rest ran in, and taking his sword from him, sent for his palankeen, and had him carried into the fort. Next morning, having come to himself, Hearsey told him what he had done, on which he sent for the soldier he had wounded, and gave him 500 rupees. He also wrote an apology to Bourquoin, expressing his concern for what had happened.

On the 29th Thomas marched out, and encamped near us; and on the 1st of January he marched with a battalion of ours, under Captain Smith, who escorted him safe to Anoopsheher. He carried with him about a lakh and a half of rupees in ready cash, and above a lakh more in shawls, jewels, and other property.

A few words more will suffice to conclude the history of this remarkable man, whose enterprise and energy seemed to merit a happier fate. In the middle of January 1802 he reached the English frontier; and having inspected the state of his funds, and the wreck of his property, he found himself possessed of no more than might suffice to procure the decent comforts of life in his native country, whither it was his intention to retire. But this was not granted to him. He left the upper provinces, and, after a residence of some time at Benares, was proceeding down the river, when illness, probably brought on by his late severe exertions and exposure, arrested his progress near the military cantonments of Berhampore,—and there he died, and there he lies buried.

Chapter Ten
The Coming of the Mahratta War 1803

"About the 25th of January," continues Skinner, "after placing a battalion, as garrison, in the fort, we marched to Futteeabad, in order to settle the Bhuttee country, while I, having received a letter from my father at Berhampore, desiring that I should come and see him, applied to Perron for leave to do so. This being granted, I left the brigade at Futteeabad on the 15th of February, and marched to Cawnpore. From thence I embarked, in a budjerow, for Berhampore, and joined my father in the end of April. After spending a couple of months with him, I went to Calcutta to see my sister, Mrs. Templeton, and then returned to Berhampore for another month. On the 1st of July I took leave of my father, and rejoined General Perron, at Coel, in January 1803: at my own request I was posted to the second brigade; and having received command of my old regiment, joined them in the country of Meerut.

Perron was now sent for by Sindea to Oojeine, and ordered the second brigade to accompany him. He joined us at Khoshalghur, with 500 sowars, and from thence we reached Oojeine on the 20th of March. His reception here was not of a nature to gratify an officer like Perron. It was not until the 25th that he was invited to call on the Maha Raja; and then, having proceeded to the Durbar with 200 horsemen, he was kept waiting in the kutchery (or office) at the gate for two hours, while Sindea was amusing himself by flying kites. Not a chieftain came out to meet him, while he sat in company with certain discontented chiefs of note, among whom was old Gopaul Rao Bhow, who was at the head of the army. This officer, addressing Perron, said, "Observe to what the old Pateil's reign has come: good soldiers are all forgotten,—none but dirty time-servers and flatterers can get on; but mark my words, he will soon find out his error, but not until too late to mend it." To this Perron replied, that he was but a servant, and all he knew was to obey. This sort of conversation went on until the Choleedars announced the approach of Sindea, when we all rose, and Perron went up and presented his nuzzur. Sindea just touched it, and asked him if he was well; to which Perron made the usual reply of "by your favour"; and then we all, in turn, presented our nuzzurs, and were desired to sit down.

In half an hour Sindea dismissed the Durbar, and desired Perron to return to camp, which he did, completely disgusted with the cold and slighting treatment he had received from his master.

Eight days now passed without the slightest notice or message from Sindea to Perron; and Gopaul Rao, a great friend of the latter, signified to him that he had best be on his guard, as the Maha Raja had resolved to lay hold of him. Several secret visits passed at this time between Perron and Gopaul Rao, whilst Colonel Sutherland and Major Brownrigg were intriguing against the former.

Perron, aware of the intrigues of his enemies, became depressed and perturbed; when, at length, matters seemed likely to be brought to a crisis. A day was appointed for holding a durbar, to which Perron and all his European officers were invited. At this durbar Sindea, together with his father-in-law, Surjee Rao Ghatkea, had formed a plot to lay hold of him; and had employed 500 Pathans, belonging to Bahadour Khan (a chief then at Malaghur), and several others of his own favourites—his companions in vice and debauchery—to carry this purpose into effect.

Perron, however, was made aware of this plot, and ordered all the native officers of both brigades, as low as the rank of jemadar, as well as all the European officers, to come fully armed to attend his visit to Sindea. Our full uniform included a brace of pistols attached to our sword-belts, and these he directed us to bring loaded. We amounted in all to 300 native and thirty European officers; and in this state of preparation we marched to the durbar, a large tent pitched for the occasion.

At the hour of nine in the morning, headed by Perron, we reached the tent. Sindea rose to receive us, and we all presented our nuzzurs. We were then directed to sit down on the left side of the presence, the right being occupied by the Pathans, who regarded us very fiercely. When we were seated, Sindea, turning to Perron, observed that the invitation had only been extended to himself and his European officers, to which Perron replied, that in arranging his suite he had only followed the old rule laid down by himself and his uncle; and this answer silenced him. All this time we sat quiet, eyeing each other, whilst much whispering went on between Sindea, Gopaul Rao, and Surjee Rao. I believe it was Gopaul Rao who persuaded him not to attempt any violence, for that not only himself, but the whole party would be cut to pieces by the fine body of men whom Perron had brought in.

Sindea then ordered the Pathans to retire, and they all got up, looking at us as if they would eat us, while our men sat laughing at them with the most perfect unconcern. When they were gone, Sindea and Surjee Rao began to flatter, and endeavour to throw him off his guard; but he, assisted as he was by his old friend Gopaul Rao, was too old a soldier to be so cajoled; and so khiluts were ordered for us all, and after receiving them we presented our nuzzurs, which he graciously accepted. Betel was then handed round, and we received leave to retire.

Perron then got up, and taking off his sword, laid it down at Sindea's feet, saying that he had grown old in his service, and that it did not become him to be disgraced by dissolute knaves and bullies; that all he wanted was his discharge. Then, addressing us, he said, that henceforth we must look to Sindea, for that he, for his part, was too old now to brook affronts, and must retire. Sindea, on this, rose and embraced Perron, telling him that he regarded him as his uncle, and that he had no idea what had offended him. Compliments without measure passed between both parties, but, on taking leave, Perron cautioned Sindea to beware of Surjee Rao Ghatkea, for he would be his ruin,—a caution in which all the old Mahratta chiefs joined cordially, and applauded the part which Perron had taken.

At length we returned to camp, where several days were occupied in the transmission of messages to and from the court, and in visits from chieftains who were sent to make matters up. But Perron was too indignant to be pacified. Colonel Sutherland, in the mean time, was sent to the 2nd brigade, and Colonel Pholman to the 1st, while Major Brownrigg was put in arrest under fixed bayonets. On the 15th of April, Perron marched with the 2nd brigade, having requested Sindea to send Ambajee to take charge of the troops in Hindostan, to which I believe he agreed.

On the 1st of June we arrived at Alleeghur, Perron still persisting in his purpose of retiring from the service, and Ambajee being appointed commander-in-chief, or soobah, of Hindostan. Our brigade was now ordered to cantoon at Secundra, near Dehlee, when news arrived that Holcar had defeated the Peishwah, and cut up four battalions of our 1st brigade, under command of Captain Dawes, at Poona. The Peishwah, thus situated, had flown to the English for protection, and the whole Mahratta empire was thrown into the greatest agitation. Rumours came from Sindea's camp of disagreements between himself and the English Resident, and alarms of an English war began to be spread. Great preparations took place in all the armies; and Sindea, in these circumstances, succeeded in persuading Perron to remain a year longer in the service.

About the 1st of July, it became publicly known that Sindea and almost all the native powers had fallen out with the English. The 4th brigade was now completed, and sent to join Sindea at Oojeine. Perron, on his part, made great preparations at Alleeghur. His plan for acting against the English was as follows: — Gholaum Mahomed, the Rohilla chief, was engaged to commence in the Katahoor, and overrun the country towards Lucknow; while Umbajee, with all his horse, should cross at Cawnpore, and march down to Allahabad. The brigades under Perron's command were to assemble at Dehlee; while Perron himself, with about 20,000 horse, composed of his own regular cavalry, the Sikh chief's contingent, and all the horse belonging to the petty Rajahs of the Doab, were to occupy that country, and harass the British troops forming at Cawnpore under Lord Lake. The Mahrattas were to hoist the King's imperial colours. Sindea, with all his own forces, undertook to watch and harass General Wellesley in the Dekhan. The battalions of the Nagpore Rajah were to march through the Rewah country towards Calcutta, each commander being instructed to burn and destroy everything in their course in the countries through which they passed.

Although it is not the purpose of this narrative to enter on the wide subject of the Mahratta war of 1803, it may interest the reader to learn here generally, what the condition and relative force of the respective parties was, at least in Hindostan, where Skinner himself was exclusively engaged. The Mahratta princes themselves were so utterly at variance, that little of combination was to be looked for among them; the hereditary enmity between Sindea and Holcar prevented any coalition on their part; and it was the growing power and hostility of Holcar that had led the Peishwah to seek the assistance of the English government, and which led to the famous treaty of Bassein. Thus the principal confederates against the English were, Dowlut Rao Sindea, and Rughoojee Bhounslah, with Shumshere Bahaudur, and their forces have been estimated as follows.

Sindea and Rughoojee together, had about 100,000 men, of whom 50,000 were Mahratta horse, generally good; 30,000 regular infantry and artillery, commanded by Europeans; the rest were half disciplined troops belonging to Rughoojee. Sindea is understood to have had more than 500 pieces of cannon, all in excellent order, and manned by stanch artillerists. Shumshere Bahaudur's troops have been estimated at 10,000 to 12,000 men of all sorts.

Of these, the army of Hindostan, under Perron's command, consisted of 16,000 to 17,000 regular infantry, and from 15,000 to 20,000 horse, with the usual proportion of artillery, not less than twenty pieces. To oppose this force, Lord Lake had but 10,500 men, all ready to march, at Cawnpore, besides which, 3,500 under his orders were stationed at Allahabad, to oppose Shumshere Bahaudur. It is to be remarked, that though Holcar had not as yet joined the Mahratta confederacy against the British, and that the Rajepoot princes had taken no active part in what was going on, there is little doubt that had the British been unfortunate at the outset, they would soon have had these additional powers to cope with, as well as the Sikhs of the Punjab and the states of the Desert, which would have added a force of 100,000 more men to that of their present enemies.

Skinner continues:-

On the 28th of August, a most important change took place in the condition of all the English and country-born officers in the service of Sindea. Captain Stewart, a country-born, and Captain Carnegie, a Scotchman, having signified that they would not serve against the English, all of us, nine in number, were summarily dismissed, our arrears were paid up, and we were ordered to quit the Mahratta country. This was a most unexpected blow to many of us, but there was no help for it. My brother went off to the Begum Sumroo, and I, with five more country-borns, resolved to go to Sindea himself to seek redress. On the 29th we arrived at Alleeghur, just as General Lake was marching up with his army. Perron had made a show of hostilities with his cavalry, but they quickly dispersed, and General Lake encamped before the fort. For our parts, we found ourselves surrounded all in a garden near the Sasnee gate of Coel, from whence in the evening we went to General Lake, and were very kindly received.

Captains Stewart and Carnegie were, as Skinner remarks, the first of the officers who tendered to Perron their resignation, declaring that they could not fight against the British arms,— a measure which enraged Perron so much, that he gave a general discharge to all British and British country-borns in the service. Skinner and several others remonstrated against this, but in vain; and having been warned not to be found within reach of the Mahratta camp after certain time, he went off, with four others, to Agra, whither he had previously sent his family. On the day of the battle of Alleeghur, he and his companions had pitched in a garden, on the way thither, during the heat of the sun, when, hearing of the battle, Skinner proposed still to go to Perron, to press their remonstrances in person, and declare their intention of sticking by him to the last. But by-and-bye they saw some of the Mahratta horse passing by in a disorderly manner, and in a little Perron himself, in confusion, without his hat. Skinner went up to him immediately, and told him that he had come to remonstrate against his dismissal, and had determined to remain and share his fortunes. "Ah! no, no!" replied Perron,— "it is all over; these fellows" (the horse) "have behaved ill: do not ruin yourself, go over to the British; it is all up with us." "By no means," replied Skinner; "it is not so; let us rally yet, and make a stand,—you may depend upon having many yet to fight for you." But Perron still shook his head, and after a little said, in his bad English, "Ah, no, Monsieur Skinner,—I not trust—I not trust; I fraid you all go." Skinner, on this, got angry, and retorted, saying, that in that case it was he that was the traitor, if he meant to proceed in that way; if, on account of one or two ingrates, he should lose to his master the services of many faithful persons, this was the way to ruin the cause; but that, if he persevered in doing all for the best, no doubt he might still hold the country and effectively serve his master. But Perron, who had made up his mind upon the matter, still refused to have anything more to do either with him or any of his brother officers; on which Skinner declared he would go to Sindea himself and complain. Perron answered impatiently, and biding no further parley, shook his head, and rode off, saying, "Good-bye, Monsieur Skinner; — no trust— no trust." "Then you may go to the devil!" roared Secunder, and rode back to the garden, where he related all that had happened to his comrades, saying that he was resolved to go to Sindea and relate to him the whole case.

Skinner had, in fact, at this time not the smallest idea of entering the British service, or even leaving that of Sindea: he was a complete native,—sought nothing better than to live and die in the service he had been brought up in. He had no tie to Britain; his father was dead, his brother provided for in the Begum Soomroo's service; he knew little or nothing of his other relatives, and was himself a soldier of fortune— at large, and free to choose for himself—and he desired to stick to the colours he had hitherto served under.

Carnegie, a sensible man, who was one of the party, then came forward:— "No," said he "Sindea would never place any confidence; we should be suspected by all, and there would be an end to all promotion, if not to safety. Let us seek for protection from the British commander, who will be glad to afford it to us." Long did Skinner oppose this plan, for he did not then know his countrymen, and reposed little confidence in British faith; but at last he gave in, and they all proceeded to a fort near at hand, in possession of the British, there to demand protection.

They were met by an officer (named Clark) who had command at the gate, and who told them, somewhat rudely, they could have no protection there, and that they had better go on to the camp. They left him, in considerable indignation at the treatment they had received, and, on proceeding, were overtaken by, or overtook a gentleman, attended by two orderlies, who, seeing they were strangers, inquired who they were. On being informed that they were Mahratta officers, who had quitted the service and were seeking protection, he also said he could do nothing for them, and that they should go to the camp of the commander-in-chief, who alone could give them an answer. They then mentioned the repulse they had already met with, and begged that a soldier might be sent to secure them a better reception, which, without such an introduction, they feared might not be afforded them. This, Colonel Everard Brown, for he it was, somewhat ungraciously, as they thought, refused to do; telling them, rather cavalierly, to find their way as they best could. On this they left him, and Skinner, complimenting Carnegie upon the politeness of his countrymen, led the way towards their tents. Carnegie, a little piqued, said he would at least make one more trial; and taking with him Ferguson, another of their comrades, rode on to the British camp. Near this they were met by Captain ------, who, having inquired who they were, received them very kindly, and took them into camp. He then inquired whether they did not require some food, as they looked exhausted; and then said he would take them to Lord Lake, the commander-in-chief. When they were refreshed, he inquired after the two Skinners, who, he said, were sons of his particular friend; and hearing James was of their party, he sent a letter off immediately, to request, in the most urgent manner, that he would come to him at once.

This letter overtook Skinner just as the sun was going down; and, though he put little faith in its professions, it induced him to delay his departure; and soon afterwards came Carnegie and Ferguson, calling out to him that they had now found out the right way. Still it was with difficulty they persuaded him to go to the camp, very dubious as to the event. When they reached it, they were first introduced to Lord Lake, who received them with great good will and kindness; and were then ushered into the mess-room, where they dined, and met with so much attention as seemed to them perfectly marvellous,—in short, they were as capitally treated as they had at first thought themselves ill-used.

Next morning, after breakfasting they were again taken to Lord Lake; and then Skinner's doubts recommenced, for, on being asked which of them was the senior officer, he was at once pointed out as such by the rest. He was then questioned particularly as to the force and numbers of Perron's troops, on which Skinner was by no means disposed to be communicative, and he confined himself to such matters as were easily to be discovered without betraying what might be regarded as secrets. After some time, he was asked if he would take service, and raise a troop of horse in English pay. But this he at once and decidedly refused,—for he never, he said, could fight against his old comrades, nor draw sword against Sindea or Perron. He was then requested to write to the different officers serving under Perron, and to inform them that, if they came over, they should receive favourable terms. This he declined doing, assuring those who proposed it that it would be perfectly useless —they never would come over, or believe him; moreover, he warned them that, if messengers were sent with such letters, their lives would not be safe. His comrades, however, did not see the same difficulties; and at length he, as well as they, did write some letters, which were accordingly, sent. But the hucarrahs who carried those of his comrades were put to death; while the general attachment felt for Skinner's name proved the safety of his messenger.

The result of this experiment, and of a longer acquaintance with Skinner, was, that he became a great favourite with Lord Lake, who consulted him much on all occasions; while so greatly prepossessed was Skinner himself by the affability and kindness of his lordship, that he attached himself very sincerely to his person and the service,—insomuch that, after the battle of Dehlee, little more than a fortnight after his joining the camp near Alleeghur, we find him accepting the command of a body of horse, on the express stipulation that he was never to be employed against his old master, Sindea, This command took its origin in the coming over of a body of Perron's horse, after the dispersion of Bourquoin's force at Dehlee. These, when they were asked whom they would choose for their commander, with one voice said, that if the "Burrah Secunder" was there, he was the man. He was accordingly employed, as will be seen, in keeping the Doab open until the war with Holcar commenced, when he became again more actively engaged.

One anecdote will show Skinner's character in its true light, and show how he stood with Lord Lake. A Patan soldier came to him one day saying provided that a jagheer and a lakh of rupees were insured to him, he would assassinate Holcar. Skinner, indignant at so cowardly a proposition, was at first disposed to spurn the villain; but considering that false reports might get abroad, he thought it best to go at once and communicate the proposition to Lord Lake. "Well," said his lordship, "and what do you think? Do you believe he will do as he says?" "I think," said Skinner, "he very likely may; but there is little faith to be reposed on the word of a man who proves once a traitor." "What, then, do you think I should do?" inquired his lordship. "Does your lordship wish me to speak the truth freely?" asked Skinner. "Undoubtedly, I do," replied Lord Lake. "Then," said Skinner, "I repeat that it is very likely the man may do what he says: but what will be said in Hindostan of Lord Lake and of the English?—they will say that, not being-able to succeed against Holcar by fair means, they had recourse to treachery and, assassination. If you will be advised by me, let the man be publicly told that we give no encouragement to such acts, and let him meet the contempt he deserves: for a much smaller reward I will undertake to find a hundred men who will engage to carry off the head of Holcar from the field of battle. Let the man, however, be saved from the ruin which would inevitably befall him if abandoned after such a disclosure—let him be furnished with what will keep him from want." "You are right," said his lordship; "it is the fit way to deal with him: send for the man, and do as you have yourself proposed."

The man was accordingly sent for, and, in the presence of his own corps, and in public, Skinner told him that the English neither encouraged nor desired treachery—they could well do without it; that as to him, he was a traitor and merited death; but that, on account of the feeling he had manifested to be useful to them, they would give him 100 rupees for life, if he chose to stay in their honest service. "And now, my friends," said he, addressing the corps, "whoever brings me Holcar's head from the field of battle, fairly slain, shall have a splendid reward from me."

In an instant the man's character was gone in the opinion of all who heard the disclosure—he never could hold his head up afterwards. And, strange to say, he was not long after slain in battle of when far in the rear, and before any other man had been touched. Skinner, who with Lord Lake witnessed the circumstance, exclaimed,—"Now, Lord Sahib! See how treachery has met its deserts. That shot surely had its orders,— you see, not a man has yet been hurt, and yet that fellow, though skulking in the rear, has got the blow intended for him."

The game was now up, and Sindea's cause was lost. But had the conduct of Sindea himself been more marked by prudence and ability, and had Perron been honest and sincere, instead of a traitor as he was, the Mahrattas would have given much trouble to the English.

Sindea had abandoned himself to luxury and debauchery, and had destroyed or disgusted all his old experienced generals, while his chieftains were faint hearted, and by no means inclined to fight. Perron, in whom he trusted much, had not only disgusted all the Sirdars in Hindostan, by his pride and overbearing deportment, but had bestowed the command of the troops, the forts, and the districts, upon his own relations and connections, most of whom being men of low extraction and without education, thought only of making money, and looking after their own interests. These, like Perron himself, so far from being sincerely attached to his service, only affected a shew of zeal, in order to blind the natives until they should have an excuse to be off to the Company's provinces, whither they had already remitted the greater part of their wealth.

To name a few of those who thus made a shew of being staunch, while inwardly treacherous, I must begin with Perron himself, who not only was at the head of Sindea's infantry, but commanded all the tributary Rajahs of Hindostan.

The important fort of Alleeghur he had placed under the command of Colonel Pedron. Agra, the key of Hindostan, had been bestowed on his nephew, Colonel George Hessing. Major Deridon, Major Bourquoin, Lieutenant Felose, and others of his relations, had respectively command of brigades in the Dekhan, and had much influence with the troops.

The use they made of this was to derange in every way they could the system of the army, with a view to making their escape the more easily. They endeavoured to shake the confidence of the men in Sindea, and intrigued to have all the English and other European officers dismissed, declaring that they would assuredly go over to the British; and thus secured to themselves the undivided control over the army.

Perron made a great display at Alleeghur. He pitched the royal tent, and proclaimed to the troops, that Sindea had taken up arms in the king of Dehlee's cause, to defend his throne and country from the tyrant English, who wished to deprive him of it. He kept with himself at Alleeghur only 5,000 horse, and ordered all the brigades in Hindostan to march to Dehlee for his majesty's protection, and he invited the king to head these troops, and defend himself against the usurpers. His Majesty accepted this offer, and great preparations were made for the royal reception. Hursook Roy, Perron's chief banker, was sent to Dehlee, to advance such money as his majesty might require. The 2nd and 3rd brigade from Hindostan, and the 4th from Oojeine, were ordered to Dehlee, and all independent powers were summoned by his majesty to that city, to defend the throne of Hindostan. All these measures were taken only a month before Lord Lake appeared before Alleeghur.

But the jealousies existing in the Mahratta councils overthrew every scheme. The generals with Sindea, most of whom were in the interest of Holcar or the English, particularly Ambajee, resolved to leave the brigades to be destroyed. Runjeet Singh of Lahore also determined against making any effort in Sindea's favour. In fact, there was no unity among the powers of Hindostan who had to oppose the English. Holcar, the Nagpore Rajah, and Sindea, all of whom promised to coalesce, never joined or worked in concert, and thus were destroyed singly. The regular brigades, unassisted by any of the Mahratta horse, and shamefully deserted by the French officers who had headed them, were also destroyed by themselves.

Perron, upon the arrival of Lord Lake at Alleeghur, retired to Mendoo, a large village five côs south of Coel, with his 5,000 horse; the rest of the large body he had assembled there all dispersed to their homes, or returned to join their respective chiefs. These 5,000 were placed by Perron under the command of Mr. Fleurea, with orders to go towards Cawnpore, destroying the country as they went. He himself went off to Agra, where his family was, and a great part of his wealth, in precious stones and jewellery.

Lord Lake, on reaching Alleeghur proposed terms to the garrison, which Colonel Pedron★ was inclined to accept, but the garrison putting themselves under command of Bajee Rao,

---

★ *Perron had placed the utmost confidence in this officer, and relied on his defending to the last a fortress which, as was the case with Alleeghur, had been fortified with all the skill and pains which science could bestow upon it; and the following letter, which he wrote to Pedron, shows both the importance he attached to the defence, and his confidence that it would be maintained:—"You will have received," he says, "the answer you are to make to the propositions of General Lake. I never could have believed that for a moment you could have thought of a capitulation. Remember, you*

a Bahadourea Rajepoot, confined the colonel, and resolved
to defend the fort. This garrison was composed of a regular
battalion, 800 strong, commanded by a native, named Meer
Shadut Allee, 1,000 Bahaclourea Rajepoots, 500 Mewattees,
and about the same number of recruits, a rissalah of horse, and
200 Golundauz. The Bahadourea Rajepoots with Bajee Rao
had charge of the gate and outer fort, and the rest were all in
the inner chowbourgee.

Skinner continues:

On our second visit to Lord Lake, I was offered the
command of 2,000 horse; but I refused it, declaring that I
never would fight against Sindea. On the 4th of September
1803, Lord Lake assaulted the fort with 500 Europeans of the
76th, and two and a half battalions of Sepoys. They started
from camp about two hours before daybreak, and reached
the place a little before dawn. A piquet of fifty men, with a 6-
pounder, had been stationed, by Bajee Rao, about fifty yards
from the fort, at whom this handful of heroes ran like lions.
The piquets immediately ran away to the wicket, and got in.
The assaulting party attempted to get in along with them,
but were shut out. Instead, however, of retreating, these brave
fellows stood upon the goonjus for a full hour, under one of
the heaviest fires of musketry and great guns I have seen, and
only at sunrise did they fall back about a hundred yards; on
which the brave Lord Lake, who was standing near Perron's
house, at one of his batteries, called out, "They run!" They
were rallied, however, by some of their gallant officers, and
in going back they carried with them the Mahratta gun. I
was close by Lord Lake, and saw and heard everything that

---

are a Frenchman; and let no action of yours tarnish the character of your nation. I
hope, in a few days, to send hack the English general as fast or faster than he came;
make yourself easy on this subject. Either the Emperor's army or that of General
Lake's shall find a grave before the fort of Alleeghur. Do your duty, and defend the fort
while one stone remains upon another. Once more—remember your nation; the eyes
of millions are fixed upon you." It is known how Pedron fulfilled the expectations of
his commander.

passed. The God of heaven certainly looked down upon these noble fellows, for with two shots they blew open half the gate, and, giving three shouts, they rushed in. The Rajepoots stood their ground like brave soldiers, and from the first to the second gate the fight was desperately maintained on both sides, and the carnage very great.

As soon as he heard the shout, the countenance of Lord Lake changed from anxiety to joy, and he called out, with the greatest delight, "The fort is ours"; and turning to me, asked what I thought of European fighting? I replied that no forts in Hindostan could stand against him. Then spurring his horse, he galloped to the gate. But when he saw his heroes lying thick there, the tears came to his eyes. "It is the fate of good soldiers!" he said; and turning round, he galloped back to the camp, and gave up the fort to plunder. I must here declare that the courage displayed by the 76th surpassed all I had ever seen, and every idea I had formed of soldiering.

The inner garrison immediately threw down their arms, and began to fly in all quarters. A vast amount of plunder was taken by the troops.*

---

*The storm of Alleeghur is so remarkable a feat of military daring that we cannot refrain from adding to Skinner's spirited sketch a somewhat more particular account of this most gallant affair:— "Much dependence," says Mr. Grant Duff, "was placed on this fortress. It is very strong, situated on a plain surrounded by swamps, having a good glacis. It was well garrisoned, fully provided with cannon, ammunition, and provisions, and the Mahrattas expected, as they had a right to expect, that it would sustain a long siege. The only passage into the fort was by a narrow causeway across the ditch, for which the French commandant, by gross neglect, had omitted to substitute a drawbridge. General Lake, apprised of this circumstance, determined to hazard an attack by the gateway; and Mr. Lucan, a British subject, one of the officers who had come over from Sindea's service, offered to conduct the storming party. Break of day, on the 4th of September, was the time appointed for the purpose: on the firing of the morning gun, the party, who had been lying for some time within four hundred yards of the gate, immediately advanced; and Colonel Monson pushed forward, at the head of the flank companies of the 76th, in hopes of being able to enter the fort with a party of the enemy that had been stationed outside, behind a breastwork. This had been abandoned, however, and the gate closed, while the entrance was raked by two or three guns, and flanked by the bastions, which poured upon it a most destructive fire of grape.

As I was returning to the town I saw a European passing through the avenue with a bag of dollars on his shoulders; he was attacked by two native troopers, who sought to deprive him of what he had bought so dearly. When he found that blows would not keep the fellows off, he just took and tore the bag, and scattered the cash. The rascals believing their booty thus secure, began to gather them tip, upon which he took his gun, shot the one and bayoneted the other; then coolly taking off his jacket, he fixed a knot upon the sleeves, and filling them with the dollars, threw it across his shoulders. He next loaded his gun, and seeing me, called out to me to come near; when I came he offered me fifty dollars if I would escort him to camp. To this I agreed, and went with him to the party that was in charge of Pedron, which was about two hundred yards from us, and here he tendered me the dollars. I, of course, refused to take them; on which he thanked me, and I returned to the town. I am sorry to add, that the gate by which these gallant fellows entered was pointed out to them by Lieutenant Lucan, an Irishman, and an officer in the Mahratta service,

---

Scaling-ladders were instantly applied to the walls, and Major MacLeod, of the 76th, with the Grenadiers, attempted to mount; but an impassable row of pikemen above prevented their succeeding. A six-pounder now was brought up to blow open the gate, but it failed of effect; a twelve-pounder was then procured, after some time, but four or five shots were required before the gate would yield; and during this space of twenty minutes the storming party was exposed to a raking fire of musketry and grape from the great guns and wall-pieces. The enemy even came down the scaling-ladders to fight their assailants hand to hand; — here was the principal loss, and here was the most critical point, but nothing could appal the determined spirit of the British troops, who, as soon as the first gate was blown open, advanced, round a circular bastion, loopholed for muskets, to a second gate, which was easily forced. They then had to run along a narrow causeway, constantly exposed to the same raking fire; but succeeded in entering a third gate, at the end of it, along with the fugitives. But at the fourth gate, which led into the body of the place, they were again stopped, under a tremendous fire, until the 12-pounder could again be brought up. This, however, failed, so strong were the fastenings of this last gate; and again was the situation of the party most critical, when, most fortunately, Major MacLeod succeeded in forcing the wicket, through which he was followed by the Grenadiers. The rampart was mounted, opposition gradually ceased,

139

who received for the job 24,000 rupees, and a commission in H. M.'s 76th. On the 25th, intelligence reached Lord Lake that Fleurea had surprised Colonel Cunningham, at Shekoabad, and compelled him to sign a capitulation, by which he bound himself and party, consisting of five companies, not to carry arms against Sindea during the war; in consideration of which they were permitted to retire with their arms to Futtighur or Cawnpore. It appeared that these five companies had defended themselves for twenty-four hours against 5,000 horse, and did not give in until their ammunition was expended. All the officers were wounded, and a great number of the men killed; while Fleurea, on his side, lost seven of his best rissaldars, and about 500 of his men.

As soon as Lord Lake was informed of the direction which Fleurea had taken, he detached some regiments of cavalry in pursuit. But information of the fall of Alleeghur having that very day reached Fleurea, and his men refusing to believe it had been taken by assault, but maintaining that it was treacherously surrendered by Perron, they immediately took the way to Agra, where they expected to find that general. He had, however, removed with his family and effects to Muttra, taking with him his body-guard of 800 horsemen, mounted from his own stable, and 500 Mewattees; and here Fleurea's horse joined him.

In the mean time, Mons. Bourquoin got up an intrigue at Dehlee, which occasioned no small confusion. Asserting that Perron had turned traitor, and had gone over to the English,

---

and the British troops—by a happy combination of indefatigable courage and good fortune—found themselves masters of the supposed-impregnable fortress of Alleeghur, after a single morning's bloody work: it was indeed bloody,—223 officers and men were killed and wounded of the British; six officers of the 76th alone being among the first; under the circumstances, it is wonderful that the loss was not still more severe. The loss of the Mahrattas was far more severe, 2,000 being killed, besides those drowned or smothered in the ditch, in their endeavours to escape: amongst the slain was the brave Bajee Rao, the Rajepoot commander of the place.

he invited the troops at Dehlee to make him their commander, and that he would lead them on to glory. Having succeeded in persuading them to agree to this proposal, he next stirred up a mutiny in the 2nd brigade, and got them to place Mons. Zellon, their commander, along with all their officers, in arrest, under fixed bayonets. In vain did M. Zellon, who was an honest man, assure them that Bourquoin's assertions were false, that Perron had not gone over to the English, and that Bourquoin was only misleading them; all was fruitless, they would not listen to him. Bourquoin then called upon the king, and procured from him a khilut of investiture as commander-in-chief of Perron's infantry. His next step was to demand from Mr. Drugeon, the governor of Dehlee, all the public treasure. This Drugeon refused, and his garrison of 5,000 men proving staunch, he turned Bourquoin out of the fort, and told the king that he would obey no one until he should hear from Perron.

Bourquoin immediately laid siege to the fort with his brigade, and placed eight battering guns at one of the bastions near the Rajghaut; seized Hirsook Roy, and took from him some lakhs of rupees. The siege lasted two days, during which he levelled the bastion to the ground: and then the king begged of him to suspend operations, and that he would contrive to make Drugeon obey his orders.

Not content with this, Bourquoin wrote to the sowars of the cavalry at Muttra, informing them that Perron was a traitor, and enjoining them to seize him. Perron suspected that this was going on, and in order to save himself he had recourse to a stratagem. Mustering the cavalry, he complained to them of Bourquoin's conduct, assured them of the falsehood of all his assertions, and declared lie would immediately go and punish him for his treachery. He assured them that if they would follow him faithfully, he would drive this Lord Lake out of the Doab; and distributing three lakhs of rupees amongst the rissaldars for their sowars, declared he would that evening cross the Jumna with his body-guard; while they, taking money for their expenses from their rissaldars, should follow in the morning.

The rissaldars finding so much money in their hands, began to quarrel about the division of it, while Perron crossed in the evening with his body-guard. When it became dark, he gave the Mewattees five thousand rupees, desiring them to keep all the boats in their own hands during the night, and in the morning give them to the Sowars, while he should march on about five côs. But he lost no time in sending an express to Lord Lake, to say he had resigned Sindea's service, and requesting that he would receive and assign him charters; while, instead of five, he made a march of twenty côs during the night, and reached Sasnee in the morning.

No sooner did the Sowars discover that Perron had fled, than their faith in Bourquoin returned, and, believing him a true man, they all marched for Dehlee to join him. In the mean time, Lord Lake, having sent an officer, Captain Brownrigg, to escort Perron to Lucknow, and leaving a battalion to garrison the fort of Alleeghur, marched on the 7th September towards Dehlee. On hearing this, Bourquoin endeavoured to persuade the troops to march with him to Hurriana. This opened their eyes, and finding that he was as bad as Perron, they put him in confinement, and one of the native commandants, named Surwur Khan, taking the command, twelve battalions from both the brigades crossed the Jumna, with 100 pieces of cannon and all the horse, amounting to 5,000 or 6,000 men.

This force came up with Lord Lake on the 9th of September at Suddur ka Serai, and so badly off for information was the British troops, that the sepoys were cooking their dinner on the banks of the Hindun river, when they perceived a large body of Bourquoin's cavalry coming up. These were beaten on the 10th; but the plan and circumstances of the battle of

Dehlee* are so well known, that I need not describe it. About 2,000 men made good their retreat to Tupple, and crossed the Jumna, carrying off four pieces of cannon, the rest were all cut up by the British cavalry. Lord Lake arrived at Dehlee with the army, and was very kindly received by the king, who had long suffered from the Mahratta reign. Bourquoin and all the Frenchmen gave themselves lip, and the remains of the brigade made good their retreat to Agra, where they were joined by the 4th brigade, the commander of which, Chevalier Dudernaig, with all the French officers, escaped and joined Colonel Vandeleur at Muttra.

Eight rissalahs of Perron's horse came over to Lord Lake at Dehlee, and were taken into the British service, and being asked to choose one of their own officers as their commander, they named me. Lord Lake, on my second visit, had offered me the command of 2,000 horse, but I declined it, declaring that I would never carry arms against Sindea. At Coel, where I was left during Lord Lake's march to Dehlee, proclamation was made to all the British and country-born officers, late of Sindea's, informing us that we should meet with punishment, if we were found again in arms against the British; but that whoever chose to accept and serve, should receive the same pay he had from Perron; and now, my old comrades having asked for me, I received a letter from Lord Lake appointing me to the command, with a promise that I should not be

---

* In this memorable battle 4,500 British troops had to encounter 19,000 of the enemy, of whom only 6,000 were cavalry, supported by a park of sixty-eight cannon, all admirably served, and all in an excellent position. The British troops were wearied with a long march, and roused up to fight while cooking their untasted food. It was one steady but desperate charge of the bayonet against the cannon— for the men, though falling in scores, never took their musket from their shoulders till within 100 paces of the enemy, when orders were given for the charge. The British loss was 400 killed and wounded; that of the enemy not less than 3,000, besides those drowned in the Jumna. Both Lord Lake and his son had horses shot under them; and the same order pervaded all ranks and classes of the troops. Dehlee, of course, was abandoned by the enemy, and Bourquoin and many of his officers surrendered themselves immediately after the action.

employed against Sindea, but that my duty should be to keep the road from Alleeghur to Dehlee clear of all marauders. I accordingly joined my corps at Secundra, having arranged that Lieutenant Scott should be appointed my second in command.

When Lord Lake arrived at Secundra, my brother Robert was sent from the Begum Sumroo to make terms for her. His lordship immediately sent him back with a treaty, and directions to stand fast, and not to move from Sirdhana, in which case she should be treated favourably by the British government.

The name of this lady and of her husband, the notorious Sumroo, have been several times mentioned, and as they were personages of some celebrity, and who played no inconsiderable part in the changing scenes of those days in India, it may be proper to explain rather more at large who they were and what they did.

Chapter Eleven
Serving the British

Walter Reinehard was a native of the Electorate of Treves, who came out to India as a carpenter in the French sea service; but having served for some time in the south of India he came to Bengal, where he enlisted in one of the companies of Europeans employed at Calcutta, Deserting from thence after a few days, he repaired to Chandernagore, and became a sergeant once more in the French service. Here, however, he did not continue long; and flying to the upper provinces, he became a private trooper in the cavalry of Sufder Jung, the father of Shujah-u-Dowlut, the Nawab Vizier of Oude. But this service seems not to have suited him either; for he soon left it, and he is next heard of in 1760 as in that of the rebel Foujedar of Purnea, Khadum Hoosseen Khan; but this officer having been expelled from Bengal, Sumroo left him, and took service with Gregory, an Armenian, at that time high in favour with Meer Cossim, the Nawab of Bengal, and distinguished by the name of Goorgeen Khan. From this person, Sumroo received command of a battalion of sepoys, and to this was soon after added another conferred by the Nawab himself.

It was at this time, when Meer Cossim, furious and half disordered in his mind, at the bad success of his arms against the English, on hearing of the taking by them of Monghir, where he had deposited much of his stores and treasure, ordered Sumroo to put to death all the English prisoners that had been taken some time previous at Patna, an order which he obeyed.

When Meer Cossim's affairs appeared desperate, Sumroo, came with his troops, and surrounding the tents of Meer Cossim, clamorously demanded their pay. This the Nawab told him he had not to give, that he must now discharge him, but that he must deliver over the arms and cannon to the officer of his arsenal. Sumroo insolently replied, that they now belonged to those who possessed them, and deserted from him, with all his corps, to the service of Shujah-u-Dowlut. But upon the defeat of that prince at Buxar, Sumroo was entrusted with the care of the Begum's, and he remained in the Nawab Vizier's service until he made peace with the English. One of the conditions of this peace, which, however, never was fulfilled, was that Meer Cossim and Sumroo should both be given up. He was allowed to escape, however.

Meer Cossim, escaped, with some of his family and a few friends, into the Rohilla country, where he died some time afterwards. Sumroo not disposed to trust the Vizier, secured his arrears of pay, by surrounding the Begums and Zenana of that prince in Rohilcunda, and forcing at last his dues from them, after which he retired to Agra with his corps, and entered the service of Jowahir Rajah, the Jhat prince of Bhurtpore, and then took service with the Rajah of Jeypore. But on a remonstrance from the English authorities, he was dismissed and after another short service with the Jhats, he left them finally, and came to Dehlee. There he was discharged after four months, from fear of offending the English. He was, however, immediately retained by Nujjuff Khan Zulficar-u-Dowlut, at that time supreme at Dehlee, who, while reducing the Jhats to obedience, had probably become aware of Sumroo's value. It was he who assigned to the fortunate adventurer, the purgunnah of Serdhanah, in Jeydad, for the maintenance of his corps, and in the service of this nobleman Sumroo remained until he died, in the year 1778.

This man, at some period of his life not exactly known, became attached to the female afterwards known as Begum Sumroo. There are various origins attributed to her. Possibly the daughter of a decayed Moghul noble. The natives, say she was a Cashmerian dancing girl. She was regarded as his wife, and succeeded at his death to his corps and his jaedad,—the former having been increased by the command of a body of Moghul horse, assigned to him by Nujjuff Khan. Aided by this force, the regular portion of which, amounted to five battalions of sepoys, about 200 Europeans, officers and artillerists, and forty pieces of cannon, she preserved her country nearly unmolested, during a period of unrest. The Moghul court supported her while it could; and Sindea had so high an opinion of her capacity, that he not only added to her possessions some lands south-west of the Jumna, but, while engaged in war with Purtaub Sing of Jeypore, he intrusted the western frontier to her protection, by stationing her force at Paneeput.*

To the court of Dehlee she always adhered with fidelity, and showed her attachment strongly in the hour of need during Gholaum Kawdir's atrocious attack upon his sovereign in his own palace at Dehlee. Rejecting contemptuously that powerful miscreant's offer of marriage and equality of power, the Begum repaired to the palace with all her force, resolved to defend her sovereign. In answer to a summons to quit the city on pain of immediate hostilities, she erected a battery in aid of the fort, and replied from it to the heavy cannonade of Gholaum Kawdir; and had the Moghol troops seconded hers with equal spirit, the Rohilla would have been forced to retire. But treachery prevailed, and her efforts were rendered in vain.

Soon after this, the Shah, made a progress through the neighbouring districts, to reduce certain rebels to order, and commenced operations against Nujjuff Koolee Khan, who held the strong fort of Goculghur. Certain officers of the royal army, having neglected their duty were surprised by the enemy in a sortie, which threw the whole of the royal troops into a dangerous state of confusion. The Begum, who was encamped near, came again to his assistance; and, ordering up three battalions of her sepoys, with a gun, under command of a European,† and accompanying them herself in her palankeen, she commenced a fire of grape and musketry.

The king's troops rallied, and Nujjuff Koolee Khan was forced to retire, and then to humble himself to his sovereign. All agreed that the royal arms were saved from disgrace by the Begum's presence of mind; and the. Shah himself, in full durbar, honoured her.

Her power, however, no more than her good will, was able to save her sovereign from the misery and distress which

---

*It is a remarkable thing, and much to the credit of the Begum's troops, that some four or five of her battalions were the only part of Sindea's army that went off unbroken from the field of Assaye: they were charged by our cavalry towards the close of the day, but without effect; Colonel Maxwell, who commanded, being killed in the charge by a grape-shot. The people in the Dekhan, who knew the Begum by reputation, believed her to be a witch, who destroyed her enemies by throwing her chadir at them; the word chadir meaning "chain-shot" as well as a "woman's veil."

† It was George Thomas, who used to tell the story himself.

were poured on his devoted head by the Rohilla chief and his traitor nobles, —and we hear little more of her till about the year 1795. Amongst the principal European officers of her army, was an officer named Levasso, or Le Vaissaux, who she married. He brought about the disgrace of one Legois, an officer, so called from being a native of Liege, and to whom the soldiery had been long attached. The matter terminated in a conspiracy, which they formed to depose both the Begum and her husband, and to place in command of the troops, and on the "musnud" of Serdhanah, a son of Sumroo, though not by the Begum, Zaffer Yab Khan, who at the time resided at Dehlee. It was not at once that the Zaffer Yab Khan agreed to accept the dangerous honour; for he had a very serious dread of the ability and intrigues of his mother-in-law. But at last he did consent; and either so unexpected or so sweeping appears to have been the revolt, that we find the Begum and her husband at once preparing for flight, and proceeding towards the Ganges, in order to seek refuge in Oude. They were overtaken, however, by a party of cavalry sent by Zaffer Yab Khan especially to intercept them, — and they were surrounded, at the village of Kerwah, in the Begum's jagheer.

A free pardon was proclaimed by the usurper to her few attendants, provided they would lay down their arms, and give up the Begum and her husband—and great confusion ensued. The infantry surrounded her palankeen, demanding her to surrender; while the cavalry did the same to her husband. From whatever motive, the Begum drew her poniard, and, striking it across her breast, the blood gushed out, though the wound was a mere scratch. On hearing the tumult and the cries for assistance, her husband called out to know what it meant. They told him the Begum had killed herself.—twice again he repeated the question, and, receiving twice the same reply, he very deliberately drew a pistol, put it to his mouth, and shot himself.

The motive of the Begum in this strange proceeding is not very clear. It is said by some that, before her husband and she left Serdhanah, they made an agreement, in case of accident, that neither should survive the other: and Levasso's suicide may be held to give this some colour. It is not impossible, if any such compact had been entered into, that the Begum, a selfish and artful woman, seeing in what extremities her imprudent marriage had involved her, might choose this way to relieve herself of her self-imposed fetters. However this may be, she was conducted back to Serdhanah as a prisoner, and Zaffer Yab Khan assumed the government of her jagheer.

Like many other persons, however, the Begum in her adversity recollected those who had been her true friends in prosperity, and among the first to whom she applied was George Thomas. To him she wrote in piteous terms, declaring her apprehensions even from poison or the dagger — affirming that her only dependence was on him, and offering any terms, either to him or to the Mahrattas, if, through his intervention, they would come and reinstate her in her jagheer.

Thomas, as we have already seen, like a true cavalier, was not slow to listen to his former mistress's woes. He generously laid aside ancient animosities, and bribed Bappoo Sindea to move upon Serdhanah, and setting on foot a negociation to corrupt Zaffer Yab Khan's men—saying that no mercy would be extended to those who continued to resist the Begum's authority. The Begum was reinstated accordingly, and Zaffer Yab confined. But such is the fickleness of scoundrels like these, that before Thomas could reach the place, there was a counter-revolution. Zaffer Yab was set at large: and, seeing Mr. Thomas appear but slightly accompanied, he ordered an attack upon him and his fifty sowars. Fortunately, there were 400 more just behind: this altered the case—the mutineers submitted—the Begum was fully reinstated—oaths of allegiance administered— and the unfortunate usurper, plundered and a prisoner, was conducted to Dehlee and there confined.

From this time we hear little of the Begum, save that she appears, as formerly stated, to have held her contingent ready at the Mahratta call, for guarding the frontier. And in 1799, especially, she accompanied their army to the Sikh country, returning from Paneeput to Serdhanah. The brilliant successes of the British arms, however, and the events of the Mahratta war, so convincingly proving the superiority of the English over the native power, was not to be overlooked by so shrewd an observer as the Begum. The overture made by that lady to Lord Lake, mentioned above, took place almost immediately after the battle of Dehlee, and it was not long before she came to pay her respects in person; upon which occasion an incident occurred of a curious and characteristic description. She arrived at headquarters, it appears, just after dinner, and being carried in her palankeen at once to the reception tent, his lordship came out to meet and receive her. As the adhesion of every petty chieftain was, in those clays, of consequence, Lord Lake was not a little pleased at the early demonstration of the Begum's loyalty; and being a little elevated by the wine which had just been drunk, he forgot the novel circumstance of its being a native female he was about to receive, instead of some well-bearded chief, so he gallantly advanced, and, to the utter dismay of her attendants, took her in his arms and kissed her. The mistake might have been awkward, but the lady's presence of mind put all right. Receiving courteously the proffered attention, she turned calmly round to her astonished attendants— "It is," said she, "the salute of a padre (or priest) to his daughter." The Begum professes Christianity, and thus the explanation was perfectly in character, though more experienced spectators might have smiled at the appearance of the jolly red-coated clergyman, exhibited in the person of his lordship.

Since that time the Begum has lived much in habits of social courtesy and friendly intercourse with the English, receiving them at very handsome entertainments, and very frequently appearing at the residency table, where she freely participated in all the good things it afforded. Of her character and dispositions somewhat may be judged from what has been said above. Her best qualities were those of the head—her sound judgment, her shrewdness of observation, her prudence, and occasional fidelity to her trust—chiefly as exemplified in her conduct to the unfortunate Shah Allum. For those of the heart, we fear much cannot be said. She was cruel, unforgiving, relentless, deceitful, liberal only where self-interest required it, and courteous too often merely to hide enmity. One anecdote—it is given by Bishop Heber, and we believe is in the main correct—will serve to show something of her ruthless and implacable nature. A slave-girl had offended her—an affair, we believe, of jealousy. The poor creature was brought before her—a hole dug in the earth under the floor of the room, in which she was buried alive — and, as if it. had been a trifling occurrence, her mistress smoked her hookah unconcernedly on this living grave.

In her youth, the Begum must have been handsome — her features and person small and delicate, like most of the women of India; even when the writer knew her, in 1815-16, she had the remains of good looks, and a beautiful hand and arm, which she used to be rather proud of as she smoked her hookah, When the bishop saw her, in 1825, she was "a very little queer-looking old woman, with brilliant, wicked-looking eyes." She never had any children, but adopted several slave-girls as daughters, whom she bestowed as such upon her favourite officers. She died very wealthy, and her jagheer has reverted to the Company.

Skinner continues:-

After settling matters at Dehlee, Lord Lake marched on the 24th of September with the army for Agra. He appointed Colonel Ochterlony Resident at Dehlee, with two battalions of the line as garrison; and ordering two Nujeeb battalions to be raised for its further protection, the command of which was given to two Mahratta officers, Lieutenant Birch receiving the one, and Lieutenant Woodwill the other.

I had been engaged for about a month in settling the country under my charge, which was much infested by petty robbers, when all of a sudden, Madhoo Rao Falkea, a Mahratta chief, who possessed Malaghur in jagheer, summoned me to quit the country. My reply was, that he must make his application to the British Resident at Dehlee, whose orders alone I could attend to. On the other side, Bappoo Sindea had approached Soonput, only twenty côs north of Dehlee, with 5,000 men, and five or six guns. To oppose this inroad, Birch was ordered off with both the Nujeeb battalions, and I was ordered to Dehlee. The same day I began to cross at Putpurgunge, news arrived that Bappoo had beaten Birch, and cut up both battalions. In the evening he arrived in Dehlee, safe himself, but accompanied by Lieutenant Woodwill wounded, and the few men who had escaped. Bappoo, after this exploit, went off to Kannund, his capital, fifty côs west of Dehlee. I was ordered back by Ochterlony, and on reaching Secundra, received information that Madhoo Rao was prepared to attack me, with a battalion consisting of 800 men, 500 horse, and two guns. Hearing this, I wrote to the Resident, and aware that he could not assist me with troops, requested him to send me a couple of field-pieces, with which I would try a battle. His answer was that one of my countrymen had already lost four of the Company's guns, and he would not trust me with another; but that I was by no means to retreat.

Much hurt by this ill-natured remark, I resolved not to retreat, but rather to die; and on being again summoned by Madhoo, replied that I should not stir. His troops were led by a chief of his own, and Malaghur being only eight côs from Secundra, he came up to me about four in the morning. On becoming aware of his march, I caused my men, about 1,200 in number, to mount, and remained till sunrise drawn up in front of my camp.

Madhoo's general remained about a côs from me, and finding he would approach no further, I moved on towards him. When within reach, he fired a few rounds, on which I formed my men into two gholes* and sending Lieutenant Scott with one on his left flank, took to the right myself, the enemy being drawn up in a line with his guns in the centre, and the cavalry in his rear. Both gholes attempted to turn his flanks, but the men behaved ill, and we were repulsed. I collected them and attempted to charge, but they deserted me. I passed between the guns with about fourteen men, and just as I did so, my horse was shot under me, by a matchlock ball, and one of the troopers carried me off behind him.

I then rejoined my party, harangued them and got them together again, mounted another charger, and brought my men a second time to the charge. Madhoo's infantry gave us a volley and then turned; we dashed in and cut them to pieces. The cavalry fled to Malaghur; we took their guns and gained

* *Dense bodies.*

a complete victory. Lieutenant Scott received eleven sabre cuts, and was not expected to recover, and we had 200 men killed and wounded. The battle was gained by great exertion, for my men, just entered the service, did not fight with zeal. I wrote an account of the whole affair to the Resident at Dehlee, begging him to send assistance for Lieutenant Scott, which request he immediately complied with, laying a dak for him to that city. He also wrote me a public letter of thanks, and I received a very handsome one from Lord Lake, a few days afterwards, assuring me of his sense of my exertions. The Resident then ordered me to Dehlee, and directed me to try and get Madhoo Rao out of the fort of Malaghur, and away from the country, even at the expense of a lakh of rupees if required.

On my return to camp accordingly, I marched to Malaghur with my horse, and encamped at a place called Bagwallah, three côs to the north of the fort. There were in garrison with Madhoo, about 2,000 infantry, 300 sowars, and several guns.

I offered him terms, but he refused them with contempt, on which I commenced harassing him with my horse, cutting off all his supplies, and attacking his cavalry whenever I could meet them out of reach of cannon-shot. This was continued for fifteen days without effect, when I found out that all the forage in the fort consisted of two stacks of grass, which would last the horses about three months. These I resolved to destroy, if possible, and for this purpose agreed with a Goojur spy, who volunteered the service for 300 rupees. This man having some brethren in the fort, pretended to desert from me, and fled into the place, where he was well received. He returned in a week, after assuring me that he had done the business; upon inquiring how he had managed it, he told me he had put a slow match to each stack, an assertion which I was slow to believe at first, but in the course of twenty-four hours we saw them both on fire, on which I gave him the money agreed upon.

Three days after this the horse made offers to come over, but I refused to receive them alone. Several attempted to escape, but they were pursued and put to death by my horse. At length Madhoo Rao sent a vakeel to make terms with me, and the following were proposed and accepted. The fort was to be given up, but all his private property was to be secured to him, except the guns and provisions, which were to be left, and the soldiers were permitted to march out with their arms. I told him also, that I should take him to the Resident at Dehlee, who I was sure would take him into the service.

The fort and the purgunnah, consisting of twenty-eight villages, were then given up and added to the Company's territory, and I marched Madhoo Rao with all his troops to Dehlee, where he was received very kindly by the Resident, and afterwards handsomely pensioned. His son, Ram Rao, was taken, with 600 sowars, into the British service. For my part, I received the thanks of the Resident and Lord Lake for this service, which, though it did not involve much hard fighting, was yet a duty of great fatigue and hard work. Of my force, there were never less than 300 or 400 men mounted day and night, and amongst them I constantly required to be. By this close blockade, the enemy was forced to come in within the month, and the cash I was authorized to give for the surrender of the place was thus saved to the government.

Returning to camp, I resumed the measures which had been resorted to for settling the country, so that, in the course of a month, peace and tranquillity was restored from Alleeghur to the gates of Dehlee. Several mud forts were taken, and many parties of desperate marauders were destroyed; so that collections of revenue began to come in from the country. The Resident continued. his kindness to me, rewarding me liberally for services well performed, and sending favourable reports of my conduct to head-quarters.

On the 4th of October, Lord Lake arrived at Agra. At Muttra he was joined by Colonel Vandeleur and Colonel

Clarke, with a large detachment of troops. On the 10th October, he attacked the battalions of Perron's 3rd brigade, who were posted under the fort, and who defended the town bravely against the British. After the town had been carried, Lord Lake attacked the fort, towards the Taje. Hessing, who commanded the fort, was too rich a man to defend it well; he soon found means to dissatisfy the garrison, and the troops being offered service by the British, Colonel Hessing's five battalions, under command of Major Brownrigg, first came over; and then, on the 17th October, the Colonel got the garrison to give up the place. For himself he made good terms, carrying off four or five lakhs of rupees, besides what he had in the Company's funds; and twenty-four lakhs of Sindea's cash were taken by the English commander.

This conduct of the Europeans in the Mahratta service totally ruined their own character, and led to the destruction of their comrades who had remained stanch to their master's cause. These were all seized and put to death, or tortured in prison until they died. Among the former was Colonel Tickers, who, with seven of his officers, was beheaded in one day, by Holcar. Captain Mackenzie and Lieut. Langeman, with several others of Perron's brigades, were confined and tortured at Gwalior; others perished in the service of different petty rajahs; while all those traitors, who were the cause of their deaths, were well treated by Lord Lake, and suffered to go whither they chose.

Surwar Khan, with fourteen battalions and 100 pieces of cannon, still kept in a body; but he could get no Mahratta chiefs to join him. Several tempting offers were make by Lord Lake, both to himself and his troops, but he would not listen to them, but marched from Futtehpore Seekree to Bhurtpore to seek protection from the Rajah. This, however, was refused, so he prevailed upon a Mahratta pundit to join him with 4,000 or 5,000 horse, and they commenced their march towards the Mewat hills. Lord

Lake, after settling matters at Agra, marched in pursuit of these faithful but unfortunate men, who, deprived of their officers, were commanded only by natives, assisted by a few European and country-born gunners among the artillery.

They were overtaken at the pass of Lasswarrie, on the morning of the 1st November, by Lord Lake, with his cavalry, who attacked the rearguard of four battalions, 1,000 horse, and twenty guns. The contest was severe. A regiment or two of the British cavalry made its way through some of the Mahratta battalions; but though they put them into confusion, they could not destroy them, and British and Mahrattas got into a mess together. The cavalry charged repeatedly up to the very bayonets, but could not penetrate them, until the main body, which had marched in the morning, hearing the cannonade, returned and joined their rear-guard; on which the British cavalry retired, with a severe loss, particularly in officers and Europeans.

Surwar Khan now took up a position, determined to fight it out. He drew up the remains of the 2nd and 3rd brigade upon the right; and placed the 4th brigade, which, not having yet suffered, was complete, upon the left. The cavalry was stationed in the rear, a small tank of water was in front, and the flanks were each supported by villages, having in front long chopper grass. Had he cut the brind, or dam, of the water-tank, he might have saved himself a few days longer; but fate had decreed otherwise. The British infantry came up about two o'clock, and after refreshing themselves a little, their brave commander led them to the attack. The contest was fierce and firmly disputed, as all who were there know full well. Again did the heroes of the 76th distinguish themselves, doing credit to their nation; and so also did the 12th sepoy infantry. Lord Lake's son was wounded, and his lordship had two horses killed under him. On the British side the loss was great, but the remains of Perron's infantry was this clay totally destroyed.

As Lord Lake was returning from the battle, some of the Europeans cheered him. He took off his hat and thanked them, but told them to despise death as these brave fellows had done, pointing to the Mahrattas, who were lying thick around their guns. All of these guns were captured, with several thousand prisoners, besides killed and wounded, the number of which on the Mahratta side was very great—but it never was properly ascertained, as I believe the field was never cleared, and the poor fellows were left to the wild beasts.

Lord Lake, after sending the captured guns to Agra, marched towards Jeypore, from whence some correspondence took place with Holcar; and, in consequence of some threatening letters from that chief. Colonel Monson, with a large detachment, including Bappoo Sindea and the Baraitch horse, and 2,000 irregular horse under Lucan, was ordered to march towards his capital: while Colonel Murray, of the Bombay establishment, was directed to march from Guzzrat to co-operate with Monson. The army then, after taking Rampoorah, marched to Agra, and broke up on the 7th June, Lord Lake and the Europeans moving on to Cawnpore.

At this period, intelligence being received that a considerable body of Sikhs had assembled on the bank of the Jumna, opposite to Saharunpore, where Colonel Burn then was, I was directed to join him with all expedition. While on my way, I received orders to proceed and assist Captain Birch, formerly of the Mahratta service, but now commanding a battalion of Nujeebs, who had been pushed on to the banks of the Jumna, with instructions to prevent the Sikhs from crossing, and had taken up a position at one of the fordable ghauts. On my arrival, I perceived a numerous body of Sikhs upon the opposite side; and, after reconnoitring their position, and consulting with Captain Birch, I suggested that, if he would occupy their attention from his position, I would cross the river with my horse at some other fordable ghaut in the vicinity, and take them by surprise.

This was effected about three in the morning, about five côs below; and, having come up before daybreak, I succeeded in completely surprising them. The result was, that the party, consisting of about 5,000 horse, was totally dispersed, with the loss of 400 men and two surdars killed, and about 100 horses taken. On our side we had about 100 men and horses killed and wounded —my own horse having been shot under me.

In a month afterwards, I prevailed on the Sikh chieftains to accompany me to Colonel Burn, with whom they entered into terms. The chieftains who came in on this occasion, were as follows:—Shere Sing, of Boorea; Doolcha Sing, an owner of several villages; Goordut Sing, of Ludwah; and several other commanders of bodies of 500 men each. For this service I received public thanks from the Resident of Dehlee; and from his excellency, Lord Lake, as also from Colonel Burn, with whom I continued six months, to his perfect satisfaction.

*Lt Col James Skinner & Major William Frasier
leading Skinner's Irregular Horse in review*

Chapter Twelve
An Overview of the Monson Disaster

The expedition and disastrous retreat of Colonel Monson is an event too interesting to be dismissed with the imperfect notice taken of it by Skinner, though his information is authentic. It was, in fact, the first important incident of the new war, in which Skinner took a very active part; and therefore, we think it proper to explain how it arose and was carried on.

The first Mahratta war, which was virtually terminated in one campaign by the battle of Laswarree in Hindostan, and that of Argaum and the capture of Gawilghur in the Dekhan, was waged only against Sindea and Bhounslah. Holcar, whom Sindea had in vain invited to join the confederacy, held aloof, though he had vaguely promised assistance. His conduct, was precisely that of a cautious, designing Mahratta. Dreading as he did the power and hereditary enmity of Sindea, he was by no means ill-pleased at the chance of his rival being somewhat crippled by a collision with the British; and even should they be worsted.

Now he hoped to accomplish what both Sindea and Bhounslah could not effect together, not only to withstand, but to defeat the power which had defeated them in a single campaign.

He sought alliances on grounds of mutual interest, from the Rajepoots, the Jhats, the Rohillas, and the Sikhs; and, though last not least, from Ameer Khan, the Pindarree chief, one of his own dependants. He even attempted to persuade Sindea to renew the struggle, and though fruitlessly at the time, either Sindea or his ministers appear to have left the matter open so far as to be able to act as circumstances should determine, though they communicated the overture to the British authorities at the time.

The British suspicions of Holcar, though it would have been inconvenient to bring matters to a head while their hands were otherwise full. He had made inroads on districts they regarded as under British protection, and had ruined Malwa. From the town of Mundissore, the emporium of commerce from all quarters, he forced a million sterling. He was paused by accounts of the course of victory by which the English had delivered Hindostan, and he now resolved to act, though still maintaining the tone of negociation. His letters, indeed, were of a very inconsistent character; at one time breathing threats, at another protesting his friendship. As he moved towards Rajepootanah he wrote to Lord Lake, requesting him to retire towards Agra, "as his near approach to his victorious army might lead to unpleasant circumstances;" and almost in his next he declares that the General shall never have from him any language but that of friendship; but if any other than friendly words should come from him, then he, Holcar, would be helpless. To General Wellesley he wrote, threatening that, though unable to face his guns, "countries of many hundred côs shall be overrun, he (Lake) shall not have leisure to breathe for a moment, and calamity will fall on lakhs of human beings by a continued war, in which my army will overwhelm all like the waves of the sea."

Questions and negotiations succeeded each other, and the savage murder of his three English officers, Tod, Ryan, and Vickers, aggravated the growing quarrel. It was obvious that further temporizing was but playing the enemy's game, and that, unless something were speedily done, Rajepootanah would be rendered a waste, like northern Malwa. The inevitable war was commenced, and the first measure taken was that of the celebrated expedition under Colonel Monson, which was sent on the 23rd of April to drive Holcar from the territory of Jeypore. This was soon effected, Holcar rapidly retired to the southward as the detachment approached; and on Lord Lake making a demonstration with the rest of the army, he continued his route across the Chumbul, and regained his own frontier.

On the 6th of May, the fort of Tonk Rampoorah was gallantly stormed by Lieutenant-Colonel Don: on which Lord Lake sent the main army back to cantonments, leaving Colonel Monson with five battalions of native infantry, and about 3,000 irregular horse, under Lieutenant Lucan and Bappoojee Sindea, to keep Holcar in check. It had been intended that a detachment to co-operate with Colonel Monson should be sent from Guzerat under Colonel Murray; but the junction never took place. Trusting to this, however, it appears Colonel Monson entered Holcar's country by the Mookundra pass to the southward of

Kotah, took the strong hill-fort of Hinglaisghur by escalade, a most gallant and brilliant exploit, and advanced fifty miles south of the pass, into Malwa, where he expected to communicate with Murray; then, hearing that Holcar had recrossed the Chumbul, probably on hearing of General Lake's return to quarters, the Colonel made a forward movement to meet and fight him. But shortness of provisions alarmed him; and having now learned from Colonel Murray, that, instead of advancing to effect a junction, he meant to fall back upon the Myhie river, Monson resolved also to retire by the Mookundra pass.

On the 8th of July, this disastrous retreat commenced. The baggage and stores were sent off at four in the morning, while Monson remained in order of battle, on the ground of his encampment, till half-past nine. No enemy appearing, he commenced his march, leaving the irregular cavalry behind, with orders to follow in half an hour, and bring intimation of what the enemy was about. The detachment had marched only six côs, when intelligence came that the irregular cavalry had been attacked and defeated by Holcar's horse, and while orders were given for the troops to form and support the rear-guard, Bappoojee Sindea rode up to say that the force had been cut up, and Lieutenant Lucan with the other officers, after a brave defence, were wounded and made prisoners. On this, the order was countermanded as useless, and the march was continued to Sonara which the baggage had already reached. On the following morning, the 9th, the army moved again, and reached the Mookundra pass the same day at noon.

On the morning of the 10th, a large body of the enemy's cavalry made their appearance, and increased in numbers until noon of the following day, when Holcar summoned the detachment to surrender their arms. This being contemptuously refused, he divided his force into three bodies, with which he vigorously attacked the British in front and flanks. But he was gallantly and successfully repulsed in every effort: till, at the approach of night, he drew off some three miles distance, intending, as was supposed, to attack, with the aid of his infantry and guns, which had now come up.

Monson, not deeming his post tenable against such a force, and fearing to have his retreat cut off, resolved to march and reach Kotah in two days, much harassed by unfavourable weather and the flooded state of the country; but the men behaved well, repeatedly repulsing the enemy with material loss, while suffering little themselves.

At Kotah, Zalim Sing declined to admit the troops within the walls; and it is said, would not supply them with provisions of which they were much in want. Colonel Tod denies that, on the part of Zalim Sing, and asserts, that he not only offered to furnish them with food, but did send troops to assist and protect their rear, when a brave chief (of Coelah) and many of his party were slain.* However this may be, Monson continued his route towards the Gaumuch ford, a distance of only seven miles; but which, from the depth of the mud and incessant rain, took a whole night to accomplish; and when they did reach it, the rivulet was too much swollen to be fordable. They therefore halted here, not only until it should fall, but to procure a supply of provisions from the neighbouring village of Puttun. On the 15th, the march was resumed; but the guns sunk so deep in the mud that they could not be extricated, and were therefore rendered useless, and abandoned, but they were recommended to the care of the Rajah of Boondee, who remained stanch to his engagements, in the face of Holcar.

On the 17th, the troops reached the Chumbulee rivulet, which was not fordable; but the artillery-men were crossed the next day on elephants, with orders to proceed to Rampoorah. For nearly ten days was the gradual passage of the detachment effected by elephants and rafts, and some by a "ford" lower down, during which time they were constantly harassed by attacks of the enemy, and still more distressed by privations of all sorts; many of the men were drowned in crossing the Chumbulee, and many of the poor sepoys had to deplore the loss of their wives or children, left, often necessarily, on the opposite banks till the last, and then murdered within sight of their husbands by the Bheels from the neighbouring hills, who were in Holcar's interest. On the 21st, Captain Odonnel destroyed a camp of the enemy's, and took several camels and horses; and as the troops were crossing on the 24th, Colonel Monson, with only 700 men, maintained a sharp contest with the enemy's cavalry, who withdrew at sunset with considerable loss, the British only losing twenty in killed and wounded.

* Tod's "Rajepootanah," vol. ii. p. 549.

163

It was the 27th of July before Colonel Monson and all the troops arrived at Rampoorah, which they reached in a most exhausted state. Here, however, the Colonel had the satisfaction of being joined by two battalions of sepoys, with four 6-pounders and two howitzers, and a body of irregular horse, under Major Frith, with a supply of grain from Agra, all sent by General Lake, on hearing of the situation of the detachment at the Mookundra pass. Yet, notwithstanding this relief, and all that could be procured at Rampoorah, the Colonel resolved to pursue his march to Khooshalghur, where he expected to find a further reinforcement of six of Sindea's battalions, with twenty-one guns. Leaving, therefore, a strong garrison at Rampoorah with the field-pieces, the detachment, now consisting of five battalions of Bengal sepoys with the two howitzers, reached the Bunas river at daybreak on the 22nd of August. But it was not fordable, and three boats having been found, one of the battalions was sent across by their means with the treasure, with orders to proceed to Khooshalghur.

Next morning the enemy appeared, and pitched their camp about four miles distant from the British detachment. On the morning of the 24th, the river having fallen, Monson began to transport across his baggage. The greater part of this, along with four battalions, had crossed, and the 2nd battalion of the 2nd Bengal sepoys, who, under command of Major James Sinclair, had been left as a rear-guard, were preparing to follow with the piquets, as soon as the rest should have passed, when the enemy, many of whose cavalry had by this time crossed above and below the British position, brought up their infantry and guns, and about four in the afternoon opened a heavy cannonade on the small body of English still on that side the river.

They were led to the charge by the gallant Major Sinclair, and drove the enemy from their guns as fast as they formed in battery against them. But fresh troops poured in, and fresh batteries showered grape upon them, until, thinned and overpowered, they were forced to retreat, and the remnant of this gallant band crossed the river under the fire of the battalions on the other side, who came down to the bank to check the enemy. But the loss was calamitous; thirteen European officers, with their brave commander, having fallen in this desperate charge. The whole detachment, indeed, suffered severely; and the enemy pressing his advantage, Monson was forced to abandon his baggage, and fly to Khooshalghur, which he reached on the night of the 25th of August, after repulsing several desultory attacks of the enemy's cavalry.

At this place, they found that Sedasheo Bhow, who had been sent to their assistance, intended, as a preliminary in the way of his vocation, to levy a contribution on the town of Khooshalghur, which Captain Nichols, who had escorted the treasure thither, resolved to prevent. The Bhow, enraged, opened his guns upon the place, and then attempted an attack with his infantry; but both were repulsed by Captain Nichols, with a severe loss to the Mahrattas.

On the morning of the 26th, the whole of the enemy's cavalry encamped in separate bodies around the detachment. But the most disheartening circumstance in their case, was the discovery of a correspondence between some of the native officers and the enemy, and, though immediate measures were adopted to check the mischief, two companies of infantry and a large proportion of the irregular cavalry deserted to the enemy. On the same day Monson quitted the fort, having spiked the remaining howitzer, and forming his troops into an oblong square, resumed his march. During that night and the following day, the enemy's cavalry, supported by some guns, attempted, but unsuccessfully, to penetrate the square. On the night of the 27th, they took possession of the ruined fort of Hindoun, and at one o'clock nest morning continued their retreat towards Agra. They had no sooner cleared the ravines near Hindoun, however, than a desperate charge, in three separate bodies, was made upon them by the enemy's horse; but the sepoys reserving their fire till the enemy had come up almost to the bayonet points, it told with great effect, and they fled in all directions. At sunset on the 28th, they reached the Biana pass, where, from the exhausted and suffering condition of the troops. Colonel Monson halted, and would have passed the night; but the enemy brought up his guns, and opened so galling a fire that he was forced to prosecute the retreat, which was continued to the town of Biana. But the night was dark, the camp followers and baggage got mixed with the line, the troops were thrown, into inextricable confusion, order could no more be restored, the troops fairly broke and fled; and such as escaped the straggling parties of the enemy for there was

165

no further regular attack made their way to Agra, which they reached, in flying and detached groups, on the 31st of August.

Such was the disastrous retreat from Mookundra, the result of which, though certainly occasioned in some degree by unavoidable misfortunes and the untowardness of the season for military operations, cannot, we think, be viewed by those who know the sepoys, as free from mistakes, which a more intimate knowledge of that gallant body of men might have avoided. And there is the greater reason for believing this, from the fact, recorded by Skinner himself, of a serjeant having marched into Agra with about 1,500 of the sepoys, whom he and some native officers had rallied and collected into a body when the flight took place.

To remedy, so serious a disaster, and to prepare, not only to repulse a victorious enemy, but to repress the rebellious spirit of those already subdued, yet still discontented, became now an imperative obligation; and the courage and resources of the Commander-in-chief were equal to the emergency. Even the cruel dispositions of the tyrant turned to his own loss, for the mutilated sepoys who escaped his hands roused the indignation of their brethren, and not only excited a spirit of retaliation, but caused even deserters to flock again to their colours. But while the various arrangements were in progress, Holcar, with 60,000 horse of all sorts, 15,000 infantry, and 192 guns, advanced rapidly to Muttra, which was abandoned at his approach. Parties of his horse even crossed the Jumna, but were soon driven back, and on the 1st of October, Lord Lake, with his army, marched from Secundra, where it had been assembled to attack Holcar's camp at Muttra. But that chief had no intention whatever of making a stand. He fled immediately at the first discharge of a galloper gun; and though many efforts were made to surprise his camp, the vigilance of fear and habitual predatory precaution prevented his sustaining any serious loss.

"At an early hour on the 10th," says Major Thorn, "another attempt was made to bring the enemy to an engagement, for which purpose the infantry moved in the same direction as before, whilst the cavalry made a greater circuit to the right to cut off their retreat; but they were so much on their guard since the last affair, that they had posts out in all directions, who by firing matchlocks and burning lights gave the signal of alarm.

Our cavalry formed in two lines, moved in columns of half regiments at regular intervals. In this order, we swept clear the whole plain where the enemy were encamped, at a full gallop; but we could not succeed in our endeavour to charge them, for they scampered off in all directions, dispersing as usual. When we halted, they did the same, rallied, and stood gazing at us, and when we turned our backs to return home, they dashed on, attacking our rear and flanks, firing long shots from their matchlocks, while those who were armed with spears and tulwars, flourished their weapons, making at the same time a noise like jackalls, by way of bravado. On this occasion, about thirty of the enemy were killed, and several made prisoners, who naturally enough expected to meet with the most severe treatment, in retaliation for the perfidious cruelties committed by the master, of whom they gave this curious account, that he was the first to run away. Instead, however, of that vengeance which these men looked for at our hands, they received each a rupee by order of their general, who dismissed them with this message to their chief, that none but cowards treated their prisoners with cruelty."

The unavoidable delay of our army at Muttra had, however, afforded to Holcar an opportunity of striking a blow, which, if successful, might have had serious consequences. This was no less than, by a coup-de-main, to surprise Dehlee, and get possession of the emperor's person, to which, fallen as he was, public opinion in Hindostan still attached much of veneration and traditional importance. For this purpose the whole of his infantry and artillery were detached from his army, under command of an adopted son, Hurnaut, and on the 8th of October commenced their attack upon the Moghul capital. Colonel Ochterlony, the British resident at the emperor's court, with his usual sagacity, had suspected this intention of Holcar, from the time he reached Khooshalghur, and had prudently called in Colonel Burn and his detachment from Seharunpore, a battalion, late of Sindea's, under Major Harriot, from Rohtuck, and one of Nujeebs, under Lieutenant Birch, from Paneeput; and to these were added, about 1,200 matchlock-men of various sorts, and four companies of the 17th regiment. But this force, after all, amounted only to two battalions and four companies of sepoys, about 800 Telingas of Sindea's, two corps of irregular

167

cavalry, and Birch's Nujeebs, with the matchlock-men. Of these troops one-third, or 800 of the regular sepoys, were required by the resident in the palace itself, to guard the emperor's person. One of the corps of irregular horse went over to the enemy at his approach: the second, being found utterly useless, and not to be depended on, was sent off across the Jumna into the Doab, and the Nujeebs mutinied on pretence of want of pay, though only fourteen days' pay was due to them. The mutiny, indeed, was suppressed; some were blown from a gun, others were flogged; but the corps was annihilated. The other corps remained faithful to their duty. And to the honour of all be it recorded, that not another desertion occurred during the whole of this most remarkable and arduous defence.

This, with but few and very insufficient artillery, was, as will be admitted, a most inadequate garrison for a city seven miles in circumference, with no works, save an old ruinous wall of the worst description of masonry - in many places, without a parapet fit to mount a gun upon, or able to stand the shock of one if fired - without a ditch, and surrounded on all sides by ruins and cover, up to the very foot of the wall; add to this, a most turbulent and idle-disposed population, and it will not be denied that its defenders had no enviable task in having to protect it against an army of 15,000 regular infantry with nearly 200 guns, and backed by 60,000 horse.

The question was, whether, with such inadequate means, the defence should be limited to the fort or palace, abandoning the city to its fate? But Colonel Burn, who, as senior officer, had assumed the command, considering the evil effect it would have upon the British name were the city given up, resolved, on his own responsibility, to defend both as long as possible.

Although the enemy did not take this brave garrison unaware, there was yet but scanty time to make the needful arrangements: but redoubts were erected at the Ajmere and Toorkoman gates, and some part of the rampart was strengthened for guns. On the 7th, Holcar's horse made their appearance, and after an attempt at reconnoitering and driving them back, on the part of Lieutenant Rose, Captain Carnegie, and Lieutenant Hunter, which was defeated by the cowardice of the irregular cavalry, the troops retired within the walls. Next day, the 8th, the enemy's infantry and artillery approached in force, and commenced a heavy cannonade upon the south-east angle of the city wall: and, though compelled to withdraw by the fire from the garrison, some thirty or forty feet of the parapet had fallen from the concussion of its own guns, or been levelled by the enemy's shot. During the night, breaching batteries were erected, which totally destroyed the parapet and made partial breaches in the wall: and, as it was probably here the first attempt would be made, it was resolved to check the enemy's progress by a sally. This did not, however, take place until the 10th, when Lieutenant John Rose, aide-de-camp to Colonel Burn, with 200 sepoys, 150 Nujeebs, a reserve of fifty men and a 6-pounder, moved out to the attack. It was eminently successful; they gained the battery, spiked the guns, and retreated with very little loss, leaving the enemy fighting each other in the confusion and the darkness.

A battery of two heavy guns had been erected the same day by Captain Keating; and, when the enemy again opened their guns from the battery which had been stormed, both it and the more distant ones were silenced by the Captain's well-directed fire. On this the enemy drew off, and commenced operations on the southern face of the city, and all within the walls remained watching with vigilant anxiety for the next attack. Their heaviest guns were now placed opposite the curtain between the Toorkoman and Ajmere gates, under cover of some gardens and ruins. A breach was soon effected; but a work thrown up inside, cutting off the breached part, rendered that of no use to them, and the men worked hard and willingly to accomplish this important operation.

On the 14th, at daybreak, the enemy's guns opened from every direction, and, under cover of this cannonade, an escalade by infantry in large numbers was tried at the Lahore gate; but they were driven back with much loss in men; and all their ladders. Unfortunately, Lieut. Simpson, of the 17th regiment, was killed by a cannon-shot. After this, no further desperate attack was attempted. A show was made at the Cashmere gate, but, before the morning of the 15th, the enemy's whole force had moved off, and at daybreak their rear-guard was seen at a distance by the weary garrison, who for eight days and nights had been incessantly but cheerfully struggling to save the place. Such is a short narrative of the chief events of this memorable defence; but it is not easy to convey an idea of the persevering exertions by which success was attained. The fatigue suffered by both men and officers could only be equalled by the cheerful patience with which it was borne. And when we consider not only the defenceless condition in which this small body of men was exposed to the assault of an organized and well-supplied multitude, but the state of feeling in the country from the late triumph of that enemy, and the disastrous defeat so recently sustained, it may give some idea of what the sepoy really is, and what he will do when led by officers whom he loves and confides in. And little often is the trifle which will cheer them to extra toil and extra danger. A small allowance of sweetmeats, in addition to their daily provisions – for they had no time to cook food – was found on this occasion to have the happiest effect upon the men, and half a month's pay of gratuity, when the enemy was repulsed, rendered them grateful and happy.

Kindness and firmness on the part of their officer, and a full reliance on his judgment, will kindle the zeal and devotion of the sepoy to any exertion. Both Colonel Ochterlony and Colonel Burn knew them well, and richly did their country reap the fruits of their knowledge, and of their intrepid firmness, in the siege of Dehlee.

We do not pretend to give an account of the war, and though we cannot refrain from adverting at some length to remarkable feats of gallantry, our purpose in these notes is merely to follow the course of Colonel Skinner's career, and to give so much of the general current events as may serve to explain and illustrate it. We therefore pass over the rapid movements which took place on either side by the contending parties, and in which it will be seen that Skinner had his share. Even the celebrated battle of Deeg must not detain us long, although there, in spite of a position deemed impregnable, and chosen by his own generals, Holcar, in one morning's work, lost nearly a hundred of his guns; his two best commanders, more than 2,000 of his infantry, with the field, and his character for good fortune. But we must drop one word of regret for the loss of the gallant General Fraser, and many other brave officers, for the field was not won without the loss of 643 killed and wounded, of whom five officers were among the first, and seventeen among the second list. Nor can it be uninteresting to mention that, among the captured artillery, Colonel Monson found fourteen of his own guns, and several ammunition tumbrils, lost during his unfortunate retreat.

Four days after this brilliant success, Holcar received another check to his pride, in being surprised in his camp, in spite of his boasted alertness. After a rapid and destructive run through the Doab, burning, plundering, and destroying, Holcar came to Futtehghur, and had encamped there in safety, as he believed, being thirty-six miles ahead of the pursuing force. But General Lake, by a forced night march, and led by excellent intelligence, reached the outskirts of the enemy's camp just as day was breaking, on the morning of the 17th. Holcar had heard, just the evening before, at a nautch, the news of the battle of Deeg, but he said nothing to his chiefs, and retired to his tents as usual. An artillery tumbril blew up towards morning in the British line of march, and started him; but they told him it was the morning gun from Futtehghur, and he believed it. Even when the firing commenced, such confidence had he in his spies, that he could not believe it was Lord Lake, as they told him.

All seemed to combine to lull his usual acuteness to sleep. The men, wrapped in their blankets, were still sleeping by their piqueted horses, when they were roused by showers of grape; and before those who had not been sent to their last slumber could rise and look about them, the King's 8th Light Dragoons were amongst them, cutting them down right and left; the other regiments soon galloped up and did the same, so that the plain was soon covered with the bodies of the dead.

Holcar, too late convinced, mounted his horse, and never stopped till he was eighteen miles distant, on the road to Mynpooree. The rest, left to themselves, dispersed or were cut up. Some, whose horses were even more jaded than ours, by their desperate marches, climbed into the mango trees, and thus escaped for the time. But some of them, unable to resist firing on the dragoons as they passed, were discovered and shot among the branches. For ten miles did the pursuit continue, and as the night march was good fifty-eight miles, the cavalry had thus ridden over a space of seventy miles in twenty-four hours, an almost unparalleled feat, especially after a most harassing march of 350 miles within the previous fortnight. The loss of the British was trifling—scarce twenty men.

171

That of Holcar, severe in itself, being not less than 3,000 men upon the ground, was infinitely more so from its consequences. By desertions and dispersions, his force, on that morning reckoned at 60,000 men, was so reduced that he never mustered half that number again, and, what was still worse, he lost his *nam*, his prestige, which, from his first successes, had risen high in Hindostan.

Among other fortunate consequences of this victory, was the saving of the European civilian and merchants, who, abandoning the open cantonment, had taken refuge in the fort. There they defended themselves bravely, but could not have long held out; and happy were the almost despairing gentlemen of Futtehpore and Mynpooree, when the yellow coats of "Skinner's horse" made their appearance as their deliverers.

There yet remained one blow to complete the fall of Holcar, and that was the capture of the strong fortress of Deeg. This, as well as Bhurtpore, was the stronghold of the Jhats, and the Rajah of the latter place, so well known in Indian warfare, had been the dependant rather than the ally of Holcar ever since the rise of that chieftain to power. The loss of his guns and infantry, and his subsequent defeat near Futtehghur, had reduced him to a change of condition; he had now become rather dependant on the Rajah, and the fortress of Deeg was manned by their joint forces: for their interests were now too closely united for one to fall without bringing down the other.

On the 13th of December, the batteries opened against Deeg; on the 23rd, the breach was stormed in the usual gallant and irresistible way: and though the enemy's men, particularly the Golunduz, or artillerists, fought with the most resolute bravery, never quitting their guns till bayoneted at them to a man, and though a fierce and most bloody conflict was maintained throughout the whole of this most arduous day, by two o'clock of the following morning, the town, the shahbourg, and outworks, with all their guns, were in possession of the British. The garrison of the inner fort, dispirited and hopeless, were seen streaming off in parties during that day; and on the morning of Christmas 1804, both town and fort, with all the remaining artillery of Holcar, his stores of grain and some treasure, remained in the hands of the besiegers.

It falls not in with our duty or our plan, to touch upon the seige of Bhurtpore, with its four most gallant though disastrous assaults. Heavy and sad as was the loss of life before its ill-omened walls, the sacrifice was not altogether in vain: for it convinced the Rajah of his own impotence to resist a power which had pulled down princes so much his superior, and which must soon exhaust his own resources and destroy him. And though "Bhurtpore" continued for long to be a taunt and a reproach to us in Upper India, those who knew us best were well aware that a timely submission alone saved the Jhat prince from the fate of his allies. As for Holcar, baffled, beaten, and dishonoured, stripped of his guns and his troops, the fortresses of his family in our hands, with scarce a home to fly to, this freebooter who crossed the Chumbul with 70,000 men and 200 guns, breathing arrogant threats of ruin and extermination to the British, in less than ten short months fled before that power, and recrossed that river a wandering fugitive with scarce 8,000 horse and 4,000 or 5,000 infantry.

On the 21st of April, the army broke up from before Bhurtpore, and crossing the Chumbul, made a progress towards Bundelcund, forming a junction with the division, which was acting in that quarter and arranging treaties with the chiefs. They returned from thence in May, and in the beginning of June were distributed in quarters for the rainy season along the west side of the Jumna.

Thus terminated these two bright and rapid campaigns, which for the magnitude of the effects they accomplished, the brilliant succession of exploits performed in them, and the daring gallantry and intrepid resolution they exhibited, have never perhaps been surpassed. In less than two years, three powerful princes, elated with a long career of success, besides many minor chiefs, the aggregate of whose forces was at least 400,000 men, with 500 guns; possessed of innumerable strongholds, many of which were held to be impregnable, were completely humbled, their armies scattered, their guns captured, and their fortresses stormed and taken. And this by a force which, taking natives and Europeans together, never exceeded in number a tenth part of their adversaries. Nor were these successes gained over feeble enemies, as the heavy lists of killed and wounded will sufficiently testify; but neither their numbers nor their courage

173

could avail against the steady discipline and regulated valour of British soldiers.

Chapter Thirteen
Skinner's Account of Monson's Campaign

Colonel Monson, was decoyed by Holcar to his capital; but he delayed attacking the Colonel until the setting-in of the rains, a season as favourable to the operations of the Mahrattas as it was adverse to the British, for the country of Malwa is so deep in the rains that wheel-carriages cannot move, a circumstance of which I believe the Colonel was not aware. Holcar also contrived to throw himself between Colonel Murray and Monson, and kept manoeuvring about in hopes of an opportunity to strike some great blow. So bad was the information of the latter, that he was unable to effect a junction with Murray, who, thus unsupported and aware of the effect of the rains in that quarter, commenced his retreat to Baroda, without being able to apprise Colonel Monson of his intention.

Holcar, finding that he had thus gained his point, now turned upon Monson, and overtook him near Bhampoorah. The Colonel, who by this time had heard of the retreat of the Bombay detachment, resolved to fall back with his own corps by the Mookundra pass; but Holcar was too quick for him. He marched from Bhampoorah, leaving Lieutenant Lucan, who had command of all the Hindostanee horse, amounting to about 5,000 men, and some gallopers as a rear-guard; but the detachment had not gone ten miles, when Holcar's advanced guard made its appearance before Lucan.

Had Lucan retreated at once, he might have saved himself; but he desired to make a name, and thought he might acquire it by making a brilliant charge before commencing his retreat; and so he might had his troops been stanch, but they were not. Bappoo Sindea, who commanded the greater portion, at the first movement went over to Holcar, and the Baraitch horse (whose master now enjoys a large jagheer), began to retreat at once without orders, so that poor Lucan was left with only his horse, amounting to 1,500, and two brave chiefs (never named by Government), Prithee Raj, a relative of the Bullumghur Rajah, with 500 horse, and the Shekawat Rajah's son with 500 Rajepoots; these remained true to Lucan, and did honour to the field.

Lucan, after checking the advance party, which, by all accounts amounted to 5,000 horse, commenced his retreat, and continued in good order for six miles, unassisted by Gardiner's horse, who never came up or were heard of. Then, finding himself quite surrounded by Holcar's troops, he was forced to make a stand. In this situation he was charged by Wahud Allee Khan with an immense body of Bunjas, the best cavalry Holcar had; but he and the two chieftains stood the charge and repulsed the Bunjas with great slaughter, severely wounding Wahud Allee Khan. On this they cleared away a little, and Lucan again tried to retreat; but he was again charged from all quarters, and completely routed. He himself was wounded and made prisoner, and Prithee Raj and the Shekawut Rajah's son, with all their followers, were cut to pieces. The Baraitch Nawab was caught, wounded, and taken, and most of the cowardly fellows that left Lucan, on the enemy's first appearance, were overtaken and destroyed.

Monson had now gained the Mookundra pass, but thought fit to leave it for want of supplies. Had he continued in his position, he might have defied all the armies of Hindostan to drive him from it. But in making his retreat from Mookundra to Kotah, a distance of only sixteen côs, it came on to rain violently, and Monson lost almost all his guns, which were left sticking in the mud, together with all the tents. On his arrival at Kotah, Colonel Monson made application to the Rajah for provisions, and also for permission to leave two 12-pounder guns under his care. But Zalim Sing refused, declaring that he would neither furnish supplies nor take charge of the guns, unless he (the Colonel) would remain and attack Holcar; for, said he, if you march away, Holcar will take the guns, and punish me for assisting you with provisions.

Colonel Monson then left the guns to their fate, and commenced his march to Rampoorah, a fort near Tonke, which was garrisoned by British troops. This place lie reached with great difficulty, being overtaken by Holcar in his retreat at the Bunas river which had risen, and could scarcely be crossed. At this place Major Sinclair, who, with a battalion of the 2nd regiment native infantry, was left as a rear-guard, was completely sacrificed. His conduct was noble, and shewed the natives of the country what British courage could do. He charged the enemy repeatedly, taking almost every gun that Holcar could bring against him; but troops pouring in upon him by thousands, and no assistance being to be had from Monson, he at length fell a victim, with all his party except one officer, in this zealous discharge of his duty. This gallant act of the sepoys, proving what they will do when properly led, will long be remembered both by Mahrattas and by Indians.

My corps having now been increased to 1,200 strong, and being joined by my brother who had left the Begum's service, I was directed with all haste to join Colonel S. Brown, who commanded a large detachment of British troops at Muttra, and who now was ordered to support Monson. I reached Muttra without trouble, and my men were apparently quite stanch to the service. I had commenced crossing the Jumna, and got over six rissalahs under charge of my brother, when the rumours and alarm occasioned by Colonel Monson's retreat, began to damp the spirits of some of my men. Immediately on understanding this, I gave orders that 300 more should cross and join my brother. They saddled their horses accordingly and went to the ghaut; but then, believing themselves to be out of my sight, they commenced their march towards Koorjah in the Dooab. At this conjuncture I had with me 200 men, 100 being mounted on my own horses, the others on horses of their own. On the first I placed the greatest reliance; but I was somewhat doubtful of the attachment of the others; and seeing the rascally conduct of the 300, I was somewhat at a loss what conduct to pursue. Whilst meditating on the subject I saw my Bargheers saddle, which increased my uneasiness, for I feared they were going to follow the example of the 300; but from this apprehension my mind was soon relieved by their coming up in a body and requesting me to chastise the misconduct of the runaways, who were, they said, disgracing the character of the corps. To this I replied, that if they would swear upon their Koran to be faithful to me and to the service, I would then be proud to be their leader, and to this they immediately agreed. Lieutenant Boyd of the 15th Native Infantry, who, with a company of sepoys, had crossed to receive from me some treasure brought from Dehlee, was witness to this proceeding; and as soon as I was satisfied, I mounted my horse and desired my Bargheers to follow me, leaving the remainder in camp.

I overtook the runaways about a côs off, and when within 100 yards of them I ordered my yellow boys to halt, as I purposed to go forward and reason with them. When I got within hearing, the rissaldar, who was the leader of the deluded men, came up to me with four of his sowars. I tried to bring them to reason with mild words; but perceiving that these had no effect, I began to make use of abusive language and threats. On this the cowardly leader of the mutineers ordered one of his men to fire at me, and before I could draw either sword or pistol the man fired; but missing me, shot my horse dead on the spot through the head. My yellow boys seeing me fall, immediately gave a shout and charged them sword in hand, and with such good-will that about ninety of their number were cut up, the rest fled to a fort in the neighbourhood belonging to the Hatterass Rajah, who was not on friendly terms with the British Government. Of my party there were ten men killed, and several wounded.

Next morning I crossed the remaining portion of my party, and having joined Colonel Brown reported the occurrence to him. During the ten days we remained here, the detachment was much disheartened and perplexed by the alarming rumours and most painful objects coming in daily from the disastrous retreat of Monson. Poor Lucan had been tortured to death at Kotah, and two officers, left at Englaisghur by Monson, were beheaded by Hurnaut Sing, an adopted son of Holcar's; many others came into camp naked as they were born, and numbers of sepoys with their noses and ears cut off.★ The three companies left at Englaisghur entered Holcar's service, and many more, who had from time to time deserted during the retreat, also joined him, so that he had now about 1,000 of the British sepoys in his service. Holcar tried another attack upon Monson near Khoosalghur, but was repulsed by the British sepoys. Of the deserters, a great number got into the square and were bayoneted. Holcar's loss this day was severe.

Colonel Frith, who had been sent with his corps of Hindostanee horse, joined at Rampoorah; but on the first march from that place his men went over to the enemy. Colonel Gardiner also left the detachment when at Khoosalghur, and went off to Jeypore, where he had formerly been on service. Our situation thus became alarming, and the more so from the discouragement, occasioned by the incessant arrivals of the victims of Monson's misfortune. Desertions from Muttra were numerous, and, in fact, the greatest confusion I ever witnessed prevailed amongst the troops there.

The detachment consisted of five battalions of sepoys, a regiment of regular cavalry, 900 of my horse, and twenty

---

★ *It would be a great injustice to suppose that such cruelties were common to all the Mahrattas, - such, in truth, is not their real character. These barbarities were the effects of Holcar's peculiar disposition, which was jealous and revengeful in the extreme. His mutilations of the sepoys appears to have been from their refusal to enter his service; a circumstance which not only tends greatly to the credit and high character of those who endured it, hut tends to lessen the culpability of those who took the other alternative, and did enter his service.*

pieces of cannon, with three lakhs of Brinjarrahs, loaded with provisions sufficient to last the detachment for several months. However, a council of war was held to decide whether the detachment was to fall back on Agra, or to stand out at Muttra. The officers commanding corps, namely Colonel Ball, Colonel Toone, Major Hammond, Major Burrel, and Colonel Brown, were summoned to head-quarters. I, also, was honoured by a call, but did not vote. Colonels Brown, Ball, and Toone, were for falling back to Agra, Burrel and Hammond of the 2nd for standing fast at Muttra.

Next evening, about sunset, the detachment all of a sudden paraded, and in an hour after, marched off to Agra, leaving tents and almost everything behind. Being pitched at some distance, I knew nothing of all this, until my brother, who was for piquet, proceeding with 200 men to his post about an hour after they had gone, was surprised to find no piquet party; my men who were on duty, fifty in number, having gone off to Bhurtpore, followed by the jemadar with his party of regulars. On this he returned to me with the information that the army had gone off. I instantly saddled, and, striking my tents, formed my men in two columns with the two 6-pounders. About three hours after the detachment had left us I commenced my march, and soon found out the road they had taken, by the followers. Of the enemy I saw nothing, and joined the main body within two côs of Gowghaut.

Desiring my brother to remain in rear of the 1st cavalry, I went up to the commanding officer and told him all the circumstances, when he said he would halt at Gowghaut. The best of the business was, that Holcar was running off one way, while we were going another; and when we arrived at Gowghaut the troops were so much knocked up and straggling, that I do not believe any regiment could number twenty men under their colours. The officers had lost almost everything they possessed; and such was our fright and confusion, that had the detachment met with 1,000 resolute men of the enemy, we should have made a worse business of it than Monson's. My hircarrahs brought me intelligence that Holcar, who had encamped at Futtehpore Seekree, had fled that night towards Bhurtpore, believing that the detachment was coming to surprise him; while Colonel Burn's hircarrahs, on the other hand, brought him information that Holcar's brigade had arrived at Futtehpore - though they were not within 100 côs of that place - and that he meant to push on for Gowghaut to cut off our retreat. It was this that made the Colonel push on towards Agra in such a hurry, and such was his alarm that he would not stop at Gowghaut, but pushed on to Agra, where we took shelter under the fort, and so greatly was the character of the British troops degraded in the native eyes by this behaviour, that the very thieves pelted us all night with stones.*

In this position we remained for three days, witnessing the most horrible cruelties performed by Holcar on Monson's soldiers. The 1,000 men, who had gone over to him in the retreat, had begun to desert back to us from Futtehpore, and Holcar, in order to make an example that should deter the rest from following their example, cut off the noses, ears, and right hands from 200 of them. This act of cruelty was the saving of us, for our sepoys, who had been deserting by hundreds, seeing these poor mutilated wretches coming in daily, ceased at once to leave their regiments.

At length, after all the surviving officers had come in, I saw about 1,500 men march in to camp with colours flying under command of a sergeant, with a great number of soobahdars and jemadars of native corps. These heroes had kept their

---

* Nothing can be more striking, or more instructive, than Skinner's account of these disgraceful events: showing, as it does, the naked truth, stripped of the conventional form of official despatches; illustrating, too, as it so forcibly does, the demoralizing effect of even a small reverse; and the importance, in Indian warfare, of holding it a maxim at all times rather to dare the worst, and die upon the ground, if necessary, than retreat in face of an enemy. Retreat is almost always more disastrous than defeat, and the military history of our Indian empire abounds in instances where success has attended a resolute resistance even against overwhelming numbers.

ground after all the officers had left them. The poor sergeant was never noticed. This body of men had made good their way, pursued by Holcar's cavalry, to within eight côs of Agra.

This was the termination of both retreats; for Colonel Macan now arrived and took command of this unfortunate detachment, which had run all the way from Muttra to Agra without seeing an enemy. Colonel Macan marched us to Secundra, and brought the whole force into order: regular piquets were thrown out and rounds observed; cavalry regiments poured in every day, and Lord Lake, with the Europeans, was expected to arrive from Cawnpore. Holcar took possession of Muttra, assembled all his troops, and sent his brigade, under command of Harnaut, to attack Dehlee. The 2nd cavalry was reported by its commanding officer "refused to cross." Colonel Macan went to the spot determined to shoot the first man who should refuse. The regiment was ordered to parade, and move to the ghaut. The Colonel then ordered the first troop to cross, when not a man refused, and it was found out that they had never got orders to do so. Colonel Gordon was immediately removed, and a new commander appointed. Had there been a few more Macans in the service, many a disgraceful thing might have been avoided.

Holcar's horse now made their appearance, and daily skirmishes regularly took place. Had Colonel Macan possessed full powers, we should soon have destroyed Holcar, who now was enjoying himself at Muttra, revelling in the lall skraub* and brandy of the stores left there by the detachment. He gave himself up to nautching and all sorts of voluptuousness, which, luckily for us, had such an effect upon his health that he could not move from his bed. At Muttra he remained a month, issuing purwannahs and sending collectors to the Doab, and bestowing purgunnahs in jagheer to everybody who would join him. Among the rest he sent a man named Allahmeer, with 100 horsemen to Major Wood, who commanded the

* Claret.

fort of Alleeghur, with a demand to deliver up the fort to him immediately, or he would not spare a man. The Major, although he had a battalion and provisions for several months in the fort, was so much alarmed at this threat, that he actually promised to give up the fort in fifteen days, and wrote off to Lord Lake, who by this time had arrived at Mynpooree with all the European troops, informing him of the treaty he thus had made with Holcar's soobah. I need not state his lordship's answer - the world will easily judge of its nature.

In the mean time, his lordship was approaching to Agra, where our army, increased by five regiments of native cavalry, was in excellent order, under Macan's command. At the commencement of Monson's retreat, we had in our pay about 20,000 Hindostanee horse in different places and under various officers. Since then, of them all, my corps was the only one which had remained stanch, the rest had all gone over to the enemy. Dehlee was now besieged by Holcar's brigade, while our army at Agra was looking out for Lake as earnestly as the Mussulmans, after a month's fast, look out for the new moon of the Eede. At length this new moon was seen on the 3rd September 1804, arriving at the tomb of Eelimad-u-dowlut, which he reached with three regiments of dragoons, one of European foot, the famous 76th, and about fifteen or sixteen companies of sepoys.

My corps was now ordered to cross the river and join Lord Lake, which was done; and next morning they were paraded, when his Excellency inspected them, and praising them highly for their fidelity, increased their pay ten rupees per horse; and promised that they should have bread for life. He then ordered the European troops to cross, and directed Major Worsely, with the fifteen companies of sepoys to proceed to the Doab and drive all Holcar's collectors from thence, after which he was to rejoin the army at Muttra. His excellency then gave four galloper-guns to my corps, and directed me to join Major Worsely.

His lordship then joined the army, and commenced his inarch for Muttra on the 1st of October, attended by the whole of Holcar's horse, amounting, by the nearest calculation, to 40,000 men, who did their best to harass him on the way. But Holcar soon discovered that he had a very different person to deal with from Monson. Lord Lake kept the Jumna on his right, his baggage being between the river and the line, and reached Muttra in four or five marches, skirmishing all the way: Holcar now evincing great activity.

Major Worsely on his part took a round by Shekoabad, Zelasur, Coel, and Mahabun to Muttra: took several mud forts, hung up some of the soobahs who fought; and after a sharp and troublesome business, arrived in a few days at Hauseagunge opposite to Muttra. An able, steady, and active soldier, Major Worsely, received well-deserved praise for his zealous services, and was ordered to cross and take post in the town of Muttra with six companies of sepoys. The remaining part of his force with my horse were directed to stand fast at Hauseagunge, under the command of Major Munro; and as the Jumna was not fordable at this point, a bridge of boats was ordered to be made ready from the Hauseagunge ghaut to the town. Lord Lake had encamped on the west bank of the river in the old Mahratta cantonments; and Colonel Down with the reserve; consisting of the remains of Monson's detachment, amounting to about 2,000 sepoys, was pitched between the army and the town.

All this time, Holcar was actively engaged in cutting tip small detachments coming with supplies from Agra; so that in a few days provisions and forage failed, and large bodies were forced to go out for forage daily. Day and night was the camp surrounded with Holcar's horse, which were no sooner attacked than they dispersed. Several mornings this was attempted with all the cavalry and infantry; but the moment they saw us they vanished, and no sooner had we returned to camp and unsaddled, than there they were again surrounding the camp, and quietly dismounting; not less than from 10,000 to 20,000 of these horse were thus constantly hovering about the camp, and such became the scarcity, that three seers of atta,* were selling for a rupee. My corps was directed to work hard in the Doab to remedy this scarcity, and get grain wherever it was to be found. I used to go out in the morning, plunder the villages, and send in whatever I could lay hold of; but it seldom exceeded the day's consumption, and the minds of the soldiers became so unsettled, and desertions so common again, that the troopers upon duty were found galloping over to the enemy from their posts: and in order to prevent such shameful desertions. Lord Lake was forced to place a sepoy with each trooper vidette, with orders to shoot the trooper if he should move towards the enemy. This state of anxiety and hardship continued for six days, and to add to it, alarming accounts arrived from Dehlee; the President entreating Lord Lake to come to his assistance with all despatch.

This his lordship was well disposed to do; but the army was just then waiting for the Brinjarrahs that were on their way from Cawnpore. They came unmolested until within two côs of Hattrass, when the Rajah stopped them, and said he would not permit them to go to Lord Lake; but would take the supplies himself. The Brinjarrahs at first refused; but at length being bribed they promised to give up the grain. When this information reached Lord Lake, he sent for me and asked whether I thought I could bring them away. I replied, that if his lordship would leave it to me, I would either bring off the supplies or lose my life in the attempt; on this, he shook me by the hand, and declared he never would forget my services.

I took my leave; and returning to camp collected all my hircarrahs, and as the Brinjarrahs were only eighteen côs distant, I laid a dak of hircarrahs, just to let me know when they should begin loading to go into the fort. The second day about midnight, information was brought me; and I

* Coarse flour, the common food of the sepoys.

185

immediately saddled and set off with all my horse, 1,200 in number. On reaching within a côs of them, I halted until my spies gave me information that they were all ready, and would move, if I did not prevent them. I left my brother with 800 men, and with 400 I dashed in amongst them, crying out that Lord Lake had sent me to their assistance. At first, they began throwing down their loads, declaring they would not go with me; but I ordered all who should attempt throwing their loads to be put to death; and several were accordingly killed. When they saw this, and found me determined, and perceiving my brother coming up with the large body, they gave in and called out, "Dohee, Lord Lake, kee;" so I ordered them to march towards Muttra, which they did.

By the time the sun had risen, I had got a côs off clear with my prize. But when the news reached the Rajah, he ordered all his horse to saddle and pursue me. I still pushed on; but when I had made two more côs, I ordered my brother with 600 men to go on with the convoy, and if any of the fellows should attempt throwing down their loads, to put them at once to death. I halted myself with the other 600 to show front to the Rajah, and in two hours afterwards I perceived his sowarree coming on. I now formed my party into two gholes, and made them a speech, telling them that I had promised Lord Lake either to bring in the Brinjarrahs or die. They were all stanch, and declared in reply they were ready to die with me. My brother had gained some four or five côs when the Rajah came up to me with, I think, about 1,200 men. I formed and showed front, when he sent a man to me to inquire who I was, and by whose authority I had taken the Brinjarrahs?

I gave my name accordingly, and said that I had Lord Lake's hookum, which was the best in Hindostan. He sent in reply to order that I should immediately give up the Brinjarrahs, or he would instantly punish me. I replied that the Brinjarrahs and my head should go together, and that he had full liberty to do as he liked. He then sent on a few skirmishers in front, who fired at us; but some of my yellow boys soon sent their horses back without their riders. When the Rajah saw I was determined, and was not to be frightened, he asked me if I would take his vakeel to Lord Lake. To this, I replied that I would not take him now, lest the people might think that I had gained the Brinjarrahs by some false promise; but that if he would send him after, I would be his friend, and try to obtain his forgiveness. To this he agreed, and then marched back towards his fort.

For my part, I thanked the Almighty for my success, and joining my brother, arrived in the evening at Hauseagunge. The first person I saw was Major Worsely, who shook me warmly by the hand, and said that Lord Lake ought never to forget that day's work. I crossed and went to Lord Lake, who was at dinner; but hearing that I had arrived, immediately came out and asked me, "Well, have you succeeded?" "Yes, my lord," was my reply, on which he also shook me by the hand, and declared he never would forget me or my corps. He then asked me to come in to dinner; but I told him that having been eighteen hours on horseback, I was pretty well knocked up; but that I should wait on his lordship in the morning.

I returned to my tent accordingly, and ordered for all my sowars a seer of sweetmeats each, which, through Major Worsely's assistance I got from the town, and then ate my dinner. Next morning; I called on his lordship and reported the Brinjarrahs at 60,000 bullocks all loaded with atta. On this, he again shook me by the hand, and taking the sword he wore at his own waist, presented it to me with 20,000 rupees. The Brinjarrah jemadars were also all handsomely rewarded and ordered immediately to cross. These Brinjarrahs gave just seven days' supply to the army, which enabled it to march, on the 12th of October, to the relief of Dehlee, leaving Colonel Worsely with his force to guard the town of Muttra. Colonel Munro and my corps were detached towards Anoopsheher in order to meet and escort into camp a large convoy consisting of a lakh of Brinjarrah bullocks loaded with atta, wheat, and koonjah; and having met them, we accordingly proceeded with them to Dehlee, which place Lord Lake reached in eight or ten marches, much harassed all the way by Holcar's horse.

Four days previous to Lord Lake's arrival, Hurnaut had raised the siege of Dehlee, and retreated towards Deeg through the Alwar pass, and then continued on towards Paneeput. His lordship could not follow for want of supplies, till our arrival, on the 27th of October, with the Brinjarrahs. Lord Lake then detached General Fraser in pursuit of Holcar's infantry, with all the infantry except the reserve under Colonel Down, which was ordered to cross the river. On the 29th, information was brought that Holcar had himself crossed at Koongepoorah to attack Colonel Burn's detachment, which had left Dehlee a few days previous to his lordship's arrival. This detachment consisted of one battalion of the 14th N.I. and three irregular battalions under Captain Harriott, formerly of the Mahratta service, and was proceeding to Seharunpore. On this the reserve was ordered to march towards Bhaugput, and my corps to go along with it, and on the 31st, Lord Lake, "with all the cavalry, joined us, having crossed the Jumna at Bhaugput. By this time Holcar had surrounded Burn's detachment in a small fort at Shamlee, after taking their baggage and bazaar; so that, no grain being to be had, they were living on sheep and bullocks.

Lord Lake reached Shamlee in two marches, and next morning Holcar showed a fine bold front, which rejoiced his lordship, as he now believed his enemy intended to stand. He formed the cavalry in one line, and gave particular orders that no gallopers were to be opened on the enemy, but that the attack was to be made sword in hand. Whilst we were forming, however, a body of Holcar's horse made a false attack upon our right, on which the gallopers were instantly fired; and proved just the signal for Holcar to disperse, and so effectually was this done, that in less than an hour the whole of that immense body was out of sight. We trotted after them for about four miles; but it was all to no purpose - we had to return without effecting anything, and his lordship was so enraged at the disappointment, that he swore he would deprive these regiments of their galloper guns.

We encamped near the town, which was given up to plunder,* and Colonel Burn received high praise for his gallant defence of the position. After a day's halt, we commenced our march to Meerut, which was the road taken by Holcar; but when near Katowlee, we heard that he was still at that place, endeavouring to persuade the Begum Sumroo to join him, which she was not disinclined to do. On this Lord Lake turned his course towards Katowlee, and when six côs distant, he sent me off with my yellow troop to discover if he were there still. I had not gone two côs when I met 500 of his sowars, who were coming for information respecting our movements; and who immediately sent off express camels to tell that the British army was in full march for Katowlee. These fellows showing an inclination to attack me, and outnumbering my small party of eighty men so much, I thought it right to retire, which I did slowly and deliberately, sending off to Lord Lake a confirmation, of the report he had received of Holcar being still at the place.

Meantime, the 500 sowars charged me, but ineffectually, and having repulsed them I threw myself into a deserted village to defend myself until the army should come up. No sooner did they see Lord Lake's dust than they began to retire to their camp, on which I followed them for a côs, charging them twice, and capturing a stand of colours and about 100 horses. Just as I made my last charge, Holcar's army was seen about a côs distant, and the 8th dragoons came up, with Lord Lake,

* The inhabitants of Shamlee deserved this well; for, though pretending to take part with the British, they allowed the enemy, in disguise, to come into the town, from whence they fired upon our sepoys in the fort, and killed many. They refused, too, to sell the Hindoo sepoys any food, by which they were nearly starved of hunger.

to my assistance. Holcar's army having halted, and showing a disposition to attack us, we also halted to let the rest of the line come up. But a few rounds from the gallopers sent them to the right-about, and they dispersed as they had done at Shamlee. In this service I had about seven men killed and ten wounded, and my own horse received a cut on the head. Lord Lake praised the men very much, and made me a present of a pair of pistols.

We followed Holcar up to Meerut, but nothing of consequence occurred. There we left Colonel Burn's detachment, along with Murray's horse; and with the reserve alone we followed Holcar, at the rate of twelve or sixteen côs a day, until we reached Alleegunge. On the 16th November, Lord Lake, resolved to overtake Holcar and save Futtehghur, marched in the evening, leaving my corps, under Colonel Down, with the reserve, to bring up the baggage, and surprised that chief on the morning of the 17th. The execution done that day is well known to the world. On the morning of the 19th, I arrived with the reserve, and the same evening his lordship sent for me and said he wished much that, I would try to discover what route Holcar had taken, and asked, if I thought my corps would undertake the job? I replied, that my corps would obey any orders which his lordship might give; on which he shook me by the hand, and said, "Give me good information, and I shall soon be up with you."

I accordingly returned straight to camp, and leaving all my baggage, galled horses, and gallopers, with my brother (who was dangerously ill), under the care of Major Burrows, who commanded the horse-artillery, I started from Futtehghur at two A.M. on the morning of the 20th, with about 600 sowars, and reached Mynpooree that evening. Holcar, believing that the whole army was upon him, took to flight, while I, sending regular daily information to his lordship, pressed onwards, and saved Mr. Cunningham's house from being burned, as also that of Captain White, which Holcar was preparing to storm; the Sebundees, who were left under that officer to guard them, being in a great fright; and happy were both officers and civilians to see me that day, declaring, that had I not arrived as I did, they were afraid their own troops would have gone over to Holcar.

On the 21st I started again, and came up with Holcar at Aitah, where I took prisoners about 100 of his sowars. With these I practised a stratagem, which sent Holcar away faster than he bargained for. Telling them that my corps considered them as brethren, I gave them their liberty; but advised them to take care not to fall into the hands of the dragoons, who were but a few hours behind, and bade them give my salaam to Holcar.

Thankful for their release, they went and gave my message to Holcar, adding, that they had seen Lord Lake and his dragoons. This made him fly faster than ever; but I kept hanging on his rear, marching at the rate of twenty to twenty-five côs a day, until he crossed the Jumna at Mahabun, near Muttra; then I returned to Row-ka-Secundra, near Hattrass, where I halted.

In this hard seven day's work I had no provision but what the fields afforded, and neither tent; nor bazaar with us. The horses were never unsaddled, and we rested with the bagdoor (halter, or leading rein) in our hands all night, having frequently to change our ground two or three times during each night, to avoid a surprise from Holcar. In this pursuit I acquired great plunder in horses and camels. We lived on the green jowar that was standing in the fields, which we prepared by husking it out and putting it into large pots, adding ghee and meat, and boiling the whole together. It was then served out in earthen pots, my share being always brought me by the men, who showed me great love and attention, and were willing to act as my private servants, and tried in every way to please and add to my comfort; but I felt the want of my dram.

Four days after I came here. Lord Lake arrived, and the corps paraded to receive him. He came up and praised them highly, promised that their services should never be forgotten, and that they had, by their exertions, secured permanent bread for their lives. On me also he bestowed high commendations, giving me a horse with silver trappings, which had been sent him by some Rajah, and told me to go back to Alleegurh and rest for a month, and recruit my corps to 1,700 strong, for that he should soon require my services again. His lordship with the army went to Muttra, and crossing proceeded to Deeg; while I reached Coel in two marches, and commenced recruiting, in which I was very successful; for most of the great powers being now nearly crushed, I was joined by a great number of my old comrades from Perron's service, who had returned to their homes in the Doab.

I had not been here a month out, when an express came from Colonel Boe, who had been repulsed at a small fort near Alleegunge. I hastened to join him; and on my arrival, the garrison attempted to make their escape by night; but they were pursued and cut up almost to a man. This service was performed on a dark night, and several of my men were killed and wounded. We then marched to attack a large mud fort named Imlanee, sixteen côs east of Alleegunge, belonging to a refractory jemadar, named Nahur Allee. We besieged it for a month, and were twice beaten back in attempts to storm it. But at length, two mines being carried under the glacis, the garrison tried to make their escape: they were pursued by my brother, who killed 300 of them; the rest, with Nahur Allee, succeeded in making good their flight. My brother had his horse killed under him.

On the 23rd December, Lord Lake stormed and took Deeg, and then marched to invest Bhurtpore. Having returned to the army, I was ordered by Major Worsely to escort a large convoy of a lakh of bullocks loaded with atta and wheat from Anoopsheher. Thither I went, and receiving charge of the Brinjarrahs passed within two côs of Kamoona, a place held in great dread in the Doab. Keeping 400 of my horse in a body, I dispersed the rest among the bullocks, when, all of a sudden, out darted Doondiah Khan with 600 sowars. I attacked him with my 400, and chased him back to the ditch of his fort, with the loss of 200 of his men killed; and delivered over the convoy safe at Muttra, which gained me many commendations from his Excellency, as well as Major Worsely.

I had returned to Alleeghur, when Colonel Gruiber, with his battalion, was attacked by the same Doondiah Khan, and obliged to fall back on Anoopsheher, where he was joined by some provincial battalions, under command of Captain Cruttenden. I again received orders from Major Worsely to join Colonel Gruiber, and did accordingly join him within two côs of Kamoona. Proceeding thence to Alleeghur, I was ordered to receive and escort 30,000 Brinjarrahs loaded with atta to the grand army, which convoy I delivered just after the first storm of Bhurtpore had failed. I met with no molestation from Muttra till within a côs of Bhurtpore, when Bappojee Sindeah was sent out to attack me. He came up with 1,000 horse; but Lord Lake having sent out a detachment to my aid, Bappoo, on seeing them, retreated.

Next morning, I marched for Muttra, and from thence again proceeded to Coel to join Colonel Gruiber, who was ordered to attack Kamoona. I came up with him at Chuttooree, a village about a côs from Kamoona, and marched next morning with the detachment to the bank of the Kalee Muddee, on the east of Kamoona, where we encamped. We besieged the place for a month, during which time my corps was hard worked, and many acts of gallantry were performed by the men in presence of the whole detachment. My brother himself had two horses killed under him.

Chapter Fourteen
Against the Pindarrees

The next portion of Skinner's memoir relates in great part to the well-known "foray" of the celebrated freebooter, Ameer Khan, into Rohilcund, his native place, having crossed the whole Doab and its two great streams, at the head of his followers, in the usual Pindarree fashion, with nothing but his horse and his arms. And it is now time to give some account of the origin and rise of this remarkable predatory chief.

Mahomed Ameer Khan was the son of Illyat Khan, a Patan of the Tereen tribe, originally from Afghanistan; and who lived at a village near Sumbhul in the Zillah of Mooradabad, named Seraee-Tereen—the abode of the Tereens. When about twenty years of age he left his home for the Dekhan, then the great theatre for soldiers of fortune, with ten followers; and entered into several services, in which he so far prospered as to increase his followers to six horsemen and sixty foot. But his first engagement of consequence was with Jeysing Keechee of Ragooghur, who, with his relative, Dourjun Lai, had been ousted from their territories by Sindea, and who now maintained themselves by pillaging the same lands they had once possessed. But a quarrel with a favourite of the latter chief, terminating in a squabble in which Ameer Khan was severely wounded, led to his quitting that service, in which he had much distinguished himself, and been presented by the Rajah with a palankin and the command of 500 men. He then entered into that of Balaram, a predatory leader of Sindea's, at that-time subsisting in Bhopal on pillage, and afterwards called in to aid one of the parties who were struggling for power in that state. By him he was promoted to the charge of 1,500 horse and of the strong fortress of Futtehghur, the citadel of Bhopal.

The course of intrigue soon occasioned the departure of the Mahrattas from Bhopal; but Ameer Khan retained possession of Futtighur, and only gave it up to one of the disputing parties on being taken into the service. But his own intriguing spirit rendered him too dangerous a character to be long retained.

After six months he left it, or was dismissed, and it was at this period that the attention of Jesswunt Rao Holcar, who was then just rising into something of importance, became directed to the Patan leader. The first meeting between these celebrated freebooters took place at Ranagunge, near Shujahalpore, and they soon came to terms. Ameer Khan entered into engagements never to desert the fortunes of Jesswunt Rao; and received a written promise from that chief that all future plunder or conquest should be shared equally between them. With men of such characters and equally desperate fortunes, it is probable that an agreement, thus entered into from mutual convenience, would scarcely have been held binding any longer than the interests of either party might seem to dictate; and yet certainly Ameer Khan did continue his fidelity to Holcar long after the latter had attained to sovereign power—a fact to be accounted for probably from the strong influence of Holcar's more energetic character, and the tact which he always exhibited in distinguishing the Patan from his other leaders, even after the relations of prince and dependant were clearly established between them.* Ameer Khan remained sole commander of his own army, and entertained or dismissed whom he would, but his followers, who were always more numerous than he had the means of paying, were in a state of constant mutiny; and for more than half of every year, their chief was under restraint. The consequence was, that his conduct was always more regulated by the clamours of this turbulent rabble, and the necessity of providing for their support, than by any regular system of policy. The excesses of Ameer Khan's Patans at Saugur have been noticed; but these were far surpassed at Poonah, where he was seized by a party of them, and not only beat and. bruised, but almost strangled with his own turban, which they fastened round his neck. Though Jesswunt Rao repressed and punished this act of violence, he, too, on many occasions was compelled to soothe and humour the turbulent spirits of the freebooters.....It was the constant object of Jesswunt Rao to employ them at a distance, and he appears to have considered them more as a body of plunderers, whose general movements he could direct through his connection with their leader, than

* *He always called the Meer "brother," and affected to regard him as of equal rank with himself.*

as an integral portion of his army, whose services he could at all times command. They, on the other hand, were sensible of the advantages they derived from acting in the name of one of the recognised Indian governments; and the main influence by which Ameer Khan retained his precarious rank as their chief, was his forming the link that attached this band of depredators to the house of Holcar.

Meer Khan's expedition into Rohilcund appears to have partly originated in the mutual disputes and taunts of the confederates, in consequence of their ill-success in their war with the English; and the Meer, perhaps, imagined that he should not only succeed better in his open system of depredation, but increase his power and forces in his own country, which was filled with desperate characters. Born a Patan, he naturally leant to prefer his countrymen, although, latterly, the great preponderance of them in his army may have tended not only to curb his own authority, but to perpetuate the mischief they occasioned. It is obvious that he was deficient in that first qualification in a captain of banditti, the power to overawe and command his men. He was, in fact, not so much their chief as their slave—only tolerated as the head to contrive their expeditions, the pilot to lead them to their prey. He was even regarded as deficient in personal courage, and more of a blusterer than a doer. The marking features of his character appear to have been, a strong turn for intrigue, indefatigable cunning, insatiable avarice, and remorseless, unscrupulous cruelty. He wanted the reckless boldness in crime, the audacious defiance of all principle, exhibited by Holcar, and he was far from being-possessed of that prince's undaunted courage. He had more of the tiger than the lion—perhaps, more of the serpent than of either; and while the sweeping devastation of the Mahratta prince seems to have been regarded as an act of destiny,—a visitation of Providence, apart from its author,—the atrocities of the Patan are held in detestation over all Hindostan, as spontaneous works of a cruel and evil-hearted ruffian.

Nor were the manners of the Meer more attractive than his character. He is represented, by those who have seen and known him, as clownish and rude in appearance and address; mean in person; of dark Hindoo-like complexion; poorly and dirtily dressed, and his language low and coarse. The result of his visit to his country seems in no respect to have answered his expectations. He came over the Ganges with 30,000 followers, and a name which, as a leader, carried terror at least with it, and might have been attractive to soldiers of fortune like himself. He re-crossed that river and the Doab, baffled, beaten, disgraced, his troops reduced to a third of their number, and his name sunk into a word of derision and contempt.

Skinner's memoirs:-

At this juncture, and on the 3rd of February, Ameer Khan crossed the Jumna; on which Major Worsely sent an express to Colonel Gruber, who, on receiving it, raised the siege of Kamoona, and retired under Alleeghur. On the 9th, General Smith, with three regiments of dragoons, three of native cavalry, and a detachment of horse-artillery, sent by Lord Lake, came to our assistance. About twelve at night we marched, and, my corps being sent in advance, we reached Meer Khan's encampment before Kamoona at daybreak, and found he had taken himself off two hours before our arrival.

We came up, however, with an alleegole★ of about 300 Rohillas, belonging to Doondiah Khan, whom we attacked and cut up, following them to the brink of the ditch. About seven in the morning General Smith came up, and gave my men high commendation for their conduct.

Next morning, while marching a couple of côs in two lines, the cavalry being on our right, Colonel Gruber was insulted by a small fort, called Annoona, belonging to Doondiah Khan, which he stormed and took, with the loss of one European officer killed, and twenty sepoys killed and wounded. On the 13th, the Colonel's detachment was ordered to proceed by Anopsheher, while the cavalry pushed on after Ameer Khan,

★ *Alleegoles were a sort of chosen light infantry of the Rohilla Patans: sometimes the term appears to be applied to other troops, supposed to be used generally for desperate service.*

who crossed the Ganges at Ahmednaghur on the 15th, and went straight for Mooradabad. We followed on his track, and on the 17th reached Amronah.

At noon the same day, I was sent off with 1,000 horse, to relieve Mr. Leicester,* who, with all the party at Bareilly, was surrounded in the gaol of that place. General Smith himself followed us. I reached the place a little before dawn of the 18th, and found that Meer Khan had just left it. We followed him as far as the Ramgunga, and, overtaking his rear-guard, cut up 300 of his sowars; after which we returned to Mr. Leicester's house. An hour after sunrise General Smith, with the cavalry, reached the place.

Our arrival at the time we did was the most fortunate thing possible, for the sebundees† who were on duty would have given up the Europeans and treasure; and it is impossible to describe the joy with which we were hailed by the whole party, which had been surrounded by the Meer in this fortified place. Next morning we marched in pursuit; but Meer Khan had led us such a dance, that, for several days, we were all in the dark as to whither he had gone, and we kept marching backwards and forwards until we reached Shereghurrie, when I fell in with, and made prisoners of, some Pindarrees, from whom I made out the proper direction. As soon as this was done, I went secretly to General Smith, and volunteered to go disguised into the Meer's camp, and learn what he was about. To this, after a good deal of hesitation, General Smith agreed; and, accordingly, putting on a native's dress, I took ten of my most confidential sowars, and, giving out to my corps that I was going upon urgent business to Mooradabad, I went straight to Sherekote, where I met with Meer Khan's foragers, and with them went into their camp.

My ten sowars had brethren in Shahmut Khan's gole, and with it we remained all night. Early in the morning Meer

*Chief of the civil service at Bareilly.
† Hired irregular troops.

198

Khan, who was pitched on the banks of the Ramgunga river, near Ufzulghur, wanted to march; but the Mahratta Pindarrees, who had all been insisted the day before by the Patans, insisted on the Meer giving up the offenders. This was refused by the Patans, upon which both parties drew up to fight. All this information was sent off by me to General Smith, by hircarrahs; and when I saw that the fellows were not likely to settle their disputes that day, I thought it would be an excellent thing if I could bring the troops upon them. A foraging party belonging to Shahmut Khan, being just about to go out, I took the opportunity of quitting camp with it, especially as Meer Khan by this time had settled the dispute, and was proposing to march next morning.

I had not gone two côs, when I met one of my own spies, who informed me that the army was just going to encamp at Sherekote. On this I galloped off, and met General Smith, to whom I gave all this information, and begged that the troops might push on, as he might never again meet with so good an opportunity. The General thanked me for my exertions, and pushed on to Sherekote, where he left the baggage under protection of the 3rd regiment of Native Cavalry, 400 sowars, and about 700 nujeebs of mine. In the mean time I changed my horse and dress, and then showed them the road.

We came up with the enemy about two p.m.; but Meer Khan had got intelligence of our approach, and, having sent his baggage on to Ufzulghur, was standing his ground with all his horse, and a small body of 300 alleegoles, which he had entertained at Rampore. As our line came up, there was a nullah just in our front, the ford of which I was directed to point out to the horse-artillery. I accordingly accompanied Captain Stark on this service, showing him the ford, where the troops crossed and formed in two lines, keeping the river on our right flank.

Meer Khan now broke up into three goles; one, being commanded by himself, advanced to our left; one, commanded by his brother* Shahmut Khan, took its way to our right; while the third and smaller one, with the unfortunate 300 alleegoles, remained in our front. These fellows opened their matchlocks upon us; but a few rounds from the horse-artillery forced them to advance to the shelter of a hollow that was in our front. The 27th Dragoons dashed forward to cut them up; but the fellows, who must have been mad, rushed sword in hand, with their flags, upon the dragoons, penetrated their ranks, and caused some confusion in the regiment. Major Dean, however, charged them with a squadron of the 8th, and cut them to pieces.

Shahmut Khan then charged the right; but was repulsed with great loss by the gallopers and the 29th Dragoons. Meer Khan in person charged my corps on the left with a large gole. My men behaved most gallantly, giving fire with their matchlocks at the word of command; and then drawing swords, they charged and repulsed them with great slaughter; we killed two of their sirdars, took one prisoner, with ten stand of colours, among which were two golden ones, carried by ackas, and 200 horses. My brother Robert's conduct this day surpassed all I had ever seen him perform before. One of my gallopers on the left having got rather far away from the corps, and unlimbered about 100 yards from my flank, an acka† of Meer Khan's, with about forty sowars, charged and took it. My brother (Lieut. Skinner) observing this, immediately charged them with twenty choice men, retook the galloper, and cut down the acka with his own hand.

The Meer now retired out of cannon reach, and formed into one mass before us; but it being now four p.m., General Smith thought it proper to retreat to his baggage. Meer Khan, on the other hand, had been so sickened with the gallopers that he would venture on nothing; but retreated to Ufzulghur. He certainly gave us fine opportunities for a charge this day;

* *The wording in the original is of doubtful meaning; but, at all events, there is reason for believing that Shahmut Khan was not a brother of the Meer's.*

† *Probably from the Turkish word Aga.—leader, master.*

but it was thought that their goles were too large, and were only kept off by our gallopers. My loss was five men killed and thirty wounded; the General gave great praise to our corps, and reported our exertions to Lord Lake, who gave orders to the resident at Dehlee to present me with a fine Persian sword.

We marched in pursuit of Ameer Khan towards Mooradabad, which direction he had taken from Ufzulghur; and arriving at six in the evening, we deposited there all our sick and wounded. My brother was ordered with 500 sowars to Anopsheher, while we marched towards Chaundousee. On arriving there we found that Meer Khan had been beforehand with us, having burned the cantonments, and laid the town under contribution; after which he took his way in the direction of Bareilly. On the 8th, we made a forced march, and took up our position on the bank of the Ramgunga, where the river was fordable, in order to prevent his crossing; and scarcely had we pitched, when the dreadful intelligence was brought me that my brother was surrounded by Ameer Khan in a ruinous serai in Sumbul, into which he had thrown himself on hearing of the Meer's approach.

From the account given me by the messenger, it appeared that when the party were thus hemmed in, Ameer Khan had written to the rissaldars, desiring them to give my brother up, and that he would give each of them three months' pay as a reward. This they refused contemptuously, upon which the Meer advanced with 10,000 men dismounted, towards the serai, and sent the same message again, to which he received the same reply.

My brother now, in order to test the men's fidelity, addressed them and told them, that if, by giving up his single life, they could save 500, he was quite willing to give himself up, and go as a prisoner to Ameer Khan. To this they replied, that when they were all destroyed he might go, but not as long as they lived. That they did not mind numbers—hundreds, they said, were daily destroyed at Bhurtpore; they also were soldiers hired to die, therefore let them die like soldiers.

My brother then wrote to Ameer Khan, declaring that he had always believed him to be a brave soldier, but that his conduct this day, in attempting to seduce and delude the soldiers under his command, whose courage and fidelity he should soon have experience of, had proved him to be a coward, that he despised him and dared him to come on. As soon as the messenger was despatched, and he saw the Meer's people moving, he told his men to kneel down and offer their last prayers to God to grant them courage, and to die like brave men. The storm now took place on all sides, but it was nobly repulsed by my men. Many of the enemy got up upon the walls, and were cut down from them in trying to get over. Three times did they assault, and each time they were repulsed with great slaughter. When it got dark the spy left my brother, having spent all his ammunition except a few rounds. During the night, he took the shoes from off his horse's feet, and cut them into slugs, of which he distributed fire to each man, which, with five bullets remaining to each, was all he had to repel the multitude around him. But the men remained stanch and firm to him, and he besought me to come to his aid without delay.

I went instantly to General Smith, crying and entreating him to march, or to allow me to go to my brother's assistance, that I would cut my way through Meer Khan's troops, and get into the serai, which was only twenty côs off, in time to save him. But, as it was three p.m before the letter reached me, General Smith declared that it was useless; that the Meer must either have destroyed the party or gone off from the place, as Colonel Burn was in that quarter. As for him, he could not, he said, leave the ford. This hope failing me, I was utterly at a loss how to act, when the following stratagem occurred to me, and I instantly put it in practice. I wrote a letter to my brother, saying I had just received his, and had shewn it to the

General, who was about to march with his whole force in an hour or two; in the mean time, he must keep the Meer in play by proposing terms of surrender. One of my hircarrahs, who had been brought up in my family, volunteered to have this delivered to Meer Khan, and ten of my sowars, who were equally confidential, took in hand to play him a trick in aid of the plan. To the hircarrah I promised 800 rupees, and a thousand to the sowars. They all left me at four p. m and General Smith himself agreed to march at midnight.

The hircarrah and sowars got within a côs of Meer Khan's position about dawn of day, and got information that my brother was still safe, and had repulsed another storm on the last evening. Being a clever fellow, he came to the following arrangement with the sowars, namely, that just at daybreak they should set fire to several stacks of khurbee (corn-straw) that were in the fields, while he should contrive to be taken by the piquets, and of course be brought before the Meer. This he easily made out, and being taken to Meer Khan, he confessed at once that he had been sent by me, who was very much attached to my brother. That he had understood the sahib had been taken prisoner, and was in his camp, so he had come to fulfil the service he engaged to perform as a faithful servant. That the Meer might do with him what he pleased, only let him be permitted to see his master.

Meer Khan had the letter read, and then asked the hircarrah when the army would move. He replied that the orders issued were, that they should move at midnight. Whilst this was going on, the sowars had put fire to the stacks, and then they chased in a few camp followers, who had gone out upon business of their own. In a moment the cry arose that the English had arrived, upon which Meer Khan immediately saddled and mounted, ordered the hircarrah to receive a few stripes, and in a few hours not one of them was to be seen. The hircarrah and the sowars then went to my brother, who welcomed them very warmly. We had marched about nine côs, when information reached us of my brother's safety and Ameer Khan's flight, and next morning my brother joined me at Circey, and was cordially welcomed for his gallant conduct, not only by me, but by the whole army. The whole affair met with high praise from General Smith, and was reported to his Excellency, Lord Lake, who wrote a Persian letter to the men, applauding them for their conduct. My brother's loss in this business was ten killed and about fifty wounded. That of Meer Khan was about a thousand in both. The hircarrah and sowars were very handsomely rewarded, and we all resumed our march after Ameer Khan, who had retired in the direction of Amrowah.

By this time, having lost his name in the country, and being deserted by many of his soldiers, every walled village opposed him, and he now pushed on towards the ford. On his way he attacked Captain Murray, who threw himself into a walled village, and repulsed the attack with a loss to his assailants of several hundred men. Colonel Burn soon arrived to the assistance of Murray, who succeeded in capturing the Meer's bazaar. On the 13th Meer Khan crossed with only about 10,000 men out of the 30,000 which he had brought with him from Bhurtpore.

Our news from that place, however, was very disheartening, and threw a damp over the whole detachment. We recrossed the Ganges at the same ghaut where we passed it a month before in our chase after the Meer. We marched at the rate of fifteen or twenty miles a day, and on the 18th came before Kamoona, the chief of which was now much humbled, and entreated General Smith to procure his forgiveness from his Excellency. This the General did obtain for this villain, who afterwards proved to be a traitor, and the cause of many valuable lives being lost. On the 19th we arrived before Alleeghur, where we learned that Ameer Khan had recrossed the Jumna. I accompanied General Smith to Hanseagunge, opposite to Muttra, from whence I was ordered back to Coel. I reached that place on the 27th, terminating a course of the severest service that any corps had ever gone through. In the chase after Holcar the army had gone 500 miles, in that after Meer Khan 700 miles, and mine was the only Hindostanee corps during all that time that continued throughout the chase. It performed all the duties of the camp, and, to the best of my belief, was never less than eighteen hours out of the twenty-four on horseback. The hardships endured by my men, who were constantly out, were well known to the commander and officers of the two detachments. On the smallest calculation, they underwent in these two chases full twice the labour and hardship endured by the regulars, and often in the chase after Meer Khan, when my men had the rear-guard, have they picked up the European dragoons who were knocked up on the march, and dismounting, put them on their own horses, and led them thus to camp, conduct which made them beloved by the dragoons: and notwithstanding this hard duty, they never murmured, nor were once accused of disobeying any order whatsoever; and never did they turn their backs before the enemy, though frequently opposed to far superior numbers. His Excellency's kindness towards the corps was great, and whenever service was to be performed, I was sure of being sent for, which was a matter of the greatest consolation and satisfaction to me, and gave me spirits to undergo my labour cheerfully, knowing that if anything were done, it would not fail of being acknowledged by his lordship. In these two campaigns, I had the satisfaction of receiving from his Excellency two swords and a pair of pistols, a circumstance which was regarded as a mark of great favour and approbation.

At Alleeghur I remained about fifteen days, when my brother, with 700 sowars, was ordered to join Colonel Richardson on an expedition against Toorkapoorah, a fort belonging to Naher Allee of Emlanee. I at the same time was sent with the remainder of my corps, to escort 30,000 Brinjarrahs to the army at Bhurtpore. I delivered my charge safe, and returned to Alleeghur, when I received orders to join the detachment of Colonel Burn, near Saharunpore, which was at this time again attacked by all the Sikhs.

I marched to Dehlee, where General Ochterlony reviewed the corps, on whom he bestowed great praise, and presented me with a sword taken from his own waist, in Lord Lake's name, and in front of the corps. I then pursued my march to join Colonel Burn; but before I could join them, which I did at Kurnaul, he had succeeded in driving the Sikhs across the Jumna; and in a short time afterwards, the whole of the Sikh Rajahs came to terms. Lord Lake had also compelled the Bhurtpore man to the same course, and having completed treaties with Sindea and several Rajahs, he broke up his camp and retired to cantonments at Muttra, Agra, and Futtehpore Seekree, for the rains. Col. Burn returned to Paneeput, where we built temporary cantonments, and Holcar, having no home to go to, retreated with the sad remains of his troops to Jhoudpore. Meer Khan, having now only about 10,000 men left, followed his fortunes.

On the 1st October 1805, however, Holcar, who had contrived to recruit his troops in Rajepootanah, and to collect some artillery, marched towards the Punjab, in hopes of receiving assistance from the Sikhs, who, it was said, particularly Runjeet Singh, had actually made some promise to that effect. Together with Ameer Khan's force, he could now muster about 30,000 horse, 10,000 infantry, and about forty pieces of cannon, and with this force he marched through the Hurrianah country. When he arrived at a point on our west, we moved out from Paneeput to give him a check, but were too late; he had passed us, so we marched after him, and on the 29th November at Rawseana, we were joined by his Excellency Lord Lake. On the 2nd December we reached Loodianah; but Holcar had already crossed the Sutlej, and was only sixteen côs from us at a place called Jullunder.

Certain political considerations prevented Lord Lake from crossing; but when he found that Holcar would not move, he on the evening of the 3rd, at dinner, observed that he wished some one would try the ford with a troop and galloper. Colonel Worsely told me that the hint was intended for me, on which I immediately rose and said,— "If your lordship will give me leave, I will try the ford to-morrow morning." He replied,— "Be there about dawn, with two rissalahs of your yellow boys and a galloper, and I will also be with you." I bowed and sat down again. Next morning, with two choice rissalahs and a galloper, I was ready at the ghaut, where his lordship, with the whole of his staff and a number of officers from the camp, soon arrived. Colonel Malcolm, who was one of the political agents, dismounted along with his Excellency, and argued the point of my crossing; but I heard his lordship reply that he took the responsibility upon himself. He then mounted, and coming up to me, said,—"Well, are you ready?" "Yes, my lord," replied I. "Well then, dash forward," said he. Upon this I made my salaam, and giving three cheers, clashed on.

Our horses had to swim for about twenty yards, after which they got footing. There was an island in the middle of the river, to which I bent my course. On reaching this, we discovered it to be a quicksand, in which my galloper stuck fast. I immediately dismounted, and directed my brother, with the two rissalahs, to cross, and then dismounting one of them, to bring the men back to relieve the galloper which had now sunk up to the wheels. In less than an hour the rissalah returned, took out the horses, and dragged the gun across; and just as we landed, I took off my hat, and giving three hurrahs, in which Colonel Malcolm and all Lord Lake's staff joined, proclaimed that the first British gun had crossed the Sutlej.

A few Sikhs made their appearance, and the rissalah was ordered to drive them off, and no sooner had it mounted than away they run. We returned and sounded the ford, putting up posts to shew the road; and the work terminated by Lord

Lake making a present of 5,000 rupees to the two rissalahs for their activity and willingness.

On the 5th, next morning, a battalion of sepoys was ordered across to secure the ford. Still Holcar kept his ground; but when, on the morning of the 6th, the whole army crossed, and on the 7th commenced our march towards the Beyah, Holcar moved on, and crossed that river. Next day, the 8th, I was sent on with 400 sowars to find out if he had actually crossed; and, after a march of about thirty miles, succeeded in getting a glance at his army which had crossed that morning. Just as I reached the left bank, his rear-guard, who were on the opposite one, fired a few shots at us from an eighteen-pounder. They had been waiting for about 1,000 Brinjarrah bullocks which had gone out for supplies; but falling in with them on my return to camp, I took them prisoners, and about midnight brought them all in with me, I had this day marched with the army twenty miles, ten more to the river bank, and ten more back to camp—in all, forty miles.

Next morning, the 9th December, I went on with the army to a point opposite to Bojepore ghaut. From this place the pillar of Secunder* was distant ten côs to the west, and my horse was the first of the British camp to taste the water of the Hyphasis.

On the 19th, Holcar's vakeels, accompanied by those of Runjeet Sing, came into camp, for such was the firmness and decision of his Excellency, that the whole business was brought to a peaceful termination. The bold arrogance of the Sikhs, and the vapouring declarations of Holcar, and his determination of making his saddle his house† until he had accomplished his purposes, were all cowed and humbled by the gallantry of a force not exceeding 1,000 British troops, and to the astonishment of the whole Indian world.

*Alexander the Great.

† Holcar had more than once, in correspondence as well as by word of mouth, declared, in Mahratta phrase, that his home and house was the back of his horse, and wherever that horse's head pointed became his country.

208

In order to give them an idea of what these troops were, his Excellency gave a review of the force to Futteh Sing Alwah, Runjeet's second in command; indeed, some asserted that Runjeet himself was present in disguise. They were amazed at the performances of the Europeans and horse artillery, and especially when the horse artillery clashed through intervals of cavalry after a charge, and fired within fifty yards of the spot where these great folks were standing. It was all astonishment, and a general cry burst from the Sikhs of "Wah Gooroo, Wah Gooroo!" "Jadoo kurdeah!" "Oh saints, oh saints, it is all witchcraft!"*

On the 9th of January 1806, we left these plains where the great Alexander of old astonished the famous Rajah Phoor, and retraced our steps to Kurnaul. On the 20th February, I was left with my corps at that place along with Colonel Burn, who was directed to remain there. Lord Lake did not come up till the 25th, but he halted here upwards of two months, discharging the irregular troops with pensions and jaghires. My corps, which had amounted to 1,700, was reduced to 1,200, the remaining 500 being discharged and all the officers pensioned; and it was the only irregular cavalry retained and made permanent, as a reward for their fidelity and exertions. Having thus arranged matters, and Holcar having passed Dehlee on his return, his lordship broke up the army and marched with the Europeans to Cawnpore.

* *Major Thorn confirms this effect of the sight of our military manoeuvres on the Sikhs, and adds, that they were heard whispering to one another, "Thank God, we did not go to war with the English."*

Chapter Fifteen
Setbacks & Encouragements

But events had for some time been in progress, which were destined sadly to damp the satisfaction which Skinner had felt at the termination of the campaign, in finding so large a portion of his corps retained permanently on the strength of the service. A change of policy at home led to a change of government in India. The Marquis of Cornwallis was sent out to relieve Lord Wellesley; and his lordship had no sooner arrived in India, than he turned his attention to establishing peace, on any terms, with all the native powers; and to the reduction of expense in every branch of the service. These measures involved a wide departure from the bold and successful policy of his predecessor, and serious sacrifices of principles hitherto adhered to, with the extensive alterations in the military establishment of the company; and though, while Holcar was still in arms, and Sindea threatening, immediate reduction was impossible, the first moment of success was seized with avidity for bringing into play the purposed economical reforms.

On the 5th of October, Lord Cornwallis, worn out with age and illness, expired at Ghazeepore, and was succeeded by Sir George Barlow, the senior member of council, who adopted to the full all the cautious and conciliatory principles of his predecessor. His views were entirely adverse to defensive alliances and subsidiary forces, and to all sorts of interference with the states west of the Jumna. With them, therefore, former treaties were abandoned,* and in the same spirit, an arrangement was entered into with Sindea, on very favourable terms for the latter. The same indulgence was also extended to Holcar, who, from his treacherous hostility, still less merited such leniency.

In all these measures his Excellency differed very widely from the opinions entertained by the Commander-in-Chief, Lord Lake, who failed not to remonstrate strongly against their

The Rajah of Jeypore, in particular, was desirous of British protection; but he, as well as the rest of the Rajepoot states, was refused.

impolicy and evil tendency. Nor did events long fail of proving the correctness of his views, and how ill a timid or vacillating policy was suited for dealing with the native powers of India. The rapid growth of predatory bands, and general anarchy and confusion in Central India, indicated the justice of his lordship's calculation and prophetic fears.

Meantime, peace and economy being the order of the day, curtailment of expenditure and reduction of the military followed of course, and among the rest, Skinner's remaining corps of 1,200 horse, though guaranteed as permanent by Lord Lake, was ordered to be paid off. This very unpleasant order was communicated to poor Skinner by his lordship himself, in a manner which shows the high regard he felt for that officer, and his sense of the injustice of which he was compelled to be the instrument towards him. The general order for discharging the corps is dated the 11th April 1806, and their pay is thereby ordered to be made good only to the 20th. It terminates by the following testimony to their good and faithful service: —

"On this occasion, the Commander-in-Chief is pleased to record the high sense which he entertains of the valuable services rendered by Captain Skinner, and the corps under his command during the war; and his lordship will not fail to report to Government the zealous and successful manner in which Captain Skinner has invariably discharged the duties of his important station.

"As a further remark of his lordship's estimation of the fidelity and good conduct of the corps, he authorizes a gratuity equal to a month's pay each, to be given to all the native officers and men now ordered to be discharged.

(Signed)   "T. Worsely,
"Deputy Adjutant-General."

Skinner's memoir:-

My mind had been made quite easy by the late arrangements, when suddenly an express arrived from Lord Lake, desiring that I should immediately repair to head-quarters. I immediately overtook him at Secundra, where he was sitting at breakfast, and was very kindly received. After breakfast, his lordship retired to his tent, whither I was soon sent for, and found Colonels Malcolm and Worsley with him. With tears in his eyes he gave me the despatch from Sir George Barlow, which contained the order to discharge my corps. I read it, but said nothing, when his lordship catching me by the hand, said, "Skinner, I regret this much—what can I do for you?" "My lord," I replied, "if you are satisfied with my conduct, I am repaid for all my exertions. The character you have already given me will procure me bread; and some just man may hereafter come to the head of affairs, who, from your recommendation, may again take me by the hand." "Well," said he, "but how can I satisfy you now?" I replied that I should be contented with a small jagheer, as I did not mean again to serve as a soldier, unless obliged to do so. He asked how much would satisfy me and my brother, to which I replied, that I desired to leave it all to his lordship. He then consulted a while aside with Colonel Malcolm, and turning to me, asked if 20,000 rupees a year would satisfy both of us? I immediately thanked him, and said he was making princes of us. He laughed, and then appointed jagheers of 5,000 rupees a year a piece to four of my rissaldars, pensioned all the officers as low as duffehdars,* gave three months' pay as gratuity to the rest of the corps, and placed all the wounded men upon the Hauper establishment. I then took my leave, with a letter to the collector of Coel, for my jaghire; and returning, brought the corps to Dehlee, where the painful task awaited me of tearing myself from the men who had gained me such laurels in the British service. All those who had deserted that service at first, and then came over to it, received rewards. Those only who had proved themselves all along faithful servants were discharged from it.

Poor Skinner, however, had not, as he says, learned the worst of his hard fate; no sooner had he parted from his brave comrades, and gone to Coel to take possession of his jagheer, than he

* *Commanders of ten.*

212

received a letter from Colonel Malcolm, informing him, that being a British subject, Sir George Barlow could not permit him to hold land, so that he found himself, after all his zealous services, and after many sincerely meant promises, thrown adrift without provision or reward. The orders of the Governor-General were not of course, to be disputed; but his steady friend, Lord Lake, again interfered, and he received another letter from Colonel Malcolm in the following terms:—

"My dear Skinner, — Lord Lake has recommended you in the strongest terms to government, and I have no doubt but you will be placed upon the footing of Lieutenant-Colonel in the Mahratta service, whatever that may be. With respect to your wishes for land, Lord Lake will authorize me to speak upon the subject when I go to Calcutta, and you may be satisfied of my hearty endeavours to accomplish the object you desire, and that I shall rejoice if I am at all instrumental in promoting the success of a person for whose character I entertain the sincerest respect, and of the validity of whose claim upon the public service, I have had the best opportunities of forming a correct judgment.
(Signed)   "Jno. Malcolm."
"Cawnpore, 7th June, 1806."

It appears that subsequently Skinner himself, doubtless acting by the advice of his friends, wrote to the Governor-General on the same subject, and the result of the negociation was a communication from Mr. Edmonstone, secretary to Government, to Captain Skinner, intimating that the Governor-General in Council, with reference to the claims of those officers who had quitted the Mahratta service in conformity with the Governor-General's proclamation of August 1803, had authorized his drawing the allowances to which he had been previously entitled up to the 1st of October; and further, that considering the sacrifice of prospects in the Mahratta service, and the circumstances under which it was made, he is satisfied that the grant of a pension for life, equal to the amount of retiring allowances of officers of equal rank in the Company's service, would constitute an adequate remuneration for officers in that position. But, with reference to the special services rendered by the applicant himself, since quitting the Mahratta service, and the sense which "Government entertains of your general merits and character," the Governor-General had been induced to assign to him as remuneration, the amount of the nett full pay of the rank of colonel in the Honourable Company's service; and accordingly, Captain Skinner is authorized to draw during his life, as pension, 300 Sonaut rupees per month, with permission to reside in any part of the Company's territories, or to proceed to Europe, at his option.

Skinner's account continues:–

This was all that Lord Lake could obtain for me; my four rissaldars got each of them more; but I resolved in my own mind to remain quiet, and see what further misfortunes there might be for me to bear. In the mean time, I received from his Excellency a letter, telling me that what he had obtained now was for the present only; but that as soon as he should reach home, he would get the Court of Directors to confirm me in my jagheer, and also to replace my 1,200 men on permanent service, in spite of Sir George Barlow. I wrote in return a letter, expressive of my thanks, and assured his lordship, that I had every confidence in his desire to serve me; but that fate, I feared, was against me. However, happen what might, I should always most gratefully acknowledge his lordship's kindness and favour.

I now sat myself down in Dehlee, and built castles in the air upon the promises of my kind and worthy protector; these continued for some months after his return home, when his most lamented death put an end to my hopes, and sealed my hard fate. Despairing now of any better result, I found it necessary to exert myself, and accordingly, with the small sum I had saved, I began to trade; and thus I continued from the year 1806 to 1808, when Mr. Seton, then Resident at Dehlee, took me by the hand, and renewed my hopes of better times. He obtained for us the commutation of our pension into jagheer, which by laying out a little money on the land,

and the exercise of much diligence, we found capable of considerable improvement. But I had scarcely taken possession, and got interested in my new employment, when in 1809 I was summoned to head-quarters at Seharunpore by General Hewitt, to whom Mr. Seton had recommended me, and who was assembling an army at that place, to bring the Sikhs, who had become turbulent, to a sense of their duty. Here I met with my old friend Colonel Worsely, who first recommended that I should be put in command of the Sikhs who were to join us, amounting to about 10,000 horse.

With this promise I went to Kurnaul, having with me my 300 bargheers (stable-horse), who, by the kindness of Lord Lake, had been put in the civil service with the Resident of Dehlee, and remained detached at Paneeput. The Sikhs, however, came to terms, and gave up the point we required, which was the establishment of a station at Loodheana.

At this time, however, Abdool Sunnud Khan, to whom Hansee and the district of Hurreeana had been given in jagheer, being unable to manage the country, was desirous to give it up; and I was ordered to attend the Hon. Edward Gardner, with my 300 sowars, on an expedition to settle it. Through Colonel Worsely's means, my corps was increased to 800 men with two gallopers, all intended for the Hurreeana district. In less than two months I completed my number, for my old comrades, who had gone to Ameer Khan and Holcar, joined me as soon as they heard that I had got again into favour. From 1809 till 1814, I worked hard in the district, and performed with my corps many acts of gallantry, as the whole army can witness. Among others, I was at the taking of Bhowannee, and in company with the 6th Native Cavalry charged the garrison who were making their escape.*

In the year 1811, Skinner's warm friend, Mr. Seton, left Dehlee to accompany the Earl of Minto, Governor-General, on his expedition to Java, and the following letter will serve to show

* *Detachment orders by Lieut.-Col. Ball, camp Bhowannee, 9th Sept. 1809.*

the esteem in which he was held by that excellent man: —

On board the Momington, 12th March 1811.

"My dear James,—My departure from Dehlee was so very sudden, that I could not write to you; even now I can scarcely find time to do so. I cannot, however, quit Bengal even for a time, without requesting you to do me the justice to believe, that my friendship for you will continue the same in whatever part of the world I may be; and that should it ever be in my power to promote you or your brother's views, I shall eagerly avail myself of it.

"Lord Minto is already well acquainted with your merits; in short, both of you stand high in the general estimation. Remember me in the kindest manner to your brother Robert, and tell him for me, that where-ever I am, he must consider me his sincere friend and agent. God bless you, my dear Skinner. Believe me ever most cordially yours,

(Signed)   "A. Seton."

"P.S.—It is most gratifying to me to reflect, that our friend Metcalfe, who succeeds me, feels towards your brother and you exactly as I do."

It seems that application had been made to Government at this time, to have the jaghire of the two brothers made hereditary, or revertible to their families after their own deaths; but this, as appears by a letter from the secretary to Government, to the Resident at Dehlee (C. T. Metcalfe, Esq.), the Governor-General in Council, notwithstanding the high esteem he professed to

---

* *GENERAL ORDERS by the COMMANDER-IN-CHIEF.*

Head-quarters, Camp Jheend, 4th Jan. 1813.

The Commander-in-Chief has seldom, on any similar occasion, derived greater satisfaction than from the review of the 1st battalion 19th native infantry, and Captain Skinner's corps of irregular cavalry, the whole under the orders of Lieutenant-Colonel Arnold, commanding at Hansee.

The performance of the battalion #### Of Captain Skinner's corps, the Commander-in-Chief considers it but justice to that officer thus publicly to declare, that the size, condition, and figure of the horses, and the arms, clothing, and appointments of the men, are of a superior description to those of any other class of irregular cavalry that have yet fallen under his Excellency's observation.

entertain for the Skinners, conceived it would be contrary to the principles on which jaghires were given to accede to, as being in effect equivalent to a perpetual tenure, and their request was accordingly refused. But the estimation in which both were held, may be understood from the three general orders given at foot.*

The services of the corps had, since their last formation, of course been restricted to local affairs, the reduction of refractory Zemindars, and such duty as arises in the settlement districts brought into order for the first time. But in the mean time, Lord Moira had succeeded Lord Minto as Governor-General, and soon found that the prospect of more serious hostilities would demand an increase of military means to meet the emergency, and accordingly the following letter prepared Captain Skinner for employment more extensive and better suited to his zealous and active disposition:—

Camp Mooradabad, 6th December 1814.
(Private and Confidential.)

"My dear Skinner,—Instead of an addition of only four rissalahs, I am now to acquaint you, that the Governor-General is determined to augment the corps under your command to 3,000 sowars; you may, therefore, proceed to take measures to raise that number as soon as you can, and let me know without delay what assistance you will require in money, that an advance may be authorized to enable you to carry the measure into effect.

Acting in brigade, their movements indicated such a knowledge of European tactics as would enable the corps to combine, whenever required, its movements with those of regular troops; while its separate performance of the various movements more peculiarly appropriate to, and characteristic of, irregular horse, satisfactorily demonstrated the superior excellence of the corps for that line of service which is more immediately the object of its maintenance by Government.

The Commander-in-Chief requests Lieutenant-Colonel Arnold and Captain Skinner will accept his best thanks, for having, by their individual and united exertions, rendered the two corps at Hansee so highly disciplined and efficient.

(A true copy.)

(Signed)   A. Gordon,
                                Deputy Adjutant-General.*

"I wish you would let me know in confidence, what number of cavalry, of the same excellent description as that under your command, you could raise, and whether you do not think that raising a large body of them would probably have the effect of drawing off a great proportion of Meer Khan's best cavalry.—I remain, my dear Skinner, yours very sincerely,

(Signed)   "G. H. Fagan."

The 3,000 horse were accordingly raised in less than a twelvemonth, and though the nature of the Nepaulese or Ghoorka war afforded but few and imperfect opportunities for the use of horse, small parties of this corps were attached to several of the detachments employed against the Ghoorkas, as at Kalunga and Jytock, with Generals Gillespie and Martindale, with Generals Nichols and Ochterlony, and they were eminently useful in assisting the regular troops in overawing the powers of Hindostan, especially Sindea and Holcar, who were looking anxiously to the event of our contest with the Nepaulese, and who, upon the unsuccessful opening of that war, shewed very significant symptoms of the spirit which animated them.

Detachment Orders by Lieutenant-Colonel Arnold, commanding at Hansee.
29th Jan. 1813.

The commanding officer having, at the inspection, this morning, of the corps of irregular horse commanded by Captain Skinner, experienced singular satisfaction in the performances of their various evolutions, both regular and desultory, he begs to add his testimony to their extraordinary attainments in discipline, to those already awarded them by that experienced and veteran officer Lieutenant-Colonel Adams, whose sentiments were so fully acquiesced in, at the recent review of the troops, by his Excellency Lieutenant-General Champaigne.

Lieutenant-Colonel Arnold returns his most cordial thanks to Captain Skinner, for the result of his unwearied exertions so ably exemplified in the exercise this morning, and entreats he will explain to the corps at large the high ideas he entertains of their merits.

(Signed)   *J. Arnold,*
Lieut.-Col. commanding.

Detachment Order by Colonel Arnold, commanding at Hansee.
6th Oct. 1814.

Colonel Arnold, in quitting the post of Hansee, where he has commanded for nearly three years, performs a grateful duty in returning his sincere thanks to Captain

This increase of force, however, had reference not so much to the war at that time in progress, and in which cavalry could take but little part as to another and more important military enterprise, contemplated even at that time by the Marquis of Hastings, and in which the services of an efficient body of irregular cavalry, such as Skinner's, were likely to prove most valuable. It is obvious, in fact, that the noble Marquis did highly appreciate the value of Skinner and his brother, as commanders of such troops, as will appear from two letters addressed by himself to that officer, and which, though marked confidential, we scruple not to annex at foot.* Alas! all who could then have been interested in their being kept private, have long since ceased to think of earthly things, and the sentiments they express can but do honour to all parties. There is another letter, however, that we shall insert here, as it happily expresses the high estimation in which Colonel Skinner was held by the most competent judges in the regular service. It is from Colonel Worsely, formerly Deputy-Adjutant-General on Lord Lake's staff.

"My dear Skinner,—You will hear of the honour lately conferred on the Indian army by the Prince Regent, in allowing the officers to participate in the Order of the Bath. Having had an opportunity of seeing the Earl of Buckinghamshire, by whom the measure was brought about, I observed to him, that if honorary members could be allowed on our side of the water, as had been done with regard to German and other foreign officers in his Majesty's service, that Captain Skinner, who commands a corps of irregular horse, possessed very distinguished claims to such notice.

Skinner, for the great and prompt assistance, in all emergencies, received from him, Lieutenant Robert Skinner, and the corps of irregular cavalry, whose gallantry and good conduct has been repeatedly recorded. The orderly behaviour of the corps in cantonment, and the alacrity and effect with which they perform all duties required of them, cannot be surpassed. Colonel Arnold entreats of Captain Skinner to make known his sentiments to his brother, Lieut. Robert Skinner, and the corps at large, which he quits with regret, both as friends and valuable brother soldiers.

* *Letter from the Marquis of Hastings to Lieut.-Col. Skinner.*
Futtehghur, 25th March 1815.

Sir,—Lieut.-Colonel Pagan has laid before me your letter containing the application of your brother for leave to retire from the service. Let me beg of you

"His lordship replied with readiness, that he had often heard of Skinner's corps; but as he feared you did not hold any commission from his Majesty, he was sorry no such extension of the measure could be adopted. I replied, you certainly had no commission from his Majesty, though you were now serving the Hon. Company. He then said the thing was impossible.

"Never mind, my friend, these things are only feathers, and at all events, no longer tickle us when once we pass the heyday of life, and exchange the tulwar for the zemeendary karkhanah, and at any rate, you may confidently indulge the reflection, that you have fully deserved this honour, though your nusseeb has not commanded or obtained it. I must now conclude. Believe me, yours very sincerely,

(Signed)   "H. Worsely."

"Isle of Wight, 15th Feb. 1815."

The occasion which, as we have above remarked, gave rise to so great an increase of demand for irregular cavalry, as is pointed at in the letter of Colonel Fagan, was no less than the contemplated movement by Lord Hastings against the Pindarree freebooters and their supporters in Central India.

The consequences of that narrow and timid policy, which in 1805-6 huddled up a peace with the Mahratta states and powers of Central India, before they had been sufficiently humbled by our arms to feel their comparative weakness, and

---

to entreat that he will suspend his determination until he may be secure against foregoing advantages which might have made the profession agreeable to him. Circumstances have prevented my being able yet (as I must carry the vice-president in Council with me on such a point) to settle the rank for officers in the irregular corps. I need not repeat to you my anxiety to put that matter on a footing which would be gratifying to officers of that description, and not much time is required for arranging it.

You mention your readiness to sever from the corps which you command a proportion which might make a separate one for your brother. I own to you I should prefer his continuing (with advanced rank) second to you; though I would station him with a party of your corps at a distance from you. The wish to keep your command as respectable as possible, is what influences my disposition on that point. Therefore, tell me frankly whether your brother can be reconciled to that plan.—I have the honour, sir, to be, your very obedient servant,

(Signed)   *Moira.*

the necessity of an honest adherence to the treaties imposed upon them, very soon began to show themselves. In fact, a sense of utter impotence could alone restrain from action haughty chiefs, whose natural jealousy had been exasperated into hatred by defeat, and whose wounded honour and soreness of crippled power could only be soothed by the hope of one day turning upon their conquerors with better success than heretofore.

Of the principal Mahratta chiefs,—the Peishwah, Sindea, Holcar, and Bhounslah,—the first, forced into a subsidiary alliance by an impulse of self-preservation in a moment of danger, was again ungrateful; jealous of our interference, secretly hostile and treacherous. Sindea, though not an avowed enemy, still cherished a sullen hatred against the power that had humbled him, checked his course of conquest, and curbed his ambitious views. His secret enmity was discovered in the treasonable correspondence he maintained against the British interests, with the Nepaulese, with the Peishwah, and other ill-disposed chiefs. The hatred of Holcar and the Bhounslah had its origin in the same source; all desired our downfall as strangers and interlopers,

---

The Marquis of Hastings to the same.
(Confidential)

Futtehghur, 15th April, 1815.

Sir,—On reflection, I know not whether I have not to charge myself with omission, in not explaining to you (as it might have had weight with your brother) the particular bearing of the arrangement which I professed to have in contemplation. My motive, however, for the reserve was a just one. I wished to avoid the appearance of reckoning decidedly on the concurrence of Council on a matter which I had referred to their opinion, though I had expressed my own conviction to them of the expediency of the measure.

What I proposed was, to confer the qualified rank of lieutenant-colonel and major upon officers of talent and experience in the irregular service. You are sufficiently aware of the jealousy with which the opening such a door would be regarded by the officers of the regular army; therefore you will be sensible it was necessary to guard this first step with ostensible restrictions. Following the analogy which was fixed for the officers of the provincial corps of Loyalists who served with the king's army in America, I proposed that the youngest major of the line should command the eldest lieutenant-colonel of irregulars; but that the field officers of the latter should command all captains of the regular service. By this arrangement, you see, it would be practicable to entrust an irregular officer with a considerable force, having only

who had placed a restraint upon their projects of devastation. Nor did gratitude for being delivered from the gripe of Ameer Khan restrain the hostile spirit of the last from acting against the power which had deprived him of Berar and Cuttack.

But, even had no hostility been evinced or suspected on the part of the Mahratta princes, the consequences of their system of government, or rather of misrule, were of themselves sufficient to call for interference on the part of the British authorities. Instead of discharging the functions of government by a system of regular departments, their only means for executing these duties lay in a lawless military force. Beyond the boundaries of his own immediate, and as it were personal domain, each chief collected what he could force from the people of the country at the point of the spear and by a system of forays; and the tribute thus collected was termed chout, or moolkgeeree, expressions equivalent to the black mail exacted by predatory bands in other countries. The country of Sindea, or Holcar, never enjoyed peace; its peasantry were never safe in person or in property. The army of these chiefs was constantly detached in parties under leaders, to raise contributions, to reduce forts, or punish refractory officers and zemindars, all over Rajepootanah, Malwah, and Bhopaul.

Such a system among the leading powers could not fail

---

the attention to place under him battalions which happened to be commanded by captains. The degree in which such a capability of distinction must raise the situation of the irregular field officers will be obvious to you; and as I had contemplated the giving the rank of major to your brother, I naturally hoped the alteration might have made continuance in the service agreeable to him. To give him the chance of availing himself of any variation in sentiment which this explanation might produce, I shall say nothing of his resignation until the answer from the Council shall arrive. At the same time, it would be improper for me to keep him in suspense, if he still wish to abide by his determination; and in that case (but in that case only), his resignation shall be understood to have been accepted by me from the 10th inst.

You will comprehend that the rank to which I have alluded would not be progressive by ordinary brevet, though any brilliant service performed in it would actually tend to advancement. Of course, these observations (though the outline merely is to be communicated to your brother) are intended to rest with yourself alone. It will, I trust, be believed by you that I have peculiar pleasure in thus manifesting to a person so respectable and meritorious as you, the light in which I consider your equitable claims.—I have the honour, sir, to remain, &c. &c,

(Signed)   Moira.

of encouraging that strong propensity to plunder so inherent in the population of all these districts; and, in fact, instead of making any attempt at putting down marauders, it became a part of the Mahratta policy to encourage such bands, for they afforded additional means to the protecting chiefs of enlarging their own sphere of military plunder. The consequence was, that, by the year 1814, the country was overspread with bands of freebooters, who ravaged, systematically, every district from the Kishna to the desert of Marwar.

It is by no means our purpose to inflict upon our readers a history of the rise and progress of these freebooters, who are best known by the name of Pindarrees. It is sufficient to state, that in 1814 they were computed to have numbered full 40,000 horsemen of all sorts, without including those who attached themselves more especially to the armies of Holcar and Sindea, or the Patans of Ameer Khan, who, counting horse and foot, is said at this time to have been at the head of 30,000 men.

The principal leaders at this time were the following:—The celebrated Cheetoo, whose durra, or horde, was estimated at from 10,000 to 15,000; Kurreem Khan, at this time, only 4,000; Dost Mahomed and Wasil Mahomed, 6,000; inferior and independent leaders, 8,000.

Two sons of a famous chief (by that time dead) named Burun, afterwards well known as the two Rajuns, had not at this time acquired their full influence, and generally acted with the other sirdars.

These chiefs all haunted the valley of the Nerbudda, and the mountains to the north and south of it. There they had their camps and strongholds, where, by sufferance of the fixed powers, they bestowed their families and property when absent on expeditions, and there they themselves dwelt and pastured their horses during the rains and hot weather. By the time of the dussera,— an annual festival occurring at the end of October or beginning of November,—each chief planted his standard in his camp, and to these flocked all loose spirits and lawless adventurers who sought to partake of their fortunes. There were formed their plans of rapine and plunder, and there they trained their horses for hard work and long marches. By the end of the dussera, when the rivers generally become fordable, they shod their horses, chose leaders, and set forth upon their projected lubhur, or foray. The party usually ranged from one to several thousands. Of these, the proportion of good and well-mounted cavalry was usually that of 400 out of every 1,000, and these were always armed with long spears and swords; besides which, every fifteenth or twentieth man had a matchlock. The rest were of all sorts, looties or common scamps, attendants, slaves, or followers of the camp, mounted as each man could manage, on tattoos or ponies, and armed with every sort of weapon they might possess. Thus, without baggage or encumbrances, their progress was so rapid as almost to mock pursuit; and the barbarous atrocities they committed, their ingenuity of tortures to extort property, and their system of wanton destruction were beyond the power of description.

Under such a progress of devastation, it is obvious that every country they visited must have become a waste, which grew wider and wider as the mere exhaustion of its resources caused the freebooters to spread further, until cultivation and cultivators alike disappeared from the land. No language can paint the melancholy scale of desolation to which the Rajepoot dominions were reduced, and that of Meywar in particular; nor did Malwah, Candeish, or the northern districts of the Dekhan, Mahratta though they were, escape much better. The sketch of a single lubhur, or foray, which was made by Cheetoo, in the end of 1815, upon the Company's territories, will suffice to give some idea of the ruin effected by these miscreants in a single season.

Mr. Prinsep tells us that the Pindarrees assembled at Cheetoo's camp, at the dussera of 1815, to the number of 8,000 of all descriptions. They crossed the Nerbudda on the 14th October, and took a southward course. But soon breaking into two masses, one, in passing the valley of the Taptee, was surprised in its bivouac by a small party of the Nizam's reformed infantry, under Major Fraser. Galloping off, however, with but little loss, they continued plundering in a southerly direction to the banks of the Kishna.

The other party went to the south-east, and passing through part of the Nagpore territories, traversed those of the Nizam from north to south, as far as the bank of the Kishna; and the territories of the Madras presidency were only preserved by the accident of that river not being fordable at the time. The freebooters, therefore, turned eastward, marking their course by a broad line of fire and blood to the frontier of Masulipatam; when they took a northward direction: and, eluding all the British posts and parties, returned along the line of the Godavery and the Wurda, to Neemawur. The booty acquired in the Nizam's dominions, in the course of this excursion, was so great, that there being no merchants of sufficient substance to purchase it at Neemawur, they had to send to Oojeine for purchasers.

This success led immediately to another expedition. By the 5th February, 10,000 men, under various leaders, again assembled at Neemawur, and crossing the Nerbudda, pursued the same track to the SSE. that had been taken by the former expedition on its return. And the first that was heard of this body was its appearance on the western frontier of the Masulipatam district in the Madras presidency, on the 10th of March. From thence it turned southwards, and next day made a march of thirty-eight miles, in the course of which it plundered ninety - two villages, committing in each the most frightful cruelties. On the following day (the 12th), after another march of thirty-eight miles, and the destruction of fifty-eight villages, the horde arrived at the civil station of Guntoor, where they plundered all the houses of the civil offices, and a considerable part of the town. The government treasure, and the persons of the British residents, were protected at the collector's office by the exertions of a few troops and invalids, kept at the station for civil duties. But Pindarrees never risk loss either of time or life; so they decamped immediately with what they could get, and before night not a strange horseman was to be seen in the neighbourhood. The whole had hurried off to the westward, making on the next day a march of fifty-two miles.

For twelve days did this body of maurauders continue pillaging within the Company's frontier; and after leaving Guntoor, they swept through part of the Kuddapa district, and recrossed the Kishna on the 22nd of March—just escaping a squadron of the Madras native infantry, which came to the opposite bank at the very time they had made good their passage. Detachments were sent out in all directions; but the lubhur split into several bodies, probably in order to baffle pursuit; and, though some of them had narrow escapes, the whole, or nearly so, of the large body that crossed the Nerbudda in February, had re-crossed it in safety by the 17th of May, having, with perfect impunity, carried off a second immense booty within the year. Of the damage done in the Company's territory in these twelve days, some idea may be formed from the report of a committee appointed to inquire into the whole matter; and from which it appears that, independent of the value taken or destroyed, there were 182 individuals put to a cruel death, 505 severely wounded, and 3,603 subjected to different kinds of torture.

Had this unequalled system of rapine and murder been confined to those provinces and states which the British, by their own mistaken policy, had placed beyond the pale of their own protection, even then so gross an injury to the prosperity of the whole country could never have been tolerated in its neighbourhood; but these daring acts of aggression upon its own territory and subjects, called imperatively for immediate punishment and measures of prevention for the future. And the Marquis of Hastings, fully aware of the intimate connection between the fixed and secretly hostile powers with the maurauders, resolved to adopt a plan of operations so extensive as at once to crush all such insidious hostility, and sweep from the face of the country every freebooter that infested it.

So early as the end of 1816, a number of detachments were thrown out from various points, with so much skill as to check the lubhurs of that season with considerable success, and great loss on the part of the Pindarrees. But arrangements on a far more extensive scale were in progress; and, while negociations were opened with those princes or chieftains who could be brought to reason, the preparations for coercing the refractory were silently but industriously carried on. During the summer and autumn of 1817, the various bodies of troops assembled at their posts. The grand army, under command of Lord Hastings in person, consisting of about 34,000 regular troops, was formed in three divisions and a reserve, and occupied positions at Agra, Secundra, near Kalpee, on the Jumna, and Kalinger in Bundelcund; the reserve being stationed at Rewarree south-west of Dehlee.

The army of the Dekhan, under command of Lieutenant-

General Sir Thomas Hislop, was formed in five divisions and a reserve; and amounted to 57,000 regulars, which were disposed so as to cross the Nerbudda simultaneously at Hindia and Hoshingabad, to occupy positions in Berar and in Candeish, and act as circumstances should indicate; while a division from Guzerat was to enter Malwah by Dohud. To this large force of regular troops—the largest by far that ever took the field from British India—was added 23,000 of irregular horse, of which 13,000 were attached to the army of the Dekhan, and 10,000 to that of Bengal.

This vast scheme, rendered complete by some subsidiary details, was calculated to embrace the whole disaffected region; and advancing inwards, like one of Timour's or Chenghiz-Khan's gigantic hunts, to converge to any central point that should prove the fittest for final action, and thus gather together and crush, without hope of escape, every refractory or treacherous power within its circuit. Never, assuredly, was any plan of military operations better concerted to effect its purpose; and never was any combination of diplomatic and military tactics more completely crowned with success. The end of that year, and the space of a single month, saw the Peishwah and the Bhounslah, with the representatives of Holcar, baffled alike in their intrigues and their efforts at open resistance. The battle of Khirkee,* and its train of consequences, sent the first a hunted

---

* We dare not trespass so far on the patience of our readers as to inflict on them even the shortest sketch of the three celebrated battles, which, if they did not actually terminate, gave that spirit to the war which brought it to its speedy issue—those of Khirkee, Seetabuldee, and Mehidpore —although in the first of these 2,800 British troops, of which only 800 were Europeans, broke and scattered 28,000 of the Peishwah's chosen troops; and, in the second, 18,000 Mahrattas and Arabs, brave and fierce soldiers, were repulsed and put to flight by scarce 1,400 sepoys. That reply of the gallant Fitzgerald, when, seeing the critical moment, he repeatedly, but in vain, besought his commander for leave to charge the cavalry which were swarming in the plain— that reply will never be forgotten in India: "Tell him to charge at his peril!" was the stern and impatient refusal he received. "At my peril, then be it!" exclaimed Fitzgerald; and dashing forward with his small party, all animated with the same spirit, they scattered the immense body of horse, took the batteries which were spreading death through our ranks, and saved the day, and the life of every being on that desperately contested ground.

Not less gallantly fought and dearly won was the battle of Mehidpore, where Sir John Malcolm, who crossed the river with scarce 2,000 bayonets, stormed and

227

fugitive, worn out and driven alike from every stratagem and stronghold, to a quiet asylum in the territories of the power he had so shamefully abused. The battles of Seetabuldee and Nagpore, in like manner, proved the deathblows to the Bhounslah, chief; for though he did at first succeed in deceiving the British authorities and obtaining too favourable terms, his innate duplicity was not long to be controlled or concealed. He fled to the Pindarrees, shared their ruin, and became a homeless fugitive in a foreign land.

The subjection of the once proud family of Holcar cost even less time and trouble. Jesswunt Rao, after his return from the Punjab in 1806, survived for five years, in a state of moody and savage ferocity, that gradually lapsed into insanity. He died an imbecile madman in 1811.

His death, as is ever the case in such circumstances, was the signal for a perfect rush of crimes and intrigues of the most disgusting and revolting description, in which the fall or murder of the principal actors served but to clear the field for a new succession of adventurers in the foul and bloody work, and the whole country became a scene of rapine and of pillage. In these crimes and intrigues, the beautiful and infamous Toolsah Bhye, the mistress of Jesswunt Rao, was the principal actress; until her own time came at length. She was separated from the young

---

took seventy pieces of well-served cannon in position, and routed 20,000 men. The desperate character of that single but conclusive charge was attested by the loss, in one short quarter of an hour, of nearly 800 men in killed and wounded.

Page after page might be filled with splendid traits and anecdotes of these celebrated battles, did we feel a right to diverge so far from the more special subject of this memoir. But there is one exploit less known to the public, which, in point of intrepid gallantry, may vie with any feat of this or of former wars, and which we cannot pass over in silence. It is that remarkable defence of Korreigaon by one weak battalion of sepoys against an almost countless multitude.

Captain Staunton, in command of the 2nd battalion of the 1st Bombay native infantry, had been summoned from Seroor to reinforce the troops at Poonah, and had left the former place 500 strong, with two 6-pounders, and twenty-six European artillerymen, at eight on the night of the 31st December. By ten o'clock on New Year's Day, after marching all night, they reached the high ground above Korreigaon, a village on the bank of the river Beema, from whence they saw the whole of the Peishwah's cavalry, 25,000 horse, on the opposite side. Unable to ford the river in the face of this formidable force, Captain Staunton took post in the village, which, though surrounded by a low and ruinous mud wall, was entirely open on the east side, and had numerous

prince Mulhar Rao, the nominal successor of Jesswunt; and the very day before the desperate and decisive battle of Mehidpore, she was taken from the prison into which she had been cast by the then dominant party, and brought, towards daybreak, in her palankin to the bank of the Seepra. Many were roused by her cries for mercy; "but no foot was stirred, no voice was raised," said an eye-witness of the scene, "to save a woman who had never shown mercy to others."

That battle broke, effectually and for ever, the force and family of Holcar. Its guns were all taken, its excellent infantry, many of them of De Boigne's old brigades, were soon after destroyed; and at Murdissore, the submission of the young chief was tendered to the British commander. On the 6th of January 1818, he entered into a subsidiary treaty, which reduced that haughty house to the rate of a secondary state, and for ever put a stop to the mischief, of which their ambitious and intriguing spirit had so long been the cause.

Sindea, by good fortune, far more than by good policy or honesty, weathered the storm which destroyed his brother princes. Equally intriguing and deceitful; in correspondence with all the enemies of the British; the near vicinity of the army under Lord Hastings, and the division under General Donkin, kept him from moving until the battles of Khirkee and Seetabuldee opened his eyes, and he accepted the subsidiary

---

way. At this moment, Lieutenant Chisholm, of the artillery, was struck down, and the Arabs charged and took one of the guns. All seemed lost, when Lieutenant Thomas Pattison—eternal honour to the hero!—lying there mortally wounded, hearing of the loss of the gun, started to his feet, and seizing a musket called upon the grenadiers to follow him "once more." He rushed on the Arabs, striking to right and left, and, well seconded by his men, scattered or slew the Arabs, retook the gun, and then, again shot through the body, fell upon the ground he had so nobly won.

The headless trunk of Lieutenant Chisholm, dragged from under a pile of dead Arabs, proclaimed to the men the fate they had to look for, if the place should fall into the enemy's hands. The slight success revived their spirits, and one and all renewed the conflict; and although towards evening nature again began to droop, and the situation of the battalion was very hopeless, yet by nightfall the enemy relaxed in their attack. The men got water. By nine o'clock the firing ceased, and the village was evacuated by the Peishwah's troops.

In the morning they were still seen hovering round the village, and Captain Staunton opened his guns again, and prepared for the worst. But they soon moved

treaty which, however distasteful, afforded him the only means of safety in his option.

The minor chieftains were easily dealt with. Separate treaties or settlements were made with each according to the nature of their respective cases; and above all, every state, large or small, in Central India and Hindostan, was guaranteed against the aggression of its neighbours or the incursions of predatory bands. Ameer Khan,—the chief of these freebooters, whose military establishment was such as to cause him to be regarded more in the light of a substantial power,—when he saw his former supporters all prostrated, all scope for future plunder cut off, felt that "his occupation was gone"; and though, with characteristic deceit and cunning, he fought for delay, he found at last that nothing remained for him but to submit to the terms of the conqueror. These were not hard; after many attempts at evasion, he gave up his guns, disbanded his Patans, some of whom were taken into the British service; and abandoning all schemes of ambition or of plunder, sat quietly down on his jaghire of Tonk Rampoorah guaranteed to him by British generosity, and worth 150,000l, a year.

With the states above mentioned, fell the Pindarrees: for them there was no longer any home or resting-place—their day was past. Of these chiefs, the famous Cheetoo, after a career of

---

breaches towards the river side. 6,000 Arab and Ghossein infantry were called in by the enemy, on the battalion making its appearance; and scarce had it taken up its position, when 2,000 of these advanced to assault it, under cover of showers of rockets. They were gallantly met and repulsed at all points; but, unfortunately, got hold and retained possession of a square inclosure in the centre of the place, from whence they were enabled to fire on the sepoys with deadly aim. On the first repulse, the village was instantly surrounded by swarms of horse and foot furious to enter, and then began one of the severest and most obstinately continued contests that India ever witnessed. The sepoys, fatigued with a long night's march, without provisions or water, had to sustain the continued attack of myriads, constantly relieving each other, and under a burning sun. The ruinous wall offered no protection—the enemy swarmed up to the very guns. Every foot of ground was disputed; several streets were taken and retaken. Half of the Europeans were speedily killed or disabled; of the eight officers they had, half were killed or wounded; and the Arabs, in successful charge, having got possession of a small temple in which three of them were lying, savagely murdered the wounded.

The sufferings from thirst, especially of the wounded, were now dreadful. The men were either fainting from fatigue, or frantic for want of water, and seemed fast giving

infinite variety and enterprize, embraced the fortunes of Appa Sahib; and after the battle of Nagpore, conducted the ex-rajah to the neighbourhood of Asseerghur, having had his followers cut up in detail by British detachments. An English party having made its appearance as he reached the vicinity of the place, his few remaining people dispersed, and he took refuge in the deep jungles of Egwass. Unfortunately for himself, he would not trust in the promises of mercy held out by the English authorities; so here, wandering alone, tracked like a hunted animal by the hoof-prints of his horse, he was sprung upon and killed by a tiger. An officer of Holcar's, hearing of this event, hastened to the spot, where the horse, saddle, sword, ornaments and part of the body, with some papers, grants of land from Appa Sahib, were found. They traced the tiger to his den, and then discovered the head still perfect, and at once recognised it as that of the celebrated Pindarree Sirdar.

The fortunes of Kurreen Khan would furnish matter for a volume. At one time exalted, by a concurrence of fortunate events, to the semblance of independent power; at another, a captive in a dungeon, or a fugitive for his life, the year 1817 found him escaped from the camp of Holcar; and at the express desire of Sindea, joining the durra of Wasil Mahomed to assist

---

off in the direction of Poonah, having heard of General Smith's approach. Captain Staunton, not knowing this, resolved to retire upon Seroor, but gave out that he still intended to continue his march to Poonah. Moving, as if with this intention, he suddenly counter-marched on Seroor, and reached that place next morning, carrying with him as many as he could of his wounded. His loss was 175 men in killed and -wounded, of which twenty were of the European artillerymen. Of eight European officers, three were killed, and two wounded severely. During the action, the Peishwah, with the Satarah Rajah, sat on a height on the other side the stream, upbraiding his officers, and asked them, tauntingly, "where were now their boasts of defeating the English, when they could not overcome one battalion."

It is a singular and a touching trait of these gallant men, so far were they from priding themselves on this wonderful defence, that, mortified at not having accomplished the purpose of their march, and conceiving themselves beaten, they came into cantonments with drooping heads and a painful sense of humiliation; nor was it until they experienced the hearty welcome and warm congratulations of their comrades that they were consoled and restored to their own self-esteem—they had, indeed, won a wreath of laurels which can never fade.—See a more detailed account of this glorious defence in Grant Duff's History, vol. iii. p. 435.

in opposing the English. But disappointed and disgusted at the refusal of that chief to assist them, from fear of detection by the British authorities, he abandoned his family, and fled, very slightly attended, back to Holcar's camp at Mundissore. From thence he was driven from similar motives to those of Sindea; and after concealment for some time, and under many disguises, he was persuaded at length to throw himself unconditionally on the mercy of the British government. By them he was sent to Goruckpore, where lands were allotted for his support. Namdar Khan, one of his chief leaders, also surrendered himself; and most of the rest followed his example. Wasil Mahomed took refuge in Sindea's camp; but being seized and imprisoned there, in conformity with that prince's treaty with the British, he destroyed himself by poison.

Thus perished the Pindarrees, a growth of the diseased times—a race that could only have existed in an atmosphere of total anarchy and disorganization. Living solely on rapine, without any peaceful pursuit, it needed but to deprive them of all field for plunder, to effect their extirpation. To do this was the object of Lord Hastings in this extensive and complicated enter-prize. How well he succeeded, we have seen. "There remains not a spot in India," says Sir J. Malcolm, "that a Pindarree can call his home. They have been hunted like wild beasts. Numbers have been killed; all who adopted their cause have fallen. Their principal leaders have either died, submitted, or become captives. A minute investigation only can discover any of these once formidable disturbers, concealed as they are amongst the lowest classes." Nothing, indeed, is more wonderful than the rapid fall and utter extinction of these marauders. All powerful and intangible as they appeared at the commencement of this striking campaign, before the year was out, they had vanished. In the month of September 1817, full one hundred thousand wild freebooters ravaged and trampled down the realms of Central India; by the end of December in the same year, they were gone—dead or merged in the peaceful mass of the people, never to reappear, leaving no trace behind them of the hordes that had desolated India. Such is one feat—one lasting and characteristic boon bestowed by the British government upon the people of Hindostan.

Chapter Sixteen
The End of the Pindarree War

In the disposition of the troops for the campaign that has just been described, Colonel Skinner, with 2,000 of his corps, had been ordered to join Sir David Ochterlony, as part of the reserve division which was posted at Rewarree as a check upon Ameer Khan and his Patans. In the beginning of December, this reserve moved southward towards Jeypore, Ameer Khan being at that time employed in reducing Madhoo Rajepoora. Negociations were in progress with him, as well as with the Rajah of Jeypore: and it is a striking proof of how distasteful to all the chieftains of Hindostan was a treaty with the British, involving, as it generally did, a subsidiary force and some power of interference, that he could prefer the tender mercies of Ameer Khan and his Patans, who had been, and were still, ravaging his country, to the protection of the British government, clogged by such stipulations.

On the 10th, the reserve arrived at Sanganere, near Jeypore; whither vakeels came into camp from Ameer Khan. But the treaty with the Rajah made no real progress, and none of the officers were permitted to go into the town.

On the 15th, the treaty with Ameer Khan being in a state of forwardness, Sir David Ochterlony with his personal staff, Colonel Skinner, the Nawab Ahmed Buksh Khan, and some other persons, proceeded to a village four côs distant from the camp, in order to meet the Meer; who on his part advanced six côs from his own camp to see the General. The first meeting of ceremony took place next morning. The Meer was attended by 500 horsemen, a company of infantry, and two galloper guns. The parties came on elephants, and the Patan chief appeared to be under great alarm. When the elephants approached each other, in order that the General might take hold of the Meer's hand—the common salute under such circumstances—the attendant who sat in the howdah behind him, held a cocked pistol presented to the General's breast; and the horsemen were all prepared with lit matches, and carbines, and blunderbusses handled. After a hasty introduction, the Meer called out hurriedly, *"chulo, chulo!"* — "get on, get on," and they separated. The General, in a few minutes, retired to his tent, and Ameer Khan went to one pitched for him by Sir David's orders, he having brought none along with him.

Meer on business, and received the customary-presents; and next day visit and presents were returned. It was remarked by the writer of this account, that neither in appearance nor in address did the Patan chief make any favourable impression. He was poor and mean looking, dressed in a blue turban and dirty white upper garment. He spoke but little, and what he said was trifling, plebeian, and in bad style. He said that he was king of Hindostan, but resigned his claim to it from friendship for the General. His attendants talked lightly of him, and abused him for truckling, as they said, to the English, for which he would get well handled on his return to camp. His followers were not insolent, but fops in dress, and ridiculous bullies in talking. Some of them were handsome, respectable-looking soldiers; men chiefly from Rampore and Mhow. The horsemen were well armed and mounted. There is no doubt that the Meer's acquiescence in the treaty, after all his evasions and subterfuges, was quickened by the news from Nagpore and Poonah. He had intelligence of these battles three days before it reached the British camp: and he remarked that it was all nonsense to try fighting, when two battalions could beat so many thousand men.

Notwithstanding the signature of the treaty, however, a final settlement with the Patan chief was not so close at hand. He was overawed by his turbulent troops, and instead of giving up his guns according to treaty, they were sent out along with his infantry to collect money in the Jeypore territory. At length, however, the mutinous state of his army, and still more, perhaps, the account which reached him of the total defeat and dispersion of Holcar's army at Mehidpore, forced him to a decision. He quitted his own camp, and came and pitched his tent within a mile of that of the reserve army. The General visited him next day, and sent him tents, camels, &c.

Skinner's memoirs:-

"And now he will lay himself up in ordinary, and enjoy twenty-two lakhs of rupees a year, the fruit of his treachery to Holcar, who had adopted him as a brother, and put his son into his arms to be to him as a child. While he was temporizing with the English, he was all along encouraging Guffoor Khan and Holcar's Mahratta chiefs to fight in the south. If they had succeeded he would have joined them; but since they have been defeated he stays where he is, and secures all his jaghires in Holcar's country, as a possession from the British Government for his son, and five lakhs in ready money for his useless guns. It was by his advice that Toolsah Byhe, one of Holcar's wives, was put to death before the late action, because she had agreed to come to terms with the English."

Skinner may possibly be too severe upon the Meer in some part of these charges; for though there is no doubt of his strong propensity to intrigue and treachery, when it served his purpose, it is equally certain that if there was a redeeming point in the Patan's character, it was his long and almost faithful adherence to Holcar. When that chief died, and his family and court became a perfect hotbed of vice and intrigue, without any of the talent required to bring their ambitious designs to maturity, or to sustain the influence or power of the government, he may have fallen off from his allegiance; but then its object was no more, and he may have thought that none was left worthy enough, or safe enough, to cling to. He was a cautious, selfish, unprincipled chief; and, when the strong motive was gone, he acted up to his character.

Although Sir David, by a happy union of address and firmness, succeeded at length in procuring the fulfilment of all the articles of the treaty including the surrender of the Meer's guns, and the dispersion or absorption of his troops, the weak and vacillating government of Jeypore still held out, the only one of the Rajepoot states that had not embraced the terms of the British Government for receiving protection and support, and, therefore, the army of reserve remained still stationed in the neighbourhood of its capital. But Colonel Skinner, with his corps, was ordered to join a detachment under Colonel Patton, who was proceeding to Colonel Ludlow's force at Rampoorah. From thence, at the approach of Bajee Rao, he was summoned, with a thousand of his horse, by Sir John

Malcolm; but before he could reach him the Peishwah had come to terms. With Sir John, at Mhow, he remained two months, when he was sent to escort Captain Low, in charge of Bajee Rao, to Bittoor, at which place he remained six months. In the course of these services, and, indeed, throughout the whole of this campaign, there occurred no opportunities for those displays of courage and gallantry, which enabled the corps to distinguish itself on former occasions; but that both corps and commander acquitted themselves to the perfect satisfaction of their superiors is amply attested in the annexed letters.

"To Lieutenant-Colonel Skinner, Commanding Irregular Cavalry.

"Head-quarters, Futtehghur, 20th May 1815.
"Sir,—The Eight Honourable the Commander-in-chief must not omit to thank you for the zeal and alacrity with which you proceeded against the refractory inhabitants of Bhowanee, on the 22nd April last, and for the timely and judicious manner in which you had previously detached the 200 sowars to the assistance of the police officers. To these prompt measures the Commander-in-chief attributes the rapid suppression of the insurrection, and he has not failed to bring the good conduct evinced by you and your corps on this occasion, under the favourable notice of the Eight Honourable the Governor-General.
"The distinguished gallantry of Runjeet Khan, and the four sowars mentioned by you, attracted his Excellency's particular notice, and he desires that his thanks may be offered to that gallant officer and his brave companions, for their meritorious services on the above occasion.—I have the honour to be, &c. &c.

(Signed)   "G. H. Fagan,
                                    "Adjutant-General."

"DIVISION ORDERS.

"Camp, Mundissore, 20th Aug. 1818.
"Brigadier-General Sir John Malcolm cannot allow

Lieutenant-Colonel Skinner's corps to leave the division without conveying to that officer, and through him to his officers and men, his sense of their uniform orderly and regular conduct. The Brigadier-General has been for many years familiar with the merits of Lieutenant-Colonel Skinner; his warmest wishes will ever accompany that officer, and the fine body of men under his command; and he trusts the latter will long continue to find, in a sincere and honourable attachment to their present leader, additional motives for the faithful and gallant performance of their duty to the government they serve."

"Mundissore, 20th Aug. 1818.

"My dear Skinner,—I have said and done no more towards you, than what a sincere regard for a warm, private friend, and a zealous servant of the public, dictated. A line was by mistake omitted in the order, which I have told Napier to correct. My right to express the feelings I have done in a general order, refer to my long acquaintance with your merits. I shall have great satisfaction in transmitting this testimony to Lord Hastings, as an honest and sincere tribute to one whom, in my opinion, he has done himself honour by patronizing in the manner he has done.

"Yours sincerely,

(Signed)   "John Malcolm."

"To Lieutenant-Colonel Skinner.

"Bittoor, 13th July 1819.

"Sir,—The Most Noble the Governor-General in Council having decided that the services of the main body of the troops under your command are no longer required at Bittoor, I have the honour to request, that, with the exception of one complete rissalah, which is to remain under my orders for some time longer, you will be pleased to place yourself and the corps under the command of Major-General Sir Dyson Marshall, from whom you will receive the requisite orders respecting your future movements.

"The sentiments I entertain of your public conduct, and of the uniformly correct behaviour of the excellent corps under your command, since you have been employed on your present duty, being fully stated in my report of this date to Government, of which I have the pleasure to inclose a copy for your information, I have little to add here, but to express my anxious wishes for your health and prosperity, and that the fullest success may attend your exertions in every service on which you may be employed, and I beg to assure you, that the many obliging acts of private friendship which I have received from you, and the very cordial and useful aid which, during the last twelvemonth, you have rendered me in my official duties on all occasions, have excited feelings of esteem and gratitude which I can never forget, and have fixed in my mind the most sincere respect for your character, and the warmest interest in your welfare.

     "I have the honour to be, &c. &c.

(Signed)   "John Low,
"Commanding with Bajee Rao."

    The Report to Government alluded to in this letter, contains the highest encomiums on Colonel Skinner and his corps; but it is too long for insertion here, and merely repeats the sentiments expressed in Colonel Skinner's favour on other occasions, and is therefore omitted.

    "Extract Division Orders by Brigadier-General
Sir John Malcolm, &c. &c.

Parole, Seronge.

            "Camp, Mhow, 5th Feb. 1819.
    "Brigadier-General Malcolm was much gratified this morning, by the review of the 2nd Regiment of Skinner's horse, who are (as far as he can judge) exactly at that point of order and discipline most calculated to maintain their utility and efficiency, and promote the reputation they have acquired. Brigadier-General Malcolm had lately occasion to express his admiration of that part of this distinguished corps, under the immediate command of Lieutenant-Colonel Skinner. He cannot pay a higher compliment to Major Robert Skinner, his rissaldars and men, than by stating his opinion that the 2nd Regiment of Skinner's horse is equal

to the first, not only in its discipline and appearance, but in those more essential principles of internal regulation, which maintain the character of a corps as high in times of peace as of war; by rendering it, from its good order and habits of regularity, a real protection to the inhabitants of the country in which it is employed. In this respect, every report Sir John Malcolm has received of Major Skinner's regiment since it entered Malwah has been the same, and it is one upon which he deems that officer and those under his command entitled to his particular praise and thanks."

"DETACHMENT MORNING ORDERS"

"Lieutenant-Colonel Smith cannot allow the attack made yesterday upon the Arab camp, however unimportant it may appear, to pass, without publicly recording his approbation of that event, the result of which reflects the greatest credit on the troops of the detachment...

"Lieutenant-Colonel Smith would be wanting in his duty, were he to omit on this occasion to express more particularly the high sense he entertains of the zealous and spirited conduct of Major Skinner, and the fine body of men under his command. The steadiness and alacrity with which they obeyed orders, the regularity of their rapid advance in two columns round the village where the enemy had been encamped a few hours before, and their subsequent gallant pursuit of the fugitives down the bypaths in the mountains, and the continuance of that pursuit to the very gates of Asseerghur, was such as would do honour to any corps, however exalted in character.

"The Lieutenant-Colonel cannot but express his admiration of the conduct of Skinner's horse, and requests Major Skinner will communicate those sentiments to the men under his command. It will be a part of the Lieutenant-Colonel's duty to bring to the notice of his superiors, the conduct of all the officers and men employed in these services.

(Signed)   "H. Coyle,
"Brigade Major.
"Camp at Kairee, 15th Feb. 1819."

A further general order, by Brigadier-General Malcolm, under date 26th of February 1819, upon Major Skinner leaving his command, speaks in the highest terms of that officer and his corps, and refers, in terms of the highest commendation, to the conduct of Major Skinner and his corps in the affair already described by Colonel Smith; but as the matter has already been given, it becomes unnecessary to repeat it.

There is, however, a letter written about this time by Sir John Malcolm to Colonel Skinner, which, containing as it does that distinguished officer's deliberate opinion not only of his corps in particular, but of the characteristic requisites of irregular corps in general, is too valuable to be omitted, and it is therefore given at length:—

"Sir John Malcolm to Lieut.-Col. Skinner.

"Mhow, 23rd Dec. 1819.

"My dear Skinner,—I should sooner have answered your letter, inclosing your reply to the 'Bengal Cavalry Officer.' Calumnies upon corps or individuals have on some occasions their uses, when they elicit that truth from modest merit which gives publicity to actions that should never be forgotten. This has been the case on the present occasion. The plain and admirable statement you have given of these affairs—which the brain of the 'Cavalry Officer' anxious to establish some favourite hypothesis, confused and misrepresented—will do you and your corps the greatest credit. You can both boast, that though there was in an hour of extreme trial some defection, never was the honour of a body of men better vindicated, than by the exemplary punishment (inflicted by the corps itself) of the criminal cowards who deserted their standards.

"The 'Bengal Officer' should have thought more before he alluded to a partial defection of a few of your men, a solitary instance of desertion; and tried on that ground to stigmatize a class. But he is, I understand, dead; and let the subject, which the imprudence of friends has used his name to revive, die with him. It will be more gratifying, and more salutary, to allow our minds to dwell upon the numerous instances of heroic valour and unshaken attachment that distinguished both the regulars and irregulars of that fine army, which, commanded

240

by our noble friend Lord Lake, conquered Hindostan, than to expose the failings of deceased worth by groping amidst old posthumous MSS. for productions probably repented of as soon as written. But with a man who has a purpose to serve, and an editor who has a page to fill, much less consideration is, I fear, given than ought to be to the feelings of others. Letters, however, like that you have sent to the journal, are calculated to do great good. Unless there is bad intention (and I acquit the parties of that), they will learn caution when they see the effect such attacks upon individuals and corps produce.

"I am glad you propose to give a short memoir of your corps. If written, as I have no doubt it will be, with the same clear conciseness, and in the same spirit of modesty and truth, which it no doubt will be, that marks your letter to the Calcutta journal, it will be a most valuable document. With respect to the merits of our irregular horse, you know my sentiments. We have, both in our own services and as auxiliaries, many excellent bodies of this class of soldiers. Yours are the best I have seen of the former description, though I believe some of the Rohilla corps are very good; but yours have had great advantages, and have made admirable use of them. I do not mean to flatter, when I say you are as good an Englishman as I know; but you are also a native irregular, half born and fully bred; you armed them, understand their characters, enter into their prejudices; can encourage them, without spoiling them; know what they can and, what is more important, what they cannot do. The superiority of your corps rests upon a foundation that no others have. Your rissaldars* are men, generally speaking, not only of character, but of family; those under them are not only their military, but their natural dependants. These are links which it is difficult for the mere European officers to keep up. They too often go upon smart men; promote, perhaps, a man of low family and indifferent character among themselves for some gallant actions; and then ascribe to envy, jealousy, and all unworthy motives, the deficiency in respect and obedience of those under him; forgetting the great distinction between regular and irregular corps in this point. Your personal kindness and generosity to your corps, has also effected much: and I have even found in

* *Native captains of troops. A Rissalah is generally a troop of 100 men.*

Hindostan, fourteen years ago, and in Malwah during the last two, that every horseman of your corps considers, whether his duty requires him to act against the enemy, or to protect the inhabitants, that he has "Sekunder Sahib-Ke-Alroo" in his keeping. This, I delight in observing, is a master-motive with them on all occasions.

"To conclude with my opinion, upon irregular horse. Independent of the policy of keeping in pay, or in the service of our allies, a considerable number of this class, I know not, on the scale we now are, how we can operate in the field without them; but everything depends on their good management. They are no more fit for the duties of regular cavalry than the latter are for theirs. They are our light troops; and as such have their distinct place: to take them out of that is their ruin. You know my opinion; that you have gone to the very verge of making bad regulars of admirable irregulars.—Yours, ever sincerely,

(Signed)   "John Malcolm."

Nor was the younger Skinner a whit behind his brother in rendering himself useful and acceptable to his commanders during this stirring period. Immediately after the rains, he was ordered by Sir John Malcolm to join Colonel Smith, then in command of a detachment from the Madras presidency; and he distinguished himself in the pursuit of Appa Sahib, the ex-Rajah of Nagpore, cutting up his people, with a small party of his sowars, to the gates of Asseerghur. And, in the beginning of 1819, he escorted Chimnajee, the brother of Bajee Rao, to Allahabad, under command of Captain Clarke; for both of which services it will be seen that he received the thanks of his commanding officers.

With this war, commonly called "the Pindarree war," the active military career of Colonel Skinner may be said to have closed. There was, in fact, no longer any field for active service on any considerable scale in Upper India. Accordingly, at the close of 1819, one-third of Skinner's corps was paid off; the second, under Major Robert Skinner, was sent to Neemuch; while the remaining 1,000 men, with the Colonel himself, continued at their old quarters of Hansee.

In the mean time, one of the favourite objects of Skinner's desire was accomplished, in the grant of the small estate he had hitherto enjoyed in his jaghire being made perpetual to his family. It was an act of bare justice, a mere redemption of a former pledge; but the manner in which it was done reflected credit on Lord Hastings, while conferring a benefit on its object; to whom the information was conveyed in the following letter from the secretary to Government:—

"To LIEUTENANT-COLONEL SKINNER"

"SIR,—It having come to the knowledge of the Governor-General in. Council, that you are solicitous to secure, as a provision for your family, the permanence of the grant of the jaghire held by you in the district of Alleeghur, in commutation of your pension as an officer retired from the service of the Mahratta states, Ms Excellency in Council has not hesitated on resolving to grant the jaghire to you and your heirs in perpetuity; desiring, by this public mark of favour, to acknowledge and to remunerate your distinguished merits and firm attachment to the British Government, which, throughout a long period of honourable and active service, have been uniformly conspicuous.

"Conceiving that it may add to your satisfaction, as well as be in itself a just reward of very considerable merit, the Governor-General in Council has been further pleased to resolve to grant, in perpetuity, to your brother, Major Robert Skinner, and his heirs, the small jaghire which he holds in the district of Alleeghur, in commutation of his pension as a Mahratta officer. You are requested to communicate this resolution to Major Skinner.

"I am directed to inform you that the necessary orders will be issued to the proper local authorities for giving effect to the arrangements of which I have now had the honour to apprise you.—I have the honour to be, &c. &c,

(Signed)   "J. Adam,
                    "Chief Sec. to Government."
"Fort William, 26th Sept. 1818."

The following letters also show the feelings with which the Colonel's most attached friends learned his good fortune:—

"Camp, Mhow, 6th Oct. 1818.

"My dear Skinner,—I have great pleasure in giving you the following paragraph of a private letter, this morning received, from Adam.

"Your friend Skinner's jaghire will be confirmed to him and his heirs. He well deserves it, and your eulogy of him is not a bit overcharged."

"One of our best Persian songs has a chorus—
'Allee Shah-in-shah Moobarik bashud!'

In sober English, I wish you joy, and feel most warmly to Lord Hastings for his just understanding of your character.— Yours, ever truly,

(Signed)   "John Malcolm."

"10th Nov. 1818.

"My dear Skinner,—I cordially congratulate you on your good fortune, for which you are indebted to the kindness of Lord Hastings, and your own merits, which have powerfully recommended you to his favour. Believe me sincerely joyful at your success, and ever yours, most truly,

(Signed)   "C. T. Metcalf."

"Dear James,—It was not that I did not receive great pleasure from your communication, but because I was unwell, and for some time past unable to write, that it has been so long unacknowledged.

"I rejoice very much in the complete accomplishment of your wishes; but, valuable as the gift is, I think it has been made much more so by the very handsome terms in which it has been bestowed, and that you may long live to enjoy, and to continue to deserve, such kindness, is the sincere wish of yours, sincerely,

(Signed)   "D. Ochterlony.
"Camp, 30th Nov. 1818."

On the death of his brother Robert in 1821, Colonel

Skinner's corps suffered a further reduction; Major Skinner's division being made over to another officer, Colonel Baddely; but we shall give the winding up of the original memoirs in the author's own words.

Skinner continues:-

"I was, however, still at the head of 1,200 horse; and in 1822 I went to Calcutta, where I was very kindly treated by Lord Hastings. He promised that he would not lessen my command by a single man; but no sooner had he left the country than my corps was at once reduced to 800 men. Rapid, indeed, has been my fall. In the Mahratta service from 1796 to 1803, I had always a well-grounded hope of rising in rank and fortune; no question was ever raised as to my birth there. When I entered the British service, I believed that I gained a field in which the fruits of zeal and fidelity would be matured and reaped in perfection; and no exertions on my part were spared to forward this object. I imagined myself to be serving a people who had no prejudices against caste or colour. But I found myself mistaken. All I desired was justice. If I was not to share in all the privileges of a British subject, let me be regarded as a native and treated as such. If I was to be regarded as a British subject, did the hard labour and ready service of twenty years merit no more than a pension of 300 rupees per month; without either rank or station? and after the distinct and repeated promises of the permanent maintenance of my corps, was it fair that I should be left liable to be commanded by the youngest subaltern in the army, deprived of the hope which I had so fondly entertained of passing my old age tranquilly in that service to which my better years had been devoted? But I thank my Creator that there remains one source of satisfaction—one consolation under every disappointment; and it is this,—that I have ever discharged my duty as a soldier with honour and credit; that during the space of twenty years, in which I have served with Europeans, no one can ever upbraid me with dishonouring "the steel," or being "faithless to my salt"; that, finally, though I have failed in gaining what I desired and deserved,—that is, rank,—I have proved to the world that I was worthy of it; by serving my king and my country as zealously and loyally as any Briton in India."

If any reader should regard the tone of sadness and disappointment which prevails in this peroration as unreasonable or misplaced, let it be observed that much allowance should be made for the circumstances of Skinner's peculiar case. It may at first sight appear that the "full retiring pay of a lieutenant-colonel in the Company's service" was a liberal provision for all that Colonel Skinner could have done in a three years' service; for no longer had he served when this was first granted to him. But this would be a very partial and imperfect view of the case. For regard must, in the first place, be had to the reasonable hopes of advancement in rank, and provision for the future, he had in the Mahratta service, as was demonstrated by the fortunes which many Europeans made in it, and which he was forced to abandon. In the next place, he might reasonably pitch his expectations high, when he saw traitors and deserters receiving splendid allowances; and even his own native officers pensioned with 5,000 rupees a year each. But he entered the British service without any sordid views, and with all the enthusiasm of a generous mind, increased by an admiration for his first commander. He had been encouraged by the commendation and the voluntary promises of that commander — promises addressed still more to his thirst for military rank and honour, than to his interest. Honest and true himself, he could not but believe that the faith kept with the treacherous and the cowardly, would be equally sacred towards the zealous and the brave.

Had even the pittance bestowed upon him been accompanied by military rank, it would have fulfilled his most ardent expectations; but when his birth was brought up as a misfortune, if not a reproach, and, like a two-edged blade, was made to cut both ways against him, it is scarcely to be wondered at if he became indignant at what looked very like a pitiful subterfuge for denying him that right to honour and reward which had been conceded and established by so many spontaneous declarations and promises in the highest quarters. It is also to be held in mind that Skinner, at the time when this was written, had not even imagined the honours which were hereafter to be wrung from the tardy justice of his country, by the powerful and reiterated representations of his many and noble friends; and we venture to say that few men, if any, in India could boast of having won so bright and distinguished a succession of hearty friends as James Skinner; and of this the correspondence which we have already given, as well as some letters we still mean to offer to the reader's notice, is a sufficient proof. At a subsequent period, this narrative was continued; and it is from this continuation that we shall now proceed with our work.

From the last-mentioned period,—that is, about the end of 1822 till 1824,—nothing occurred worth recording; nor, in fact, was the corps employed in that year, in any more serious service than that of suppressing the outbreaks of certain troublesome zemindars, chiefly in the Bhuttee country; and in driving from thence a troublesome freebooter, or cazak,* named Soorjah, a Rajepoot chieftain, who had gathered together a band of armed robbers amounting to near 5,000 men, it was said, and who did some damage before the force sent after him could overtake him.

On the Colonel's return to Hansee from this expedition, he, however, was greeted with a very pleasing piece of intelligence. This was a resolution of Government to replace under his command another corps of horse equal to that he then had.

Skinner's account continues:-

I lost no time in promulgating this good news; so that all my old men, who, to use their own phrase, " had been praying for such a day," flocked around me; and in the course of a month and a half, I mustered my new corps, equipped, complete and efficient, in all respects, men and horses; and immediately commenced drilling them. Shortly after I received orders to complete both corps from 800 to 1,000 men each. And this enabled me to admit many more of my veteran soldiers

* Robber, freebooter—probably derived from, or having a common root with, the name of the Tartar tribes, called Cossacks.

who had been disbanded, while the new appointments and promotions were filled up by seniority with men who had distinguished themselves by their gallantry.

Two months after this augmentation, I was reviewed by General Reynolds, who also presented colours to the corps with the usual ceremonies: and issued a very flattering general order respecting the appearance and performance of the men. In the evening, we gave him a grand English and Hindostanee entertainment; and he left the station much pleased and gratified. Soon after, I was directed to recruit 400 horse for Captain Hawkes, and a similar number for Colonel Gardiner, both commanding corps of local horse. This I did in a short time: and sent them well equipped in every respect to their respective commandants.

> In 1825, the state of affairs in the Jhat states of Bhurtpore and Deig called again for the interference of, the British authorities. Since the death of Rhundeer and Runjeet Sing, the chiefs of Lord Lake's day, the court had become a scene of intrigues and debauchery which produced the greatest disorder. At length Doorjun Lai, the uncle of the young Rajah Bulwunt Sing, confined his nephew, and usurped the throne; at the same time his arrogance was such as to draw on that punishment from the British Government which had long been due to that turbulent state. An army was accordingly ordered to assemble at Muttra early in the year, under command of Sir David Ochterlony; but, from some change of policy or plan, it was broken up until the ensuing cold weather, when it again assembled under the command of Lord Combermere, then commander-in-chief. Of this army, Skinner's horse was ordered to form a portion.

Skinner continues:-

We arrived, says Skinner, (the 1st corps) at Muttra on the 28th November, where his lordship and Sir Charles Metcalfe soon joined us. Immediately after his arrival, Lord Combermere inspected my corps, and expressed himself greatly pleased.

"He had frequently heard of the corps," he said, "and never but in terms of praise; and yet, what he witnessed at the inspection exceeded every expectation he had formed." The men, to whom I fully explained the sentiments thus expressed by his Excellency, felt proud indeed at having thus, at the first inspection, gained the applause and esteem of so gallant a British cavalry officer.

All preliminary arrangements for the siege having been made, Lord Combermere ordered one-half my corps (500 rank and file), under Major Fraser,★ my second in command, to join the Agra division of the army (with which it served throughout the siege), under command of Sir Jasper Nicholls; while his Excellency himself assumed that of the Muttra division; and both moved from their respective stations towards Bhurtpore, on the morning of the 10th December. On our second march, the day of our arrival before that place, my corps, supported by a squadron of H.M.'s 11th light dragoons, and another of native cavalry, with some light infantry and gallopers, was ordered to form the advance guard of the army; and had received orders to march, direct, and take possession of the water bund from which, on occasion, the ditch of the town was filled; but on entering the heavy jungle before Bhurtpore, we went straight towards the fort instead of the bund, which lay quite in an opposite direction. A troop of mine was thrown out in advance as skirmishers; and as we had got pretty near the ditch, a slight skirmishing commenced with a body of the enemy's horse, who were advancing apparently to attack us.

★ *This gentleman is the same who has already been mentioned as Skinner's most intimate friend. He was also the writer's brother, and it is not without some feelings of hesitation that he brings him so prominently forward in the narrative. His appointment, in fact, was a curious and anomalous one, and therefore may claim a few words of explanation. Mr. Fraser had, at a very early period, had much to do with Skinner's corps. It was by their aid that he had brought under control the district of Mewatt and other very wild and refractory ones in the "assigned territory"; and during the Ghoorka war, in which he was political agent with the army, under General Martindale, and made several*

On seeing this, General Reynells immediately ordered our troops to form. The gallopers, tinder that distinguished veteran Colonel Starke, first drew tip and unlimbered; and I could not help admiring the cool steadiness of this fine detachment of artillerymen, as they stood to their guns, anxiously awaiting to welcome the enemy's approach with a salvo of grape. The infantry formed on the right, and my corps was directed to deploy into line on the left of the gallopers, But the enemy seeing us thus on the alert, retired; on which the fort immediately commenced a heavy cannonade; and as we had well got under their range, so that several casualties occurred, General Reynells ordered a retreat; but we halted when out of reach, and remained under arms until the whole of the army had come up and encamped.

When our retreat was sounded, Colonel Stevenson, quarter-master-general, with his usual coolness and gallantry, rode straight up to the bund, accompanied only by a few of his hircarrahs and a small party of pioneers, under command of Captain Irvin of the Engineers. On reaching it, they found the place completely evacuated by the enemy, and in possession of Major Fraser, who had taken it. The enemy had only just opened it; and Captain Irvin immediately commenced stopping up the mouth of the watercourse, so that the ditch remained dry during the whole siege. On information of the affair of the bund being received by General Reynells, he immediately proceeded thither with some infantry, and took possession of a garden upon the bank of the Jheel, which he set instantly to work on and stockaded.

After the army had encamped, some of my men brought me word that Major Fraser, with his detachment, had

---

long and hazardous journeys amongst the mountains in the prosecution of that duty, he was constantly attended by a detachment of this corps. After the war, being appointed commissioner for the settlement of the Hill states, he found not only the military escort, but the military character, of so much use in bringing these wild countries into order, that he made it a plea for urging, what assuredly was not disagreeable to his own tastes—for he was by nature far more of a soldier than a civilian—the expediency of investing him

had a brilliant affair with the enemy; and thus gained the honour of the first engagement before Bhurtpore. Major Fraser, supported by some of the regular troops, formed the advance-guard of the Agra division. They also had received orders to proceed direct to the bund: and on coming up, found a large encampment of the enemy's pitched close to the garden; under the command of Neem Ranah Rajah, who had joined the Bhurtporeans, and had "sworn to his colours" that he would remain out to guard the bund, and have the first encounter with the British force. On seeing Fraser's detachment appear unexpectedly, they got confused; and on being charged, fled to the fort. Fraser gallantly pursued them up to the very glacis; and so very closely and determinedly were they followed, that the enemy shut the town gates against their own men, for fear that ours might force their way in with them. The Rajah being a brave man, however, and seeing no other alternative left, called out to his men to rally; and leading them himself, charged gallantly back. He fought desperately; but being soon slain by my men, his followers lost courage and either fled into the jungle or surrendered. The loss on our side was about twenty rank and file killed and wounded; among the latter was Fraser himself, who received a slight spear wound in the face. That of the enemy was much more considerable; and a number of their horses, arms, &c, were captured by our men.

On the following morning, Fraser's detachment was again ordered out upon a foraging party; and having been desired to charge some of the enemy's horse standing near the fort, the detachment galloped right up to the ditch; but the enemy

---

with military rank, as the best means of aiding the objects of his mission. To this Lord Hastings, enterprising and chivalrous himself, and willing to gratify a congenial taste in an officer who had already done his work well, gave him the option of receiving the heal rank of Lieutenant-Colonel, unattached to any corps, or that of Major, and second in command to the corps of his friend Colonel Skinner. He did not hesitate a moment in choosing the latter, which gratified Skinner as much as himself; and till the day of his death he held

would not wait to receive them, and retired into the fort, which immediately opened a smart fire on our detachment. The firmness displayed by Fraser in his retreat—not permitting the men to go out of a walk—surpassed every idea I had formed of his gallantry; and though the shots began to tell severely on the column, I was glad to learn that both on this and the preceding occasion the men behaved with most unswerving steadiness. Indeed, they could not well have done otherwise, with the gallant example of their leader in their view; and right glad I was that they proved themselves not unworthy of being placed under so brave an officer. The casualties on this and the preceding engagement were, ten rank and file killed, and twenty wounded, besides fifteen horses; and so close did they approach the fort, that the bodies of five or six of my men were left upon the glacis.

During the siege, the whole of my corps was constantly employed on escort and forage duties, as also in furnishing pickets, &c.; and in repeated instances did detached parties distinguish themselves, and by their gallant conduct elicit the applause of his Excellency the Commander-in-Chief, as may be seen by referring to the Adjutant-General's letters.* His Excellency finding the first corps so useful, ordered my second corps, then stationed at Hansee, to be relieved by Captain Hawkes's corps, the 7th local horse, and to join the army at Bhurtpore. But it only came latterly, as, during most part of the siege, it remained as a corps of observation at Dring, a place between Deig and Bhurtpore, to watch the conduct of

that rank, led his corps where-ever it was ordered on service, and bore the brunt in every affair they were engaged in. At other times he was the civilian, and discharged the duties of chief commissioner in the ceded and conquered provinces, we believe, with, unquestioned efficiency.

* The following is an extract from General Orders, by the Commander-in-Chief.
"Head-quarters, Bhurtpore, 21st Jan. 1826.

"The services of the 1st and 2nd corps of irregular horse, under command of Lieut.-Colonel Skinner, assisted by Major Fraser, throughout the siege, have frequently elicited the highest admiration and applause. Nothing could exceed the bravery of this valuable class of soldiers; and Lieut.-Colonel Skinner and Major

Madhoo Sing, the Deig Rajah, who, though openly declaring himself an ally of the British, was supposed to be secretly aiding and assisting the cause of his brother, Doorjun Lai, the usurper of Bhurtpore.

His Excellency having ordered a storming party to be formed of dismounted volunteers from the cavalry, my corps was directed to furnish 200 men for that duty. When I made known this order, and called out for volunteers, the whole corps replied, that if any selection was to be made, they wished me to do it myself, as, if left to their choice, they would all go. This praiseworthy spirit left me no alternative. To avoid hurting the feelings of any one, I refrained from all selection; but ordered the party to be told off agreeably to the "roster of duty"; but as I wanted a steady and experienced commandant to lead them, I placed at their head Shadull Khan, one of my oldest, most faithful, and trustworthy native officers; and on the evening previous to their joining the detachment of cavalry volunteers, I paraded this fine party, and thus addressed them:— "This is the first time of your going into danger when I cannot accompany you; but such is my affection for you all, that I cannot allow you to part from me without carrying with you something dear to me." Then, taking by the hand my son James, whom, on the late augmentation, Government had permitted to enter my corps as adjutant, I went on— "See, here is my son! take him, and gain for him such laurels as you have won for the sire."

Fraser fully merit this acknowledgment of his lordship's unqualified approbation of their conduct, and that of their men."

The conduct of two rissalahs employed on forage duties, under Rissaldars Amanut Khan and Zubberdust Khan, in beating off upwards of 1,000 of the enemy, commanded by several sirdars of note, and completely routing them, is acknowledged in-terms of high encomium by the Adjutant-General, by his lordship's command. As is also the gallantry of Rissaldar Meer Bahaudur, who, with, a piquet of the corps, charged and beat off a party of the enemy of 250 men, with the loss of thirty men killed and ten horses taken. The documents themselves are omitted being too voluminous.

On this the noble Shadull Khan, of whose valour I had often been an eyewitness, stepped forward, and taking my son by the arm, called aloud, in reply, — "Farewell, our own commander, trust in God, who never deserts those faithful servants who do their duty; and who, please God, will now do their utmost to maintain the honour of the corps." Having said this, the whole party gave three cheers, and went off to join the camp of the volunteers, while I and the rest returned to our lines with tears in our eyes.

The storm, however, was deferred, and the Company's European regiment, having arrived, the cavalry volunteers were ordered to join their regiments before it took place. But both the Commander-in-chief and Brigadier Sleigh, who commanded the cavalry division of the army, issued very handsome orders on the spirited manner in which the cavalry had volunteered their services for the storm.

The engineers having reported the grand mine "ready," and the breach "practicable,"* his Excellency ordered the storm on the morning of the 18th January. His orders were speedily carried round the camp, and before daybreak all the infantry corps destined for the storm moved into the trenches, and the cavalry were detached all round the fort to prevent escape. The following was the plan of attack:—

The right column was directed to escalade the breach, close to the Juggernaut gate, and consisted of two companies of the

---

*When the breach was first reported practicable by the engineer officer, Lord Combermere asked Skinner, who was by, his opinion on the subject; to which he only replied that he was unworthy to touch his Excellency's shoe, much more so to offer him advice. But his lordship, desirous of learning his opinion, repeated the question, and urged a reply. On which Skinner said that the breach was impracticable, and that, if attempted, the men would sink up to their armpits in the rubbish, and there would be a repetition of the former failures. Colonel --------, then a subaltern in the engineers, said he differed, but would ascertain the fact, and gallantly rushed forward, crossed the ditch, and found that it was as Skinner had stated. He returned untouched by the fire, patted Skinner on the back, and said, "Old boy, you are right and I am wrong." Skinner then said they must just do as the Mahrattas used to do on similar occasions, and trust to mining. They did mine, and the event proved the soundness of his opinion.

254

European regiment, the 58th native infantry, under Captain J. Hunter, and 100 ghoorkas, the whole under command of Colonel J. Delamaine.

The main column for the assault of the cavalier breach, tinder the immediate orders of Major-General Reynells, consisted of Brigadier Paton and McComb's brigades, which were to form two columns; and, after gaming possession of the breach, were directed to file up to the right and left.

A column of reserve, under Brigadier Whitehead, was left at the head of the trenches, and consisted of two companies of his Majesty's 14th, the 18th and 23rd regiments of native infantry.

The left main column was placed under the immediate orders of Major-General Nicholls, and consisted of Brigadier-Generals Edwards and Adam's brigades, with a column of reserve.

An intermediate column, consisting of two companies European regiment, and grenadier companies of 35th native infantry, light company of the 37th regiment, and 100 ghoorkas, all under command of Lieutenant-Colonel J. Wilson, was bastion between the two main columns. The springing of the mine under the north-east bastion was the signal for attack, and to this quarter every eye was anxiously directed.

The explosion took place exactly at eight o'clock, when it is supposed that the greatest part of the enemy destined to defend that point were blown up. The grenadier company of the 14th also suffered materially from the explosion, having been advanced to the foremost point in the trenches, close to the bastion. Brigadiers McComb and Paton, Lieutenant Irvine, of the engineers, and Lieutenant Daly, of his Majesty's 14th foot, were most severely wounded, and carried off; the latter officer had his leg amputated on the spot.

As soon as the dust had subsided, that brave officer Major Everard was the first who moved forward, gallantly leading his Majesty's 14th up to the breach. Major-General Reynells immediately followed, and a momentary hesitation on the part of the sepoys being remarked at this critical time, the

General gallantly stood up on the summit of the bastion, exposed to the heavy fire from the citadel, calling out for the columns to advance. This they immediately did; and as the enemy, certainly not aware of the mine, or, at least, of its immediate explosion, had suffered severely, the column met with no material resistance until they filed off to the right and left of the bastion. Then the light companies, under Major Everard, were obstinately opposed upon the ramparts, insomuch that there was a momentary check. But nothing-could long resist the bravery of that fine corps and their leader, and, surmounting every obstacle, they pushed on, clearing bastion after bastion.

My corps having been drawn up close to the fort, I quietly stole up to the walls, and witnessed the bravery displayed by the right escalading column under Colonel Delamaine; which equalled my full idea of British valour. This breach (at the Juggernaut gate) was most gallantly defended; yet, in spite of the most obstinate resistance, our men, overthrowing every obstacle, mounted the breach, and planted on it the colours of the 58th N. I. At this very time the right column of the 14th, had just reached the Juggernaut gate; and a most furious struggle took place, as was testified by the dead bodies literally lying in heaps, which we saw here next day. This column then pushed on, clearing the ramparts, and never halting until they met with their brave comrades of H. M.'s 59th, at the Koombhere gate, where both corps mutually cheered each other.

A party of this (right) column had penetrated into the heart of the town; and in driving the enemy into the citadel, they pursued them so closely that the enemy were obliged to shut the gates against a large body of their own men: thus a furious rencontre ensued at the bridge. It was here that gallant officer Major George Hunter distinguished himself so conspicuously in a single combat with one of the Bhurtpore chieftains; and had he not been well supported by his men, his bravery would have cost him his life; for in guarding a blow made at him, his sword broke; and in endeavouring to defend himself with the scabbard, he received a severe wound in the left arm; when at the critical moment, some of his sepoys ran up and bayoneted his antagonist in the act of striking another blow. The rest of them, assisted by the 14th, put all the rest to the bayonet, as the citadel bridge showed well next morning, being absolutely covered with dead bodies.

Being obliged to remain near my corps, I had had no opportunity of seeing the success of the left or main column, and the intermediate or escalading one. But from all I heard, their gallantry was not less conspicuous than that of the two columns whose valour I witnessed; for, on going back to my corps, I saw the enemy actually throwing themselves from the high walls into the ditch, to escape from their brave antagonists. A dismounted squadron of my corps under orders of Captain Martindell, my second in command, had been directed with some guns, just before the mine was sprung, to advance up to the fort, and thus divert the enemy's attention. They drew a smart fire from the citadel; but not having orders to advance, they waited until one storming party got in, and opened one of the gates, when they joined the assailants, and shared in the honours of the storm. Immediately after the mine was sprung, a perfect roar of cannon and musketry commenced, and was most vigorously maintained on both sides for three hours; by which time the town was completely in our possession. But the citadel held out till four p.m., when it surrendered.

Thus fell Bhurtpore, the pride and glory of Hindostan. That fortress, which had hitherto been considered impregnable, and had even bid defiance to British power, now lay prostrate at the foot of British valour. Nothing, indeed, could exceed the cool and steady courage of the troops, who seemed invincible; but having been an eyewitness of the bloody and disastrous scenes which passed before the fortress in the days of Lord Lake, I could not help contrasting the two sieges, and observing the shameful decline which had since then taken place in this once unrivalled state. In those days, as it is well known, we had to fight our ground inch by inch as we approached the place; while now, so different was the spirit or skill of the defenders, that we took up our ground on the very glacis, close to the ditch, without the smallest opposition on the part of the enemy; and the breach once practicable, what force of theirs could have successfully opposed Lord Combermere's fine army; a force powerful enough to conquer the whole of Hindostan. Even the brave men who fought Lord Lake would have vainly tried to oppose it, when once on equal terms. But Lord Lake and his most gallant army had obstacles to encounter which did not now exist. His acts, and those of heroes whom he led, require no mention here: they stand immortal and unrivalled, and ever must do so. And had it not been for most untoward circumstances, his success here had been certain. In the present siege, though nothing could surpass the gallantry of the veterans of Bhurtpore, the younger soldiery and their leaders gave them no assistance. These veterans did all that men could do; they only gave up the place with their lives, as their dead bodies covering the ramparts unanswerably proved; they faced the European soldiers with "the cold steel," as their antagonists themselves declared; but this was all too late: the breach once won—the ramparts gained—who could withstand the British troops? It is on others, and especially on their cowardly leader, that the blame and the shame rests. Doorjun Lai, instead of heading his veterans, as Rundheer and Runjeet did of old, and striving to oppose the storming columns, remained inactive; committing the fate of his city and his fortunes to the care of others; and when he did move out and expose himself, the time was past; the breach was carried; the British troops had gained their footing, and the town was their own. His young chieftains, followers, and flatterers all left him in the hour of need, flying as best they could; and Doorjun Lai himself soon followed their example.

Taking his two Ranees and children, and mounting them behind some of his most faithful bodyguard, he attempted to dash through our lines; but our cavalry were on the alert, and Lord Combermere's arrangements in disposing them round the fortress were too well made to admit of his escape. In a fit of despair, as a last resource, he made one gallant charge, and tried to cut his way through a squadron of the 8th Light Cavalry, under Lieut. Barber. But this proved too hard for him; and to save his life, he surrendered with his followers, and was carried into camp as a prisoner.

Since the death of Rhundeer and Runjeet Sing, the chiefs who had fought Lord Lake, the rulers of Bhurtpore had been given up to luxury and dissipation in the greatest excess. They were addicted to the lowest vices; and the young soldiery pursued the example of their superiors. Of this description was Doorjun Lai the usurper of the government, who, instead of encouraging a spirit of military enterprise amongst his young followers, was their leader in every species of vice. Inexperienced himself in the art of war, he kept them equally ignorant of military matters, and the state fell entirely into the hands of a parcel of writers of the Khyte caste, the shrewdest and most dishonest knaves in Hindostan.

No one was better aware of the state of affairs at Bhurtpore; of the usurpation of its throne, and the imprisonment of its lawful Rajah, Bulwunt Sing, by his uncle Doorjun Lai, than Sir David Ochterlony; a man who was an honour to his profession and to the Government he served. He knew of every intrigue amongst its chieftains; and, from what I know of his information, I have no hesitation in saying that he would have got possession of Bhurtpore without a shot being fired, had he been permitted to pursue his own plan of operations; but, for reasons of which I am ignorant, the army assembled under his command was broken up, and another course pursued.

The strength and reputed riches of Bhurtpore were celebrated, and almost proverbial, in Hindostan. Its imagined impregnability had been confirmed in the opinion of the natives by the repeated failures of the gallant army under Lord Lake. "Ah! you may bully us, but go and take Bhurtpore," was a common expression among the petty chiefs and refractory rajahs we had frequently to reduce. Of its riches the most wonderful tales are told; and, in fact, from the universal feeling of its security, it had become the depository of great treasures, sent there from a very remote period in times of trouble and disturbance. The writer of this has heard it asserted by several persons, but particularly by a native of high rank and respectability, who was intimately acquainted, and, indeed, connected, with all the affairs of Bhurtpore, that, while besieged by Lord Lake, the Rajah being hard pressed for money to pay his troops, in this dilemma sent for the Chowdry, or head man of the Chumars (or skinners, a low and unclean caste), and told him of his wants. The man inquired into the nature of his difficulties, and being satisfied of their reality, he took his people to a certain spot, where, on digging, they found a store of three lakhs of gold mohurs (equal to 600,000l. sterling), and a number of brass guns.

The Rajah was very thankful; but expressing a desire to know whether, if wanted, this assistance could be repeated, the Chowdy inquired what his daily wants might be? The Rajah said about a lakh of rupees a day, on which the Chumars replied, "Fight on, then, Maha Rajah, with good heart, for two years, if it be needed, and we will find you the means."

It may not be very generally known, that in India, where of old, in the often changing times, the rich natives used to bury their treasure in specie—a practice which may, in some degree, account for the remarkable absorption in that country of the bullion which has always been flowing into it — and in order to preserve the record of such deposits in case of accidents to themselves, the secret of their places of concealment was confided to the low and degraded caste of the Chumars—the skinners of dead animals— the scavengers, as it were, of the community. The reason for making this choice at first was no doubt the very circumstance of their degradation, which forbade the hope of rising, and, therefore, took away the temptation for appropriating the wealth thus confided to their charge. The event has proved the correctness of the reasoning; and the feeling of confidence reposed has given birth to an esprit-de-corps, even amongst this wretched class, which has prevented the trust from having ever been violated. The only occasions on which they were permitted to discover and make use of this ancient treasure were in cases of great state difficulties, as in that above related; and there is no doubt that there is a vast amount of buried treasure, not only at Bhurtpore, but over all India.

A circumstance of this sort was related to the writer by the same person who told him of what had passed at Bhurtpore. Not very long ago—that is, in his knowledge as a grown man—on pulling down a wall of the old palace at Biana, a town belonging to the state of Bhurtpore, there was found a slab of marble, under which were discovered a number of gold pieces, bearing the impression of the emperor Allah-u-deen Ghoree. The matter was hushed up at the moment; but for seven days afterwards 100 camels daily were sent from Biana to Bhurtpore, and 50 on the eighth day; in all 750 camel loads of some heavy substance. What it was—whether gold, silver, or lead—was not known; but my informant himself was witness to the number of loads, and the natives believed them to be of gold. This, probably, may not have been the case: but the fact was understood to be incontestible.

It may be thought strange that when these Chumars are so well known to be the depositors of so much hidden treasure, the chiefs or kings of the country should not by some means force the secret from them. But such is their fortitude and peculiar point of honour, that when this has been attempted they have always suffered torture and death in preference to betraying their ancestral trust, which, in fact, has something of a religious sacredness attached to it; and on one occasion no less than fourteen Chumars were thus put to death. It is said that Diaram, the Rajah of Hattrass, succeeded by a stratagem in obtaining some money from the Chumars of that fortress, and in cheating them out of their customary fee. They had agreed to furnish him with a small sum, on his paying them their due and granting them his protection; and this he in the first instance honestly performed. But on the next application a larger store was pointed out to him, when he refused to part with a shilling of it to them. We believe they foretold his ruin from this piece of perfidy.

After the fall of Bhurtpore, negociations were opened by Sir Charles Metcalfe with the Alwar Rajah, who had slighted and disobeyed the Resident's authority, and no satisfactory reply having been elicited, Lord Combermere marched with Sir Charles to the Alwar frontier. The demonstration was enough. The example of Bhurtpore sufficed—the Rajah came into camp, and having first paid part of the expenses of the expedition, agreed and signed every condition required of him, and then was permitted to depart in peace. The army then broke up, and Lord Combermere reviewed the several divisions. Among the rest, my two corps had the honour of an inspection, and his Excellency, on taking leave of them, was pleased to address them in a most handsome speech, intimating his high satisfaction with their services, which he would not, he said, fail to bring to the notice of the Honourable Court of Directors. We then gave his lordship a grand entertainment,* in token of our high respect, and the sense we entertained of his uniform kindness, and finally bade him adieu.

While on our march back from Bhurtpore, I learned that Lord Combermere had received from the Court of Directors an order to disband three of the new local corps of cavalry, of

* *This entertainment was given at his jaghire of Belospore, to which place Lord Combermere came to visit him, with all his staff and camp followers. It was an ample feast, and served in true Hindostanee fashion. We have heard, on good authority, that Skinner, with his own hands, carried a dinner to the lowest drummer in the camp!*

which my second corps was to be one. Alarmed at this news, I
hastened back by dawk to see his lordship, and to represent the
extreme hardship which such a measure would inflict upon
my poor men. A year had scarcely elapsed since the corps was
embodied, and the poor fellows were of course still deeply in
debt from the purchase of their horses, arms, and uniforms, so
that the present orders, if carried into effect, must cause their
utter ruin. Happily, I found his Excellency too fully sensible
of the worth of the corps and of the value of their services,
and too much alive to the obvious injustice of the measure,
to have much difficulty in securing his influence in their
favour. He made a strong remonstrance against the orders of
the Court, and procured a very favourable modification of
them. Recruiting was put a stop to in the corps ordered to
be disbanded, and they were permitted to die off, instead of
being abruptly discharged. But my first corps was reduced
to the peace establishment—that is, to 800 instead of 1,000
men; the native officers of the reduced troops being, however,
retained as supernumeraries, until absorbed by the effect of
casualties into the strength of the corps.

Chapter Seventeen
Rewards & Closings

In this year I had the gratification to learn that his Majesty, at the recommendation of the British Indian Government, had been graciously pleased to confer upon me the most Honourable Military order of the Bath.★ I understand objections were started as to my eligibility to the same, as having no other than the Company's local or temporary rank in this country: upon which his Majesty was further pleased to declare, that "this officer has so often been brought to our notice, that his services must no longer be neglected; therefore, let the gift of rank be bestowed by the Crown."

To his Excellency Lord Combermere, I feel especially indebted for this mark of his Majesty's approbation, as his lordship, after the siege of Bhurtpore, promised to bring my services and that of the corps to the particular notice of the Honourable Court of Directors; and it was at his lordship's recommendation that his Majesty was pleased to confer it upon me. But it would be ungrateful in me to omit the expression of my thanks to Mr. C. W. Wynne, of the Board of Control, for the generous interest he took in my favour, and the more especially as I was to him a perfect stranger.

When the efforts of my first most worthy and lamented patron, Lord Lake, and, subsequently, those of the Marquess of Hastings, failed of obtaining for me rank, I had little expectations of ever receiving any further acknowledgment of my past services, and far less so brilliant a reward as has now been so graciously conferred upon me; and my feelings on first receiving the intelligence may be more easily imagined than described. I can only say, that my utmost endeavours shall now be directed to render my future

★ *That is, Commander of the Bath.*

264

services equally deserving the approbation of my sovereign and my honourable employers as hitherto; and though old age is creeping fast upon me, I trust that the Almighty may yet spare me to lead my "yellow boys" again into action; for I could not desire a more honourable end to my career than to close it at their head as I commenced it. Such, too, is, I know, the ambition of my brave veterans, to whose valour and fidelity alone I owe all the honours that have come upon my age, and who would seek no better than to fall in the faithful discharge of their duty.

In the year 1828, Lord Combermere again visited the upper provinces, and coming to Hansee, in November, took occasion, after an inspection of my corps, to announce to them the honour that had been conferred on me, in the following speech:—

"I have," said he, "a most pleasing duty to perform, and I take this, I fear, my only opportunity of doing so in presence of your distinguished corps. I have to inform you, Colonel Skinner, that our beloved and revered Sovereign has been graciously pleased to confer on you the companionship of the most honourable Military Order of the Bath, for the long, faithful, and meritorious services rendered by you to the Honourable the East India Company.

"I am confident that all the officers, non-commissioned officers, and soldiers in the 1st Local Horse will be gratified, and will feel a just pride in knowing that their gallant and faithful conduct upon all occasions is not unknown to, and has been thus rewarded by his Majesty in the person of their respected and adored commander. It would have added much to my own gratification had I been enabled, by the arrival from England of the decoration, to invest you with the insignia of the Companionship of the Bath, at the head of your corps." And when all this was explained to the corps the men congratulated me with three cheers, and appeared quite proud of the honour.

In 1829 I repaired to Calcutta, to take leave of Lord Combermere on his departure from the country, and repeat my grateful acknowledgements for his unvarying kind attention to myself and my corps. By him I had the honour of being introduced to Lord and Lady William Bentinck, from whom I received, during my stay at the presidency, the most flattering attention.

I accompanied Lord Combermere on board the Pallas frigate to the Sand Heads, and never having before been on board a ship of war, was infinitely struck with what I saw. During my stay of four days on board I was most kindly treated by Captain Fitzclarence, who commanded the vessel, as well as by all his officers. Captain Fitzclarence was obliging enough to treat me with the spectacle of a sham-fight, and showed what a British frigate could do in action. To me, who had never witnessed anything of the sort before, all seemed like magic, and I was quite astonished to see the dexterity with which the vessel was manoeuvred —after a continued roar of cannon and musketry you might the next moment have heard a pin drop, on the order to cease firing being given; and everything was kept in such order, that too much praise cannot be bestowed on Captain Fitzclarence, for the discipline preserved on board his ship.

At length I was forced to take a final leave of all my kind friends, and especially of Lord Combermere, whose unceasing goodness I never can forget. As a last act of kindness, he insisted on presenting me with his own insignia of the Bath, as my own had not arrived; and he did not, he said, like to leave the country without seeing me invested. I could no longer control my emotions, but left the ship with my eyes full of tears.

About the middle of 1829, an epidemic broke out at Hansee, by which I lost a number of my oldest and most valuable native officers; while at the same time orders were received from the Court of Directors, in reply to the reference made concerning the disbanding of the three local corps, repeating their commands for this reduction. I consequently lost my second corps, and it was with great difficulty that Government, at my most earnest request and remonstrance, sanctioned the settlement of a reduced pension on those native officers and men whose service was of twenty years' standing; and as I had been obliged to draft or promote a number of men from my first to my new corps, I lost many of my most valuable soldiers by this reduction.

In the year 1831, a party of thirty sowars of my remaining corps, under command of Bajazeed Khan Jemmadar (son of a veteran who died in the corps), distinguished itself very honourably in discharge of the duty entrusted to it. Being posted at Babul, a frontier point, information was sent to tell them that a strong body of Kozaks, or plunderers, had driven off a herd of camels from our territory into that of the Baraitches. The detachment saddled instantly, overtook and cut up a number of the robbers, and rescued the camels. These being left in charge of one-half the party whose horses were fatigued, the other half continued in pursuit of the plunderers, and followed them up to a Baraitch village, from the people of which they expected that assistance which it was their duty to afford. Instead of this, however, the whole village turned out, joined the robbers, and surrounded the few of my sowars who first came up. One of their horses which was knocked up dropped down with his rider, and the Zemendars with a yell rushed on to destroy him; but his companions, nothing daunted, sprang forward to his assistance, and in spite of the enormous disparity of numbers— they being full 500, while of my men there was only about a dozen— they rescued the fallen trooper, and after a desperate skirmish made good their retreat with the loss of only one sowar killed, and another, with two horses wounded, that of the villagers amounted to fully fifty in killed and wounded; and so sickened were they of the taste of my men's steel, that they did not venture to pursue the party.

At this time Skinner records, in terms of deep feeling, the death of Shadool Khan, that old and most trustworthy officer, to whose care, at the expected storm of Bhurtpore, he had entrusted his son James. We do not venture to give the passage: but it affords a touching proof of the kindly and patriarchal footing on which he ever stood with his men, and the great interest he took in the affairs of every individual among them. On this occasion, he wished to place the son of the deceased officer in the corps as a "duffadar," or commander of ten, because he knew that it would be a gratifying compliment to the whole corps—a boon, as it were, to their esprit du corps which would have had a powerful and excellent effect—and he regrets that, from the extreme youth of the boy, it was not deemed proper to grant his request. It is difficult for official people to break through established rules, even for the attainment of a desirable but insulated object.

Skinner's account continues:-

In the latter end of 1831, I was directed to hold myself in readiness with a squadron, or two rissallahs of my corps, to join the grand camp about to be formed at a place called Hooper, on the banks of the Sutlej, where a meeting was to take place between the Governor-General Lord William Bentinck and Runjeet Sing, chief of Lahore. It was Lord William's wish to show the Sikh chieftain a specimen of each branch of the British Indian army; and previous to his lordship leaving Simlah the under mentioned troops were ordered to march to Hooper, the whole to be under the personal command of Brigadier-General Adams, viz., two squadrons of his Majesty's 16th Lancers, his Majesty's 31st Foot, the 14th Native Infantry, a troop of Native Horse Artillery, and two rissallahs of my corps, besides his lordship's body-guard.

We left Hansee on the 1st of October, and marched by Kurnaul to Hooper, which we reached on the 21st, and found General Adams already there, busily employed in clearing a large piece of ground for the encampment, in the front of which was a fine level parade, made to extend from the camp to the bank of the river, and occupying a space of at least two square miles. On his lordship's arrival, a daily piquet was put on duty, and a chain of sentries planted at night, just as if we had been before an enemy; and Runjeet was particularly struck with this strictness of our discipline. A field-officer was daily appointed for duty, and had to go the rounds regularly at night, and visit each piquet and sentry. This was the first time I had the honour of commanding British troops, as the General had ordered me to be placed on the roster of duty as a field-officer.

Preparations were likewise carried on upon the opposite bank of the river: and Runjeet's men had cleared a fine space and planted a garden, in the centre of which the royal tent was to be pitched. Wheat had been sown, too, in the shape of men, birds, horses, &c, in which forms it came up for the amusement of the chief, as well as to give verdure to this royal and magnificent encampment, as the place cleared out for the Maha Rajah's tent was under a barren rock, though on the bank of the river. A bridge of boats was likewise prepared by the Maha Rajah's people; and though the boats were very small, it was yet sufficiently strong to allow the royal sowarees, consisting of elephants, horses, &c. to cross to and fro; nor did a single accident occur during the whole time of the meeting.

After his lordship and suite had arrived from Simlah, and all our encampment had formed, the royal tent and the Maha Rajah's superb peishkhanah★ arrived, and was pitched in the centre of the newly-planted wheat-garden. The royal tent was made of red broadcloth, and the kunnauts, or curtains, which extended on each side to the river, leaving the front view open, were made of yellow silk and satin, with an entrance resembling the gateway of the royal palace at Dehlee, so that elephants with howdahs might pass under it. Besides the royal tent, there were two or three smaller ones of rich cloth, &c,

★*The people and preparations sent in advance.*

as also a silver bungalow or pavilion, something in the shape of a Hindoo temple, about ten feet square. This was placed on a hill in a very conspicuous situation, so as it might be seen very plainly from our encampment, and was carried about and placed as suited the different ceremonies and occasions.

On the 25th of October, about eight a.m., his highness inarched in, and the arrival was announced by a royal salute and discharge of 101 guns from the Maha Rajah's artillery. Their encampment occupied a large space of ground, as the troops were scattered in their tents all over the country, in order perhaps to give them a more formidable appearance. The force accompanying Runjeet was, however, pretty much as follows, viz. 16,000 horse, seven regiments of infantry, and twenty-one guns, of which, however, more hereafter. In the mean while, I shall give an account of each day's occurrences.

Immediately on the Maha Rajah's arrival, a deputation, consisting of Mr. Prinsep, General Ramsay, and two other officers, with sixty sowars from Skinner's horse, was sent over, and received by the Maha Rajah with a salute of fifteen guns. After which, his son, Khurruck Sing, paid the Governor-General a visit, and was received with a salute of seventeen guns. He took his leave at noon.

On the 26th, the Maha Rajah paid the first visit, and all our troops formed a street from the Governor-General's tents toward Runjeet's camp. He arrived at nine A.M. escorted by 1,000 horsemen, dressed in silk and velvet, and with rich armour. As he passed along, each corps saluted; the Company's colours only dropped. The Governor-General, with all his suite, received him about 100 yards from the Government tent. After going through the ceremony of talking and asking after each other's health, about 200 trays were brought forward, filled with shawls, silks, velvets, keenkhaubs, salahs, and other manufactures; together with several double barrelled guns and pistols, two horses, and two elephants; which were all presented to the Maha Rajah. About ten he took his departure, which was announced by a royal salute of twenty-one guns from our side. On his arrival at his own camp, his men received him with about fifty guns. Of the horsemen of his suite, about 200 were good, the rest very indifferent. The French Lancers were only a mockery as to discipline, their horses were inferior, and they were badly armed.

On the 27th, about seven in the morning, his lordship returned the Maha Rajah's visit. Khurruck Sing, his Highness's eldest son, met his lordship about a mile on our side the river. When he crossed the bridge of boats he was met by Runjeet Sing and all his sirdars. His lordship shook hands and went into the Maha Rajah's howdah. They then passed along a street of fully a mile long, formed by his infantry and cavalry. The Durbar was surrounded with large silk kunnauts, enclosing a space of about 2,000 yards square. In the middle of this was pitched the royal tent, made of scarlet broadcloth, and lined in the inside with yellow velvet, worked with gold; the carpets were all rich and superb shawls. Horses unmounted were arranged in ranks in different places.

His lordship, on dismounting from his elephant, received a salute of twenty-one guns, and was seated on the left of the Maha Rajah; his son, Khurruck Sing, was on his right; about twenty sirdars, richly dressed and armed, succeeded, and their own officers according to their respective ranks. Captain Wade sat a little before Runjeet Sing, and acted as interpreter between him and his lordship. He was also master of the ceremonies, as long as the interview lasted. About 300 sirdars were introduced to his lordship, good-looking men, and richly armed. After them our officers were introduced to the Maha Rajah.

When we had all been introduced, the sirdars removed to a separate tent; and then came a band of about 100 young women, well dressed and jewelled, who, after saluting us, sat down upon our left: some had arrows in their hands, and some had bows—the commandant bore a staff of order. They all wore yellow turbans inclining to one side, which gave them a very imposing appearance. After singing a short while, they also retired; and then came the Maha Rajah's presents, consisting of about 100 trays of the manufactures of the country. A string of pearls was put round Lord William's neck, by Runjeet himself, and two horses and an elephant were brought forward and accepted by his lordship.

He then got up and looked at all the magnificent tents, &c. and afterwards took leave of the Maha Rajah, under a salute of the usual number of guns. Everything was well arranged, and in the old royal fashion of India. The Maha Rajah was superbly dressed with jewels, and wore upon his left arm the famous diamond called the Koh-e-Noor. We returned to our tents about eleven in the forenoon.

On the 28th, at three in the afternoon, all our troops were paraded. Runjeet, with 200 soldiers, arrived about four, accompanied by his lordship, his body-guard, and staff. A general salute was then given, after which the Maha Rajah inspected the whole of the troops very minutely. Then the manoeuvres commenced, and his Highness was so much delighted that he went about alone amongst the troops with the greatest confidence, and asked the general to repeat some of the manoeuvre? He was particularly pleased with our squares. "They are like a wall of iron," he remarked. About sunset he took his leave under a royal salute, quite delighted with all he had seen, and presented 11,000 rupees to the troops. This evening Runjeet proved himself to be a far superior soldier to any other native. He seemed as if gifted with the intelligence of an English Field-Marshal: and, in fact, he moved about as if he was himself in command of the troops.

On the next day, the 29th, the review of Runjeet's troops took place; and it was as grand a sight as I have seen since I left the Native Service. In front of the parade was placed the silver bungalow, which I have before described; on the top of which sat the Maha Rajah, with the Lord and his staff. The rest of

the officers were seated under Shemianehs* pitched before
the pavilion. Before the whole of this Durbar were all the
movements performed. There were four regiments of infantry
drawn up three deep. Each consisted of 1,000 men, chiefly
Sikhs, but having some Mussulmen and sepoys intermixed.
This brigade, with from fifteen to twenty gallopers, was
commanded by a Sikh general; who, after they had passed
in review before the Durbar, went through some of those
manoeuvres which were practised by our troops about a
century ago. All was clone in slow-time, and each manoeuvre
took up fully a quarter of an hour. Their firing, however, both
in square and line, was very regular, and the men marched
very steadily. They were all armed with muskets, and dressed
like our sepoys.

Three or four of the guns, out of the number brigaded with
the infantry, were attached to each battalion; and, whether in
square or line, the infantry always left a space for the guns, and
both fired together. The artillery were much inferior to ours;
and all their movements were done at a walk. There was only
a regiment of cavalry, called "the Dragoons" brigade, with the
infantry; but after passing in review, they stood still on their
right flank, and neither covered nor acted with the infantry.
They were dressed in red jackets and steel helmets, and were
armed with carbines and pistols. Monsieur Allard, under whose
command they were, thinks them fully equal to our cavalry;
but as far as I could see of them, I think them much inferior.
The rest of the cavalry was drawn up in line on each side of the
temple, and occupied, from flank to flank, a space of from three
to four miles. They are by far the best of Runjeet's troops, and
I think the only ones that would be useful in the field, though
they are not disciplined. The whole of this body are Sikhs,
good-looking men, and well mounted. They were dressed in
yellow silk, and a great number wore armour. Some of these
men who have distinguished themselves, receive, as Runjeet's

* *Fly tents, or pavilions, merely to afford shade from the sun.*

own Bungars (Bargeers?), from 300 to 400 rupees per month.

On the morning of the 30th, the horse artillery was reviewed separately; and Runjeet was much pleased with the rapidity of their movements and firing, &c. Afterwards the howitzer practice was shown, and firing grape at the curtain from various distances. His Highness was quite astonished when he saw the shattered state of the target, and such was the interest he took in our artillery, that there was no satisfying his curiosity. Wishing to put their skill to a still severer test, he requested Lord William to have an umbrella put up as a mark near the target, a distance of about 1,000 yards, and direct the artillery officers to fire at it with round shot. The first two or three discharges being ineffective, Runjeet himself dismounted and laid the gun; but neither his Highness nor some of his best officers, whom he desired to try their hand, were anything more successful. Captain Campbell, of the horse artillery, then took their place, and the first shot he made sent the umbrella to pieces, on which a roar of applause arose from the Sikhs.

After this, Runjeet sent for some of his best horsemen, who went not very successfully through the following feats—viz. firing at the bottle at speed; taking a tent-peg out of the ground with the spear; and cutting at a brass-pot with the sabre. At this last exhibition, Runjeet's men made a very poor figure, upon which the Maha Rajah himself drew his sword and attempted immediately at speed to cut the brass-pot. Unfortunately he did not succeed; but I could not help the less admiring his fine spirit, and bold manner of riding and making his cuts. My men were then called upon to show their skill in firing at the bottle, in which they succeeded to the full as well as the Sikhs, though Runjeet's men had been picked for the occasion.

Yesterday evening an entertainment was given by the Maha Rajah to Lord William and his party, in which there was a great display of fireworks, See. In front of the royal tent was pitched a Shemianeh, or canopy of velvet, richly embroidered with gold, under which chairs were placed for the company. The carpeting consisted entirely of keenkhaub, silk, and other rich cloths, superbly embroidered with silver and gold. In the royal tent was placed a throne of gold, inlaid with precious stones, and two bedsteads of the same rich description, with equally magnificent cushions. Indeed, the whole inside of the tent was gorgeously decorated, and formed a most perfect specimen of Indian luxury and extravagance. The troop of Amazons also made their appearance, and sat under the Shemianeh in the centre of the company; and each set danced alternately before the Maha Rajah, who seemed very merry on the occasion, and was most attentive to his noble guests, Lord and Lady William Bentinck. Wine was brought in too, and very freely distributed in golden cups to all the guests; Runjeet taking a pretty large allowance. After he had got somewhat elevated, a quantity of gold-dust was brought and placed before the Maha Rajah, who ordered the nautch girls to throw it over the guests, in imitation of the festival of the Hooly,★ and he seemed much to enjoy the joke; for he also threw it at the ladies and gentlemen who sat near him, as well as at the dancing women. A number of his chieftains, too, were present, but none of them appeared to know how to conduct themselves; and instead of the manners of noblemen and gentlemen, displayed those rather of village churls.

Rich presents were brought in after the entertainment, and I believe Runjeet made offer to his lordship of one of his famous horses named Loylee: but of this his Excellency declined acceptance; and about ten o'clock the party broke up. On the following evening a similar entertainment was given by his lordship; and the next morning both chiefs left Hooper, and on the 1st November the camp broke up. Next day all the troops commenced their march back to their respective cantonments.

★ *When red, purple, and yellow powders, made up in balls, are thrown at each other by the guests at entertainments, like snowballs, until they get quite covered by the various colours.*

Shortly after the Hooper meeting, I was honoured with the commands of his Excellency the Governor-General to repair to his camp at Dehlee, and remain in attendance during his lordship's tour through Rajepootanah. Lord William had invited all the native chiefs of that country to meet him at Ajmere, which place his Excellency's camp reached on the 18th of January 1832. On the 23rd, Rajah Kullian Sing of Kishenghur arrived and paid his lordship a visit. Some officers of the staff were deputed to conduct the Rajah into camp, and a party of my sowars, on duty with his Excellency, was drawn up before the Durbar tent. The Rajah was received with a salute of eleven guns, and his lordship rose from his seat to meet him, and offered him and all his sirdars seats. The English band of music was in attendance, and continued playing during the interview. After the customary ceremony of "utter" and "pain," the Rajah took his leave under the same salute as on arriving.

On the 30th, Nawab Ameer Khan* arrived in camp, with a force of two or three battalions, 2,000 or 3,000 horse, and some artillery. He was received with the same ceremonies as the Kishenghur Rajah, except that the salute to him was of thirteen guns, and that his lordship took an emerald ring from off his finger and presented it to the Nawab. A concourse of full 20,000 persons assembled around the Durbar to witness this meeting. Next morning his Excellency with all his staff went to witness a review of the Nawab's troops, and were much pleased with the various feats of Hindostanee horsemanship which were exhibited. At the termination of the review, Lord William took his own sword from his waist and presented it to the Nawab.

The next visit, on the 3rd February, was from Rajah Ram Sing of Kotah, who was received in the same manner as the former chiefs; and two days after came Jeewun Sing Rajah-Rana, of Oudipore, with a grand Sowarree. The deputation

*The celebrated partizan and freebooter.

sent to welcome him consisted of six officers from his lordship's staff, and the body-guard, together with a rissallah of my corps, was drawn up in front of the Durbar tent. The Rana was saluted with seventeen guns, and met by his lordship, who advanced some steps and led his Highness to a throne on which the two chiefs sat during the meeting. The presents offered were handsome, and included an elephant and two horses all richly caparisoned.

The Rajah of Jeypore, Sewaee Sing, a lad of eighteen, was received with the same ceremonies and presents as the Rana of Oudipore. The Rajah of Boondee, Ram Sing, received the same welcome as the Kishenghur man. The Rajahs of Jhoudpore, Jesselmere, and Bickanere sent excuses for not appearing.

On the 8th of February, the Governor-General, accompanied by Lord Clare, Governor of Bombay, mounted on elephants and attended by their respective staffs and escorts, returned the Rana of Oudipore's visit, receiving similar presents to those which had been given. On the two following days the same visits and ceremonies were gone through with the Jeypore and other Rajahs, all of whom presented the same gifts, though the three first had received none — a compliment which obliged his lordship to invite those chiefs a second time in order to return them similar presents. These matters having been thus fitly arranged, the camp broke up, and Lord William returned to Dehlee by the way of Jeypore, Alwur, Kishenghur, and Bhurtpore, the chieftains of which places all gave grand entertainments to his lordship and his camp.

The various bodies of troops, both cavalry and infantry, assembled at Ajmere under their respective chiefs, amounted to upwards of 100,000 men, and about 200 pieces of cannon. When I was in the Mahratta service in the year '98, and met these brave Surajebunsees or "Sons of the Sun," as they call themselves, they were then in the full bloom of their pride as gallant soldiers courting enterprise, and fearless of danger. How changed were they now! Chief and follower alike reduced

277

to poverty; degraded in feeling as in condition; the spirit of the soldier utterly departed; all remembrance of the deeds of their forefathers vanished from their minds; a single British chuprassie might have driven them in flocks. Their chiefs, instead of brave leaders, were either boys, or men sunk in vice or debauchery, guided by women or karindahs (agents) to whom all state affairs were willingly abandoned, provided they themselves were permitted to enjoy unrestrainedly their own vicious pleasures. To this state of affairs the Rana of Oudipore offers the only exception; and he, though like the rest reduced to utter poverty by the misrule and anarchy of past times, still maintains the appearance of a prince and a Rajepoot. On this occasion, they had an opportunity of seeing and estimating somewhat of the British people and power. The reception of the various chieftains was admirably managed; and all of them left Ajmere flattered by the attentions, and delighted by the courtesy, of the British nobleman and governor.

At Ajmere I had the honour of being introduced to Lord Clare, governor of Bombay, who had come over in order to meet the Governor-General, and his lordship was pleased on this occasion to present me with a very valuable sword, accompanied by the following handsome and most gratifying letter:—

"Camp, Ajmere, Jan. 27, 1832.
"My dear Sir,—Your own sword has performed such good service to the British Government, that it is quite unnecessary to send you another; but I cannot resist begging your acceptance of that which I send by the bearer; being confident that whenever your services shall again be required in the field, you will use it in the service of Government with the same zeal and success against the enemies of England, which has in former and more perilous times than the present, so much distinguished your honourable career in India. I would also beg your acceptance of it as a small proof of my personal regard and esteem; and I assure you, I set a high value on the handsome horse of your own breeding which you presented me a few days ago on the occasion of my visit to your tent.

"I unfortunately do not speak the language of this country; I must therefore beg of you to let your own horsemen know how much pleased I was this morning with their manoeuvres, and the exhibition I witnessed of the skill of the whole troops.— Believe me to be, my dear sir, with great truth, your faithful and obedient servant,

(Signed)   "Clare."

On the termination of the tour in Rajepootanah and the return of the Governor-General and his camp to Dehlee, Skinner received permission to return to his station.

Our task is almost done. Hindostan was quiet, "soldiering was over. The fire had burned out for lack of fuel, and the ardent spirits that so long had revelled in high military excitement were forced to settle down into the calm routine of peaceful life. The duty of the gallant, dashing "yellow boys," who had so long flown at high game, was now reduced to little more than keeping the peace, and now and then chastising a troublesome robber or refractory Zemeendar.

Their veteran commander, now little called upon for active service, divided his time between his well-beloved corps at Hansee and the superintendence of his jaghire, now greatly improved by his good management: or in other affairs, amongst which were his large and systematic charities. "Nothing," says a dear friend of his, in a letter to the writer, "nothing was to me more beautiful than his great humility, to see him with the poor sitting on the floor, and conversing with them on their several cases. I had the happiness to march all over the Doab with him for near three months. We visited almost every village, and the Zemeendars used to talk freely over their concerns and of our rule; and all classes, high and low, used to come to our tents, and we went to their little forts and dwellings. At the termination of our tour all the Zemeendars came and paid the Colonel a visit for three days at his jaghire of Belaspore, and were feasted in turn. I was very ill at the time, but nevertheless enjoyed the trip much, and I think they were the happiest days of my life. Your poor brother William was often of our party, and with him we spent many happy hours. You know Lord Combermere paid him a visit at Belaspore with his camp followers. On that occasion, Secunder carried a dinner with his own hands to the lowest drummer in camp.

"Perhaps you may remember the singular end of the favourite charger that carried Skinner through Lord Lake's wars, and which, in a rencontre with the Sikhs, saved his life by leaping over some of them who attempted to stop his progress, when he got speared. This horse was pensioned, and had been so for some years. One morning he broke away from his head and heel ropes, and ran up to the window of the bungalow at Hansee where Skinner was sitting, neighed loudly, and dropped down dead, as much as to say, 'My end is near, I am come to take a last farewell!'

"Of Skinner's humility, and utter contempt of all assumption, I may mention one trait. When I was living with him, he always had an old spoon placed on his breakfast-table, to remind him, as he said, of his origin and early days."

"Skinner," writes another of his friends, "was a man of sincere piety, though one might have known him long without being aware of its extent, as he avoided all show. When I was with him at Hansee during the hot winds, we used to sleep in the verandah, for the sake of coolness. Long before daylight in the morning, I used to hear him at his prayers with most earnest utterance, half aloud, and he at all times expressed a feeling of deep gratitude to the Almighty for the worldly advantages that had fallen to his share, and an entire dependence on Him for the future."

Amongst the chief objects which lie desired to accomplish, and which he at length attained, was the erection of an episcopal church at Dehlee. There are two motives to which the writer has heard the origin of this design attributed. He has been heard to say, that on the morning of that night of pain and misery which he passed naked and wounded on the field near Oonearah, when relieved by the Chumar woman who gave him bread and water, in the feeling of gratitude to Providence for this unexpected succour, lie vowed if he should ultimately be preserved, and ever have the means, to build a Christian church. It has also been said that Skinner, when he purchased his house at Dehlee, found in the "compound," or enclosure, a mosque in ruins, which he repaired, and this having given rise to some remark, he declared, that though he respected

Mahometans, and would be the last to destroy or desecrate their places of worship, he reverenced his own religion far more, and would prove it if God preserved his life, and he became rich enough to do it, by building a Christian church, He did live to perform this votive promise, and in time the episcopal church of St. James's was built.

The active life which Colonel Skinner had always led, contributed, with a good natural constitution, to keep him in habitual good health; and though a diminution of the necessity for personal exertion had encouraged a disposition to fulness, with the exception of one apoplectic seizure, which did not recur in any serious degree, and an occasional visit of the gout, he had scarcely ever been annoyed with any illness: and so free from all such symptoms had he been for years, that when on the 30th of November 1841, he complained of a slight shivering fit, and though this was followed by daily small attacks of fever and ague for the next four days, no alarm was taken on his account, either by the medical men or those around him.

On the 4th of December, however, he became more uneasy, nor did he receive any relief from the medicines exhibited. Towards the afternoon he became sensible of pain in the region of the stomach, and expressed his fears that "the gout had got into his chest." He repeatedly now exclaimed, he "did not know what was the matter with him." Towards evening his pulse sank and his skin became cold; a slight tremor came on, and then, as appears, danger was first apprehended. There was, indeed, cause for alarm. In less than an hour after, vomiting, which had at first been vainly encouraged, came on, but with it came a quivering spasm. His pulse ceased, and all was over.

To speculate on the cause of death was useless. The medical men, we learn, could throw no light upon the subject. It was enough for the heart-stricken family, that the father and the friend was gone for ever. An account of his last moments, written by his son, then an officer in his father's corps, tells of the honours paid to the dead.

"We buried him with military honours. The Hurreeana Light Infantry under Captain Campbell formed the advanced guard. I gave no orders to our own corps, leaving it to them to come either as private mourners (as they do at their own funerals) or mounted. They preferred the latter; and the recollection that this was the last occasion on which I should ever see the "yellow boys" together with their distinguished commander (for the sight of his charger and helmet and accoutrements made all appear exactly as if he were at the head of his corps, and not in his coffin) tried my nerves sorely. And when they lowered him into the grave I could not help thinking of the conversations we frequently had about death; and the striking opinions he always expressed and maintained on that subject. 'We are just like seed, which vegetates when cast into the earth; and we return from whence we came.' Since his confirmation by the bishop in 1836, he was very regular in his devotions, and constantly studied the Bible. I sincerely hope he is now where "we all wish he may be; for if happiness is to be found in the next world, no one deserves it better than my father; for he died with an upright and easy conscience, having never injured any one, and done good to thousands. We intend removing-his remains and burying him in his church at Dehlee; so that it may form his monument; but I think it would be better to bury him by the side of poor William Fraser,* and build a separate monument, which would serve as a memorial both to the European and native community."

That this was the wish of Skinner himself, in spite of the singularly humble desire he had once expressed, may be gathered from a passage in a letter to the writer of this, written in the end of 1836:—

"Dehlee, 29th Nov. 1836.
"I came here to have my church consecrated; which was done on the 21st inst. And a most handsome white marble tomb has been put over poor William. So you see, by the blessing of God, I have served Him and my friend too, whose memory and love remains firm in my old heart; and I only wish that when I am no more I may be laid alongside of him. . . . You wish me to give a narrative of his murder; I have neither the heart nor mind to relate the melancholy event. In him I have lost the best friend I ever had in this world; and my friendship with the world ends with him. I only wish I were lying with him."

*Killed by an assassin in 1835.

282

This wish was gratified. On the 17th of January, the remains were disinterred; and were escorted by the whole of the corps and a great concourse of people to a place four côs from Dehlee called Seetaram-ka-seraee, where it was met by all the civilians and officers of the station, with a great multitude from the city.

"None of the emperors," said the natives, "were ever brought into Dehlee in such state as Secunder Sahib." And an eye-witness observed, that he never on any occasion saw such a crowd. Military honours were paid to the funeral by official command; and sixty-three minute guns were fired, denoting the years of the deceased. A funeral sermon was preached over the body, at which all the Europeans at Dehlee attended; and on the 19th of January, the veteran soldier was committed to his final earthly resting-place, beneath the altar of the church he had built, and beside the friend he had best loved.—*Placide quiescant.*

![LEONAUR]

ALSO FROM LEONAUR
AVAILABLE IN SOFT OR HARD COVER WITH DUST JACKET

Printed in the United Kingdom
by Lightning Source UK Ltd.
127256UK00001B/179/A